# Studies in Rhetorics and Feminisms

Series Editors, Cheryl Glenn and Shirley Wilson Logan

**Other Books in the Studies in Rhetorics and Feminisms Series**

Feminism Beyond Modernism
*Elizabeth A. Flynn*

Gender and Rhetorical Space in American Life, 1866–1910
*Nan Johnson*

Appropriate[ing] Dress
Women's Rhetorical Style in Nineteenth-Century America
*Carol Mattingly*

The Gendered Pulpit
Preaching in American Protestant Spaces
*Roxanne Mountford*

*Liberating Voices*

Karyn L. Hollis

# LIBERATING VOICES

*Writing at the Bryn Mawr
Summer School for
Women Workers*

Southern Illinois University Press
*Carbondale*

Library of Congress Cataloging-in-Publication Data
Hollis, Karyn L., 1948–
Liberating voices : writing at the Bryn Mawr Summer School for Women
Workers / Karyn L. Hollis.
p. cm. — (Studies in rhetorics and feminisms)
Includes bibliographical references and index.
1. Bryn Mawr Summer School for Women Workers in Industry—History.
2. Working class women—Education—Pennsylvania—Bryn Mawr—
History—20th century. I. Bryn Mawr Summer School for Women
Workers in Industry. II. Title. III. Series.

LD7069.5.B79 H65 2004
374'.186'23—dc22
ISBN 0-8093-2567-5 (cloth : alk. paper)                        2003018886

Printed on recycled paper. ♻

The paper used in this publication meets the minimum requirements of
American National Standard for Information Sciences—Permanence of
Paper for Printed Library Materials, ANSI Z39.48-1992. ∞

*For my mother, Carolyn*
*My husband, Paul*
*and my son, Marty*

# Contents

List of Illustrations / XI
Acknowledgments / XIII

Introduction: Feminisms, Rhetorics, and Materialisms at the Bryn Mawr Summer School for Women Workers / 1

1. The Bryn Mawr Summer School for Women Workers / 10

2. Composition Instruction, Labor Education, and Bryn Mawr Materialist Writing Pedagogy / 33

3. Liberating Voices: Autobiography at the Summer School / 61

4. Material Texts: Labor Drama at the Bryn Mawr Summer School / 93

5. Women Workers and Literary Discourse: Transgressive Reading and Writing / 117

6. Material of Desire: Bodily Rhetoric in Working Women's Poetry / 151

Afterword: Questions of Agency and Voice / 166

Notes / 173
Works Cited / 177
Index / 187

# Illustrations

*Following page 60*

Summer School students studying in the Cloisters, M. Carey Thomas Library, Bryn Mawr College, 1928

Teresa Wolfson teaching her economics class in the Cloisters, M. Carey Thomas Library, Bryn Mawr College, 1929

An astronomy class, Bryn Mawr College

Ellen Kennan with her English class, Bryn Mawr College, 1931

Summer School students in a social science workshop, Bryn Mawr College

Summer School students and faculty in the Mark Starr–Ture Unit around the Cloisters fountain, M. Carey Thomas Library, Bryn Mawr College, 1930

Dr. Colston Warne's economics discussion group, Bryn Mawr College, 1928

Meredith Giveus and unidentified instructor with economics class, the Cloisters, M. Carey Thomas Library, Bryn Mawr College, 1928

Mark Starr with economics class, Bryn Mawr College, 1929

Summer School students in science workshop, Bryn Mawr College

Poetry reading on the lawn in front of the M. Carey Thomas Library, Bryn Mawr College, 1928

Summer School students in the Cloisters, M. Carey Thomas Library, Bryn Mawr College, 1932

Summer School students reading, portico, M. Carey Thomas Library, Bryn Mawr College, 1929

Bryn Mawr Summer School outdoor dramatics, Bryn Mawr College

Summer School students in the science room, Bryn Mawr College, 1927

Summer School students in the library, Taylor Hall, Bryn Mawr College, 1933

# Acknowledgments

I have many to thank for helping me complete this book. First of all, Cheryl Glenn, coeditor of Southern Illinois University Press's series Studies in Rhetorics and Feminisms, provided invaluable support and advice throughout this project. Others who wrote letters of support or provided critical insights and suggestions include the other series coeditor, Shirley Wilson Logan; Southern Illinois University Press senior sponsoring editor Karl Kageff; project editor Kathleen Kageff; Susan Kates, John Trimbur, Paul Lauter, Nicholas Coles, and the greatly missed Jim Berlin. I received a generous grant and release time from Villanova University, which allowed me to get started on the research. And a grant from the National Endowment for the Humanities afforded a lengthy period for writing. And of course, I wouldn't have ever finished the book without the support and encouragement of my family far and wide, but especially my husband, Paul; my son, Marty; my mother, Carolyn, and my brothers, Duane and Earl; as well as many friends of labor and working women. Thank you all.

Earlier versions of portions of this book were published previously: Chapter 3 first appeared as "Liberating Voices: Autobiographical Writing at the Bryn Mawr Summer School for Women Workers, 1921–1938" in *College Composition and Communication* 44 (1994). Copyright © 1994 by the National Council of Teachers of English. Reprinted with permission. Another version of this essay appeared as "Autobiography and Reconstructing Subjectivities at the Bryn Mawr Summer School for Women Workers, 1921–38" in *Women's Studies Quarterly* 23 (1995) and was reprinted in *What We Hold in Common: An Introduction to Working-Class Studies,* edited by Janet Zandy. Chapter 4 is a revision of "Plays of Heteroglossia: Labor Drama at the Bryn Mawr Summer School" from *Popular Literacy: Studies in Cultural Practices and Poetics,* edited by John Trimbur. Copyright © 2001 by University of Pittsburgh Press. Used by permission of the University of Pittsburgh Press. Chapter 6 first appeared as "Material of Desire: Bodily Rhetoric in Working Women's Poetry at the Bryn Mawr Summer School, 1921–1938" in *Rhetorical Bodies: Towards a Material Rhetoric,* edited by Sharon Crowley and Jack Selzer.

# Introduction: Feminisms, Rhetorics, and Materialisms at the Bryn Mawr Summer School for Women Workers

As Cheryl Glenn writes in her call for manuscripts,

> Studies in Rhetorics and Feminisms seeks to address the interdisciplinarity that rhetorics and feminisms represent. . . . This interdisciplinarity has already begun to transform the rhetorical tradition as we have known it (upper-class, agonistic, public, and male) into regendered, inclusionary rhetorics (democratic, dialogic, collaborative, cultural, and private).

The rhetoric developed and practiced at the Bryn Mawr Summer School for Women Workers was indeed interdisciplinary, democratic, working-class, largely collaborative, and female, but it also entered the public realm, making it, even today, a rare rhetorical event. The Summer School immersion in liberal arts and labor studies was to prepare working-class women for a formidable challenge: transforming their oppressive work environment into a more humane, equitable experience for themselves and other workers. The Summer School also provided the worker students with a short respite where they could grow in purely aesthetic and intellectual realms. In writing about these pursuits, the working-class women reinscribed their identities and aspirations, resisting stifling cultural scripts and attending to both the "bread" and "roses" of their desires.

Sharon Crowley's discussion of bodies and material practices is crucial to understanding the rhetoric, feminism, and materialism in place at the Summer School. She writes: "Feminists practice rhetoric when they attempt to have a voice in policy-making and when they intervene in public practices" ("Material" 359). Such was the goal and often the achievement at the Bryn Mawr Summer School for Women Workers. Students formed a self-government and demanded representation on administrative and curricular committees where they lobbied successfully for a number of important programmatic additions: admission of African American students, as well as waitresses and housekeepers of all races; an extracurricular poetry class; an expanded dramatics program; a "proletarian" literature course; and a "Marxist" instructor. As will be seen repeatedly in the chapters that follow, decisions made by the working women had significant repercussions at the Summer School.

Most of their writing aimed to persuade an audience of the need to improve workers' lives. Occasionally their prose was gendered and raced; more frequently women used the masculinist rhetoric of male working-class empowerment for their own ends. They wrote themselves stronger subjectivities, which they embodied in labor dramas, skits, and mock hearings. They published hundreds of essays, poems, autobiographies, and short stories in the Summer School magazine. In addition, the best writers conducted surveys in their economics class involving the whole student body. These studies were published by the U.S. Department of Labor thanks to the efforts of Amy Hewes, Mount Holyoke economist and Summer School faculty member. Thus, using the rhetoric they learned and practiced at the Summer School, the women workers textualized their arduous material conditions—the low wages, the stifling factory floor, the disrupted family life—making them visible through a national, governmental forum, where the discursivity of working-class women had been and continues to be all but erased.

While in Crowley's terms, the rhetorical praxis at the Summer School is clearly an interventionist, public rhetoric, its feminism is complex and implied rather than simple and straightforward. In all the pages of woman-centered text that I read for this study—syllabi, lesson plans, student writing, faculty meeting minutes—I found only one reference in Summer School discourse to "feminism." In a calendar of events of the 1924 session, Mabel Thurlwell recorded that the school was visited by Baroness Ishimoto, "a leader of the feminist movement of Japan and much interested in workers' education." But the contents or effects of this speech were not revealed.

In explaining the complicated attitudes and beliefs about gender and class held by militant working women, Annelise Orleck uses the concept of "industrial feminism," a term coined by Mildred Moore to describe the work of the Women's Trade Union League (6). Orleck argues that industrial feminism was practiced by many working-class activists of the 1920s and 1930s, although they would not have used the term themselves. Rather, they associated "feminism" with the women of the middle and upper classes, who had the luxury of focusing solely on gender; and they refused to embrace any movement that was blind to class. Having a broader scope than the women's rights focus of many feminists at the time, industrial feminists wanted "bread" as well as "roses." Indeed, Summer School women wrote about their need for "bread" in the form of higher wages, fewer working hours, sanitary and safe working conditions, good housing, and medical care, while also voicing a desire for "roses": education, access to the arts, meaningful work, and a sense of community. Orleck asserts that industrial feminists dreamed of bringing the varied aspects of their lives, home, work, education, art, gender, class, ethnicity, religion, into harmonious relationship. This desire for "harmony" will be seen as an important theme in the Summer School poetry.

Scholars have offered many reasons for American working-class women's refusal to adopt an explicitly feminist identity. The women's movement of the early twentieth century and later is often criticized for its largely upper- and middle-class constituency and lack of interest in working-class women. In addition, many of the early suffragettes left the United States after winning the right to vote in 1920 to work in European women's rights campaigns. American women were then deprived of some of their best organizers and leaders. Working women, in general, had little access to feminist rhetoric as such, and the Bryn Mawr Summer School experience proved no exception. Earlier generations of socialist women had put the "woman question" inside a critique of capitalism, arguing for the most part, that overthrowing the capitalist economic system was prerequisite to solving the problems of women's inequality. This idea was no doubt part of the legacy many of the more politically sophisticated working women brought with them to Bryn Mawr (Weedon 138).

Still other scholars have argued that working-class women may not regard gender as central to their oppression, as many of their middle-class counterparts do. In her analysis of gender and class in German working women's autobiography of the early twentieth century, Mary Jo Maynes concludes that gender oppression was not regarded as primary by any of the female autobiographers she studied:

> Whether socialist or apolitical, whether writing for a working class audience or a middle class one, whether positing collective or individual solutions to their problems, or no solution at all, these autobiographers all seem to agree that it is mostly because they are poor and reliant on their labor that they suffer. . . . While their identity as women is certainly central to their accounts of their life courses, they do not regard solidarity with women, across class lines, as a possible or desirable tactic for improvement. ("Gender and Class" 243–44)

Similarly, it may be that the working-class women at the Bryn Mawr Summer School were well aware of the brutality of working men's lives and, as many indicated, did not aspire to "equality" with men but to a more humanized world for everyone.

However, when interviewed by Marion W. Roydhouse for her article "Partners in Progress," Hilda Worthington Smith, longtime director of the Summer School, remarked that "at the Bryn Mawr Summer School [we] never talked directly of women's problems because these were women, and we knew they were women, and we knew what they'd come for" (203). Roydhouse argues that

> the Summer Schools were certainly feminist in the early years because the students and faculty did discuss disparities in wage scales or the difficulties faced by married women in the work force, but they viewed these issues within the context of needed change in the industrial system, rather than as problems resulting from a male-dominated society. (203)

Roydhouse further maintains that "this feminism was based on an idealistic belief in women's potential for fuller participation in society, rather than in the kind of commitment that led to the introduction of the ERA during the same period" (203). Scholars have termed this approach "social feminist" (Lemons).

No matter how self-consciously it was or was not adopted, Summer School "feminism" did not rely upon "individualist, rationalist and universalist assumptions," perspectives that poststructuralists have pointed out often implicate feminisms in racist, essentialist, or other troubling narratives (Ede, Glenn, and Lunsford 407). Indeed, the school's accomplishments can be readily appreciated in poststructuralist terms since, as will be seen in subsequent chapters, an emphasis was placed on locating the difference among women workers in terms of geography, race, ethnicity, class, and religion, among other factors. The women also critiqued the inferior representation accorded them in patriarchal bourgeois textuality and reconstructed their subjectivities with more powerful, resistant discourses. They transcended patriarchal dualisms, rewriting them into more woman-friendly and inclusive syntheses; and through what I call a "materialist pedagogy," the women focused on the extratextual world to remake it in terms they articulated themselves.

It became apparent to me that the term *materialist* might be fundamental to characterizing the pedagogy at the Summer School as I was contemplating the call for papers issued by Jack Selzer and Sharon Crowley for the 1997 Penn State Conference on Rhetoric and Composition. The conference theme of "the material, the body and rhetoric" led me to write a paper on the body as a central motif in Summer School students' poetry. (The paper has been rewritten as chapter 5 of this book and was also published in the Selzer and Crowley volume of conference papers, *Rhetorical Bodies*.) As I thought about Selzer's suggestions for inquiry around the conference theme, the notion of materiality seemed to take on special significance for Summer School pedagogical activity. For example, Selzer asks "how does a 'materialist' notion of rhetoric contrast with 'idealist' notions" (10). That question led me to characterize as "idealist" writing pedagogies that largely ignore the *extratextual* context for writing, assigning subjectivity to decontextualized classroom writers, devoid of identity, geographic or cultural location, and that ask them to write within the relatively limited academic rhetorical situation. Such pedagogy has been criticized by post-process composition scholars such as Crowley and John Trimbur, to name but two, and contrasts with "material-ist" writing pedagogy, such as that practiced at the Bryn Mawr Summer School, which does not strip students or their subject matter of material cultural life. Both students and subject matter for writing are studied and situated in terms of a local, national and/or international context, given political dimensions, and related to an economic base associated with discursive power struggles. As I began to take a comprehensive look at the work and writing at the Sum-mer School, I noticed how frequently material culture either engendered a discourse, as for example, a worker's low wages prompted an essay on strik-ing for better pay; or material culture was created by a discourse, as when text was "materialized" in the form of labor plays and skits. In short, discourse was not disembodied or dematerialized at the Summer School.

As Krista Ratcliffe points out in her excellent review of the Selzer and Crowley collection, "the term *material* has a long and checkered history in philosophy, rhetoric and politics" (614). In general, I welcome all the signifi-cations and connotations the term brings with it to my study—from its ev-eryday meaning of "physicality" in opposition to the "mental," "abstract," and "ideal" realms; to the Marxist notion of "historical materialism," describ-ing the process by which concrete, physical forms of economic production are linked to a society's ideas about culture, social relations, and, in the case of "materialist feminists," gender. The term *materialist pedagogy* also leads to the poststructuralist concept of "cultural materialism," a perspective that argues for the "materiality of discourse," as when Summer School texts lead to concrete action in the political realm, as well as the "discursivity of mate-riality," as when cultural texts are interrogated and resisted because they con-struct an oppressed subjectivity among the working women or rationalize a capitalist system of exploitation. All these concepts related to the "material-ity of teaching and learning" have deep resonance in Summer School peda-gogy and will be discussed in more detail in chapter 2.[1]

## OVERVIEW OF THE BOOK

Because of the importance of recovering the working women's writing itself, most chapters in the book are followed by an appendix, which offers a se-lection of student writing related to the chapter's central issues. In this way, the women workers' voices will gain a long-deserved forum, the sparse amount of published working-class writing will be augmented, and readers will achieve a better understanding of the issues from the women workers' perspective. In addition, I have a more extensive selection of their writing on my web page at <www.homepage.villanova.edu/karyn.hollis>.

Chapter 1 places the Bryn Mawr Summer School for Women Workers in a broad historical context. I review the social, political, and economic landscape of the two decades during which the Summer School offered courses. Beginning with the early 1920s and the institutional and educational discourses that framed the call to educate working women, I show how middle- and upper-middle-class women educators joined with union women, working-class women activists, and church and civic leaders to establish the Bryn Mawr Summer School. The students also played an influential role in the Summer School's formation, making the crucial demand for its leftist underpinnings.

From the beginning, a clear direction for the newly developing pedagogy emerged: It centered on the women's lived experiences of work, family, and community with an emphasis on their important, but ignored, economic role in industrial capitalism. As discussed above, I use the term *materialist pedagogy* because of its insistent focus on improving the material environment of the women's "real lives"; the emphasis was on the world presented through, yet outside of, texts studied and discussed, on the bodily oppression experienced in the factories, on the mental and physical anguish brought about by labor strife endured as workers, union organizers, or strikers. A related materialist objective was that the women become producers and creators of material and discursive culture instead of merely uncritical consumers. Chapter 1 is followed by an appendix containing students' own accounts of their work and school lives.

Chapter 2 situates the Summer School more specifically in pedagogical history and offers examples of teaching and learning activities. I show how the Summer School project reflected trends in mainstream composition pedagogy of the 1920s and 1930s, providing an early example of process pedagogy while largely avoiding the current-traditional mold. Using Jim Berlin's rhetorical categories, I argue that Summer School pedagogy combined elements of both subjective/expressionistic and social/transactive rhetorics while keeping the worker subject at the center of all pedagogical interactions. Other influences included the workers' education movement, Deweyan educational philosophy, and socialist educational concepts, as well as principles of progressive education.

Next I describe the school's materialist pedagogical enterprise, so called because of the extratextual focus of many pedagogical activities: writing to reach a wider audience in publications such as *Shop and School,* producing cooperative statistical studies for the U.S. Department of Labor, giving a material dimension to written documents through scrapbooks or illustrated laboratory notebooks, and designing visual components to compliment textual explanations in the social science workshop. The "outside world" was continually brought into the classroom through guest speakers; current events were analyzed through newspaper reading and dramatization; students were also taken on field trips to steel mills, public hearings, and union grievances on workplace issues. In short, the education offered at the Summer School was geared to understanding and ultimately improving the harsh living conditions experienced by most working women. I also show how this pedagogy has much in common with recent post-process thinking among compositionists and the materialist feminism of Dana Cloud and Teresa Ebert. The appendix following chapter 2 contains expository essays by Summer School students, accounts of collaborative writing projects and social science workshops, as well as an interview with Jean Carter, an esteemed teacher at the school.

In chapter 3, I use concepts from literary criticism and feminist composition theory to analyze autobiographies written by Summer School students. Since locating subjectivity was an important experience for students and faculty, students were commonly given an autobiographical assignment. Several autobiographical pieces written by black women and white women of varying ethnicities complicate notions of gender, race, and class as the writers negotiate these factors in their daily life at the Summer School and elsewhere.

In writing about their families and childhood, their work and union, education and other issues, the women frequently adopted a first-person narrating "I" in the tradition of unitary, bourgeois subjectivity. As the narration continues, however, an empowered, collective "we" subjectivity is adopted, as well as on occasion a feminist stance. Through their autobiographies, the working women took the opportunity to represent newly acquired versions of more powerful selves. Although these ideas of empowered selfhood were most often derived from androcentric texts offered to workers in their Bryn Mawr classroom and other institutions of working-class culture, the women often used this rhetoric to demand better working conditions and more respect on the job. Again, the desire for material transformation motivated the women workers to struggle for better lives. Follow-up studies of alumnae attest to the fact that many went back to their communities and assumed leadership roles in unions, women's associations such as the YWCA, and churches. When surveyed, all attributed these accomplishments to their experiences at Bryn Mawr. Chapter 3 is followed by an appendix of additional autobiographical pieces.

Chapter 4 describes the most popular curricular component of the Summer School's materialist pedagogy, the numerous labor dramas students produced each session. The chapter begins with a historical rendering of the workers' theater movement in the U.S. and abroad, which provides a context for Bryn Mawr dramatics, again a materialization of ideas and concepts acquired in class or in discussions of current events. The Summer School dramatic productions included "mass recitations," "agitprop" skits, "election scripts," "living newspapers," and various annual pageants and festivals. This embodiment of textual constructs gave the women practice role-playing stronger identities and collectivities. As part of the leftist aesthetic of the times, the traditional separation of spectators and actors was often abandoned, with actors frequently sitting among the audience to deliver their lines. In turn, members of the audience were invited to participate in the plays. Frequently these dramatic creations were not written down but improvised again and again for greater verisimilitude, the excitement of spontaneity and variety, and practice assuming more forceful subject positions. The appendix to this chapter includes the prelude to *It's Unconstitutional,* a labor play written and performed at the Summer School.

Chapter 5 analyzes the working women's experience as producers as well as consumers of literary discourse, a milestone in working-class women's literary history. The women themselves initiated a turn to poetry, asking for a workshop that met with an instructor after the regularly scheduled classes were over. Their poetry was of a more personal nature than other writing they produced and allowed the worker students to use textual strategies of transcendence and transgression in breaching cultural constraints. Again revealing a focus on the material realm, their poems told about their work lives, but tributes to nature, aesthetic creation, and education also broke discursive boundaries that restrained these women. The most frequent theme locates the body and its struggle in the industrial context. The appendix provides further examples of student poetry.

In chapter 6 I look closer at the bodily motif, especially as the body is pitted against the machine in the industrial workplace. A full two-thirds of the working women's poems mention their bodies, which are frequently gendered. The women wanted a wider audience for this erased discourse of dangerous factory work and its toll on their bodies. Again focusing on the extratextual "real world," their embodied, materialist rhetoric depicts injured hands and arms, strained eyes, numbed brains. The women wrote their bodies as sites not only of social control, but also of individual and collective resistance. In this insistence on the body's liberating potential, the poetry transgresses the androcentric mind/body dyad that posits thinking as the superior path to individual liberation. Transcending masculinist cultural binaries is a frequent rhetorical move of the working women as they open their oppressive cultural texts and reinscribe a more worker-friendly cultural discourse.

I take up questions of agency and voice in the afterword and also discuss the Summer School's embattled, eighteen-year existence, attacked as it was from right and left. Finding financial support finally became impossible in the late 1930s as more conservative ideologies in the political and labor culture began to predominate, and the Bryn Mawr Summer School fell out of favor. Turning to the nature of the worker's discourse developed at the Summer School, it is difficult to assess "voice" in a poststructuralist age. Accordingly, I discuss the degree of agency attained by the writing workers. I believe the vast array of available cultural texts contributed to their construction of a heteroglossic discourse that accurately represented the needs and desires of these working women. That this discourse helped them in their lives after Bryn Mawr attests to its "authenticity" and worth.

# The Bryn Mawr Summer School for Women Workers

## 1

["]Bryn Mawr has given me a new definition of internationalism and a new feeling for the word 'tolerant,'["] writes . . . a cigar worker from a southern mill. ["]At first I thought my mother would have a fit if she knew I was going around with the cotton mill girls. Now I see that they are just as nice girls as anyone else, and I am trying to get them to come to our club [YWCA Industrial Club]. I got acquainted too with a lot of the Russian girls, and learned a lot from them. . . .["]
—Hilda Worthington Smith, *Women Workers at the Bryn Mawr Summer School*

When I first read the narratives written by students at the Bryn Mawr Summer School for Women Workers, I was moved by the growth in intellect, self-confidence, and political awareness I found in the texts before me. Clearly, these working women benefited greatly from the eight-week immersion in liberal arts and labor economics they experienced on a beautiful suburban college campus where, in the words of one student, "the scent of the honey suckles made us feel that we were in heaven" (Smith, *Women Workers* 18). The Summer School was the first of four resident workers' schools for women established in the 1920s and 1930s, and at Bryn Mawr, students were offered some of the advantages and luxuries their more elite counterparts enjoyed during the fall and spring terms. They were taken on field trips to local museums and factories, honored with teas and luncheons, taught to swim and play tennis, and treated to guest lectures by W. E. B. Dubois, Margaret Sanger, Norman Thomas, Francis Perkins, Harold Laski, Walter Reuther, and Eleanor Roosevelt, as well as many other renowned labor, political, academic, and feminist leaders. This extraordinary pedagogical experiment stands as one of the few moments in U.S. women's history of a successful cross-class alliance among upper-, middle-, and working-class women from a variety of ethnic, religious, and geographic backgrounds. And while the pedagogy developed at the Summer School was innovative by all accounts, the writing instruction was particularly remarkable.

The more I learned about the Summer School, the more convinced I was of its importance to many scholarly fields: rhetoric and composition, women's studies, education, and labor studies to name a few. This story of individuals, organizations, and their commitments and struggles in the cause of working women, provides valuable examples that lend strength and understanding to current endeavors. The Bryn Mawr Summer School for Women Workers offers an important antecedent to the feminist and activist pedagogies we strive to develop today. The faculty practiced a nonhierarchical teaching style that relied extensively on the discussion method; the student-centered pedagogy focused on students' life experiences, and student input was sought in developing a meaningful and effective curriculum and administration. Interdisciplinary approaches prevailed, and a wide range of writing genres were taught, from poetry and labor drama to the expository essay, collaborative reports, and autobiography. Differences in student awareness and experience of sexism, racism, and classism were acknowledged and openly discussed. In addition, the special needs of women workers were recognized; women were encouraged to develop their confidence as speakers and writers and to seek leadership roles in the workplace. Most significantly, students and faculty alike believed education could be a catalyst for progressive social change.

## THE 1920S AND 1930S: A TIME FOR EDUCATING WORKING WOMEN

The Bryn Mawr Summer School for Women Workers spanned two decades that in popular conceptions offer striking contrasts of abundance and poverty, yet for workers, the economic hardships endured in both decades differ only in degree (Strickler). The United States came out of World War I a heavily industrialized world power, but as is often the case, the accompanying economic boom was not shared across the population. Large groups of workers in the textile and coal mining industries, as well as southern farmers, minorities, and women saw their economic condition decline. Thus from the earliest Summer School session in 1921, many students wrote about oppressive factory conditions and meager wages.

Events in the 1920s delivered a mixed legacy to women workers. Although gaining the right to vote in 1920 supplied some of the energy and confidence needed to launch Bryn Mawr's foray into working women's education, feminist historians also note that enfranchisement disrupted the women's movement by depriving it of a central focus. Many leaders went to Europe to assist feminist struggles there, leaving American working women especially vulnerable to sexist labor practices by employers and, when organized, in their unions. And while the Soviet Revolution of 1917 gave a morale boost to many left-leaning and working-class movements in the United States, it also resulted in reactionary "Red Scares" and Palmer Raids in which working-class activists were harassed and arrested. Public sentiment against immigrants and radical activists came to a head in the execution of Italian anarchists Sacco and Vanzetti in 1927. Summer School women expressed their outrage and heartbreak at this miscarriage of justice in narratives and poems.

Racist and anti-immigration sentiment led Congress to pass severe restrictions on those wishing to come to the United States from southern or eastern Europe as well as from Asian and African nations. Thus the Summer School's explicit promotion of racial and ethnic inclusion and its integrative admissions policy (after 1926) bucked a wider public trend of xenophobia and racism. One propitious result of the severe U.S. immigration restrictions, however, was a decrease in the pool of exploitable labor, giving remaining workers more political leverage. But in striking for better pay, they were often met by violent opposition from capitalist bosses and police defenders. Ultimately, the decade's conservative backlash led to anti-labor sentiment, and union membership declined. The three postwar administrations of Harding, Coolidge, and Hoover all promoted a free-market ideology of tax breaks for the wealthy, lax government regulation, and pro-business social policies. Yet before World War I, "progressivism," which focused on educating and uplifting the needy at the expense of corporate interests, continued in the hearts and minds of many socially conscious citizens. It was a cross-class alliance of such citizens, trade union members, educators, and church and civic leaders—all women—who succeeded in establishing the Bryn Mawr Summer School, an educational experiment that went against the prevailing conservative spirit of the times, by fulfilling other more progressive cultural scripts remarkably well.

With the 1930s, of course, came horrific economic disaster for a majority of Americans, and attitudes began to favor using government initiatives to accomplish economic goals. Ever greater numbers of people began joining unions and demanding higher wages and collective bargaining rights. Distrust of business leaders grew, and they were blamed for the desperate situation. Liberal and left-wing economic theories appealed to more workers and intellectuals. Union membership increased, and members were becoming ever more militant, resulting in impassioned and bitter labor strife. Women workers at the Summer School filled their writing with strike narratives and stories of workplace struggle, unemployment, inadequate housing, picket lines, and despotic bosses. Gradually, free-market ideologies of the 1920s gave way to a broad acceptance of Keynesian economics favoring government intervention and deficit spending to stimulate the economy. Since increasing labor unrest and union activism led to an ever more supportive climate for government initiatives, legislation favorable to workers passed frequently, although many of Roosevelt's programs were ultimately weakened by Congress or declared unconstitutional by the more conservative Supreme Court. Bryn Mawr women workers, in fact, devised a skit about the Supreme Court gutting New Deal legislation (see the appendix to chapter 4). Meanwhile, the menace of fascism loomed on the international horizon, giving simultaneous rise to a growing peace movement and ominous forebodings of war.

A brief listing of bills passed during the Roosevelt administration illustrates the enormous scope of the legislation aimed chiefly at helping working people. The Agricultural Adjustment Act of 1933 gave subsidies to beleaguered farmers. The Works Progress Administration established in 1935 employed construction workers to build public roads, parks, and schools. WPA projects in education and the arts used unemployed actors, teachers, singers, painters, musicians, and writers for publications and productions in the fine arts. The 1935 Social Security Act set up a government program to take care of the elderly and disabled, while the National Youth Administration found jobs for unemployed youth and paid others to stay in college. Also in 1935, the vast National Industrial Recovery Act guaranteed workers a minimum wage, reasonable work hours, and the right to join unions. "Your President wants you to join a union!" became the organizers' rallying cry, and workers flocked to unions in the millions.

## WORKING WOMEN IN UNIONS:
### THE DISCOURSE OF "INDUSTRIAL FEMINISM" VS. SEXISM

Union membership increased from 17 percent of the labor force in 1929 to 34 percent by 1934 (O'Farrell and Kornbluh 66). This increase in the 1930s reversed the previous decade's decline. From five million union members in 1920 (20 percent of the workforce), the number had decreased to 2.9 million by 1929 (Altenbaugh 40). Labor historian Alice Kessler-Harris believes that women were driven away from the labor movement in the 1920s by the climate of anti-unionism that prevailed in the larger culture as well as the sexism in unions themselves ("Problems" 121). Many male trade union leaders perceived women rank-and-filers as weak and unreliable despite the firebrand militancy that had characterized women's unionism during the textile worker strikes of the 1880s, the 1909 "Uprising of the 20,000" (inspired by New York's Triangle Shirtwaist Factory fire), and union women's invention of mass picketing during the twenty-thousand-strong Lawrence, Massachusetts, textile mill strike of 1912 (Ryan 58). In spite of this early militancy, the prevailing belief was that adding women to the workforce would lead to lower wages and a weakened labor movement.

Comparing male and female union goals of the 1920s, Kessler-Harris asserts that men strove for "unity, discipline, faithfulness" while the female rank and file longed for "community, idealism and spirit" ("Problems" 129). As will be seen, these very terms were used by Summer School women when writing about the significance of their Bryn Mawr experience. Furthermore, Kessler-Harris maintains that what many male leaders feared most was union women's undisciplined "spirit," believing it would detract from their "faithfulness" to the labor cause ("Problems" 129). Playing on the stereotypical fear of women's over-emotionalism, more politically conservative male leaders exposed women unionists' real or imagined socialist and communist party affiliations whenever it seemed politically expedient to do so. When these women were forced out, the labor movement lost many of its most talented and fervent female leaders.

Women who did climb to leadership positions in unions, such as Fannia Cohn (a Summer School alumna) of the International Ladies Garment Workers Union, often faced constant struggle and harassment. Kessler-Harris praises Cohn's extremely popular education programs aimed at building community in the ILGWU by offering women courses in philosophy, literature, writing and labor history ("Problems" 129). Cohn was also very supportive of the Bryn Mawr Summer School, coming to speak to the women workers on numerous occasions over the years. However, as Education Director of the ILGWU, whose members were 80 percent female, Cohn had to battle continuously for what she thought was best for women workers against the male leadership's vision for the union. After fifteen years of building a nationally acclaimed workers' education program and nourishing women members with the "spirit" they longed for through "dances, social hours, education and entertainments," she was unceremoniously ousted by the primarily male leadership with no recognition of her great success as Director of Education ("Problems" 129).

In another incident reported by Kessler-Harris, we see sexism as well as ethnic prejudice coming from the male leadership of the ILGWU over the possibility of organizing "Gentile girls." Immigrant European Jewish women tended to dominate the needle trades, and they often arrived in America with academic backgrounds or intellectual interests more advanced than those of their American-born counterparts. Also, many had been exposed to leftist political ideologies here or abroad and were predisposed to joining unions. The women born in North America were more suspicious of the labor movement. When male leadership focused on the harder-to-recruit U.S.-born women, they sent in male organizers; however, women organizers had a greater degree of success with them. In 1921, three locals in Toronto criticized the ILGWU's General Executive Board for sending male staff members to recruit women workers. They complained that "Only women organizers can have access to this unorganized element" ("Problems" 124). Not all the ILGWU male leadership opposed this more woman-centered, woman-run approach. A vice president (presumably male) quoted by Kessler-Harris remarked that the "Gentile girls" were readily organizable since "[m]ost of them are married which makes them independent and full of fighting spirit" (124).

Kessler-Harris points out that sometimes questionable attitudes came from the women themselves. Female rank-and-filers often requested male representatives from the international union. No doubt many pragmatically recognized the greater influence male leaders had within the union's power structure, but others, having internalized the wider culture's androcentrism, discounted their own gender's abilities. Furthermore, many women members were reluctant to publicly condemn the sexism within their locals on "the theory that a poor union is better than no union," ("Problems" 122). Indeed, most of the evidence from Summer School women's writing indicates that they may have consciously put class solidarity with working men over allegiances of gender; nevertheless, an occasional complaint against sexism in unions is voiced in Summer School writing (see Sarah Gordon's piece in chapter 3).

In 1925, the American Federation of Labor took the progressive step of passing a resolution calling on its affiliates to develop organizing campaigns directed at women workers. However, the AFL's characteristic lack of power and influence over national and local unions meant that most affiliates refused to carry out the directive (Kessler-Harris, "Problems" 122). Thus, without the strong backing of organized labor, more and more women workers turned to the organizations that would give them the workplace support they needed. "Activities that continued to develop community, such as women's summer schools, women's locals, the U. S. Women's Bureau and the Women's Trade Union League, persisted on the edge of the trade union structure" ("Problems" 131).

## A SCHOOL FOR WOMEN WORKERS

The Summer School's founding was an indirect response to the favorable climate for women's rights and worker education that prevailed during the

Progressive Era, but it was more directly due to the efforts of the National Women's Trade Union League, which in 1916 called on the women's colleges to educate working women. Two feminist educators connected to Bryn Mawr College answered this call: M. Carey Thomas, suffragette and president of the college for thirty-five years; and Hilda Worthington Smith, Bryn Mawr graduate, dean, and eventual director of the Summer School for thirteen years.[1] During its seventeen-year history, approximately fifteen hundred working women, eighty to one hundred each summer, attended the school. Appointed by Thomas to head the school, Smith attracted the upper- and middle-class Bryn Mawr alumnae to the cause of worker education through a flood of promotional publications and presentations. While alumnae committees did the bulk of the fund-raising, the school was also assisted by Industrial Departments of the Young Women's Christian Association, the National Women's Trade Union League, the National Consumer League, and unions such as the Amalgamated Clothing Workers of America, the International Ladies Garment Workers Union, and the Textile Workers Union of America. Churches, corporate and private benefactors, and Summer School student alumnae groups also helped to find students and financial assistance for the Summer School.

Since Summer School policy explicitly called for a diverse student body in terms of trade, geographic region, religion, and eventually, race, students were recruited from all over the United States and even Europe. Scholarships paid for by full-term Bryn Mawr students and alumnae made it possible for "American-born" cotton mill girls from the South to study alongside immigrant Jewish dressmakers from Eastern Europe or Italian Catholics from the Northeast. Typically, the women were unmarried and under twenty-five years old. Most had attended school only until the eighth grade. It was policy that half the student body should belong to unions, and at their own insistence, the worker students were given a big role in administrative and curricular matters. For example, they had representatives on the Joint Administrative Board, the policymaking body for the Summer School. The students themselves also requested a curricular focus on English (composition and literature), economics, and labor studies. These primary subjects were accompanied by various combinations of psychology, health education, history, art, dramatics, physical education, science, astronomy, and music. In 1926, students demanded that African American women be recruited to the Summer School. The diversity among the student body often brought uncomfortable tension and debate, but testimonies from students and faculty indicate that a more sophisticated, empathetic, and tolerant graduate was the result.

Lillian Herstein, faculty member during the early years of the Summer School, remembers such tension during the founding meeting in her memoir for *Rocking the Boat: Union Women's Voices.* Herstein, herself a prolific writer and speaker for the labor cause, was also a high school and junior college teacher and leader of the Chicago Federation of Teachers and the Women's Trade Union League. She recalls that the varying class backgrounds of students, faculty, and administration lead to mistrust at the first meeting of Summer School supporters in Chicago, around 1920 (20). Gathered at the Hull House, those attending were M. Carey Thomas, Bryn Mawr College president, women labor organizers such as Herstein herself, and several rank-and-file women union members. Thomas presented her idea for the Summer School and asked for a response. Hilda Shapiro, a member of the Amalgamated Clothing Workers of America, said, "Do you think that we working women would fall for a fake like you're talking about? We know all about the welfare plans of employers. The game is to break up unions. I'm on to your game" (21). According to Herstein, Thomas identified her class affiliations and with great dignity and patience, replied that "I don't blame you for being suspicious. My class certainly has not been fair to you working people and has tried many schemes to subvert trade unionism. All I can give you is my own word that this is a sincere effort as I have described it" (21). Thomas must have convinced Shapiro, because the latter enrolled in the first Summer School class at Bryn Mawr the following year (21).

Herstein also describes the "hot fight" that erupted over the admission of "Negroes" to the school (22). The whole student body was called together to discuss the issue. Herstein, one of two instructors from the labor movement in 1924, recalls "one lovely red head from the South," who claimed she had no prejudices against African Americans, but who pointed out that if they were admitted, many white girls from the South would not be allowed by their families to attend the school (12). Herstein admits that "[s]he had a point" (23). Nevertheless, arguments in favor of integrating the school prevailed, and "students voted to admit Negroes." When the black women arrived, Herstein recalls that "everybody held their breath as to what would happen" (22). Her account reveals much about the ethnic diversity at the Summer School and the important but racialized role played by the black students there:

> Students were always having "buzz sessions" [heated discussions] in their rooms. These Negro girls would go to one buzz session after another. They'd go to the white girls from the South and they said, 'Look, you must realize the background of these Jewish girls, the things they've suffered in Europe.' Then they would go

> to the radical bunch and say to them, "Now, you've got to picture a southern town
> where the center of the town is the church, where even the YMCA is controlled
> by the employers and where there are company schools." (22)

Although Herstein portrays these interactions positively, implying that black women played an important role at the Summer School by acting as interpreters and peacemakers among antagonistic ethnic groups, Elaine Richardson has pointed out a more sinister aspect of this behavior for the black women involved. Drawing on classroom research, Richardson explains that these roles are coping strategies, "helping those inside and outside of the Black community to feel less threatened" in uncomfortable social situations (695). From early in their girlhoods, black women are culturally inscribed to "protect and serve," often performing roles of "messengers," "caretakers" and "enforcers" in classroom and other social situations (695). Richardson maintains that teachers often rely on the "social literacy" skills of black girls to help maintain order. Thus, their own academic and social needs go unmet as they attend to the needs of others. Indeed, African American girls and women may be valued more for their socialization skills than their academic abilities, and thus are channeled "into service jobs" rather than professional careers (695). "For all intents and purposes, Black girls are reinscribed as Mammy in the classroom," (695) asserts Richardson. Such may have been the unfortunate reality—in this instance—at the Bryn Mawr Summer School.

Herstein recalls another important dispute over admitting waitresses to the Summer School. They were considered "immoral" by some students because they "made dates with the men they waited on" (22). Herstein, as one of the labor representatives on the Joint Administrative Board, recounts that the argument to admit waitresses was won by a "working girl" from New York who explained that

> if they are immoral, it's because of the conditions under which they work. If they
> got wages instead of tips, they wouldn't have to smile at every man they waited
> on. . . . We should not keep them out of the School. . . . We should change the
> conditions of their work. (22)

As years passed, students and faculty pushed for a stronger alliance with progressive elements of organized labor. By 1938, the connection to labor had alienated a great many Bryn Mawr trustees and alumnae. After an incident in which the school was falsely accused of supporting a strike (forbidden in the administrative agreement with the college), it was asked to leave the Bryn Mawr campus. The school then moved to the Smith family estate in New York and continued there as the coeducational Hudson Shore Labor College from 1939 to 1952. Its demise occurred as workers nationally began to have their educational needs met in other ways: short-term, after-work classes offered by unions, university and community college residential and nonresidential courses, and university labor education programs.

## DEVELOPING A PEDAGOGY: FACULTY AND STUDENTS TOGETHER

Based on their own accounts, faculty considered it an honor to teach at the Summer School. Included among them were distinguished professors from colleges and universities across the nation, many of whom gave up their summer research opportunities to come to the Bryn Mawr campus; others were high school teachers or YWCA Industrial Department administrators; still others had eschewed traditional careers in education to devote themselves year-round to teaching workers. The majority were women with a strong commitment to women's education and the labor movement. They formed a close-knit, cooperative academic community, drawing on each other for disciplinary knowledge, teaching techniques, and administrative skills. Perhaps there had been a precedent for this type of faculty cooperation in the Vassar English department, which maintained strong supportive ties with the Summer School over the years.[2] Laura Wylie, chair of the English department at Vassar from 1895 to 1922, was also an English instructor at the Summer School, as was her Vassar colleague, Helen Lockwood. Wylie's closest friend and colleague at Vassar, rhetorician Gertrude Buck, influenced the Summer School curriculum through Wylie. Other faculty members had ties to Fred Newton Scott and John Dewey.

The educational and political philosophies guiding the school were left of center, ranging from liberal and progressive to more radical left-wing views, with students and faculty demanding a practical and politically relevant curriculum. Several educational discourses contributed to what I am calling the materialist pedagogy that evolved at the Summer School: worker and adult education movements in the United States and abroad, Deweyan educational philosophy, leftist and liberal social thought, and to a certain extent, feminist principles. Curriculum committees met almost daily during the summer session and frequently during the year to work on issues of instruction at the school.

The institution was not geared toward turning the working women into middle-class college students. When asked about the goals of the Summer School, Smith frequently explained that

> this is not a vocational course, and it does not lead to better jobs. There is no promotion in most industries. We try to give the students a wider understand-

ing of industrial and social problems, and hope they will make some intelligent use of education in solving them. (*Opening Vistas* 209)

Democratic participation in administrative and curricular matters by faculty and students alike, a cornerstone of the workers' education movement, was much promoted by Smith, and, as previously pointed out, students had an equal vote on all governing committees (Smith, *Women Workers* 41). The policymaking Joint Administration Committee adopted the mission statement of the Summer School in 1923, according to which, the School was to provide

> young women in industry opportunities to study liberal subjects and to train themselves in clear thinking; to stimulate an active and continued interest in the problems of our economic order; to develop a desire for study as a means of understanding and of enjoyment in life. The School is not committed to any theory or dogma. The teaching is carried on by instructors who have an understanding of the students' practical experience in industry and of the labor movement. It is conducted in a spirit of impartial inquiry, with freedom of discussion and teaching. It is expected that thus the students will gain a truer insight into the problems of industry, and feel a more vital responsibility for their solution. (Smith, *Women Workers* 7)

Another formulation of Summer School aspirations was offered in a book on workers' pedagogy by Smith and Jean Carter, also a Summer School teacher who succeeded Smith as director. They wrote that

> the curriculum should afford the worker opportunity for (1) the discussion of current social and economic problems as a basis for intelligent action; (2) the building up of a background for these problems through material from the fields of economics, history, philosophy, ethics, literature, social psychology and science; (3) the attaining of greater proficiency in the use of English as a tool for understanding and expressing ideas accurately and effectively; (4) an appreciation of a richer life through the creative arts; (5) instruction in basic principles of mental and physical health with special attention to workers' problems. (16)

Students and faculty alike at the Summer School believed that education could be a catalyst for progressive social change, and over the years, through experimentation and constant debate, pedagogical principles and methods arose which, although continually evolving and being called into question, provided a general direction for the Summer School. The curriculum was critiqued and amended in response to students' suggestions and criticisms and faculty's perceptions of what worked and didn't work. However, one basic principle remained constant: Workers' own experiences should be central to their education. Regarding the importance of using workers' own lives as a starting point for intellectual inquiry, Smith and coeditor Carter contrast "learning" with "teaching."

> It may seem like an illogical arrangement of material, but . . . learning is strangely illogical. It is only teaching which aims to be logical and in so doing it often misses the necessary contact that results in learning. The contact must be with the experience of the worker and the starting point—logical or illogical—must be there. (Carter and Smith 25)

This meant first of all that student input was sought in developing a meaningful and effective curriculum. Students also had a strong voice in administrative decisions. Second, instructional materials and classroom activities focused on students' life experience, most typically their work experience. Abstractions and theory that did not clearly relate to workers' expressed needs were avoided. And third, the student-centered approach also meant that the largely middle-class faculty had to examine the lives of their working-class students and begin to see the world through their eyes. Instructors who were not able to undertake this educational journey into working-class ways were not encouraged to become teachers of workers. This requirement for faculty transformation was constantly stressed in articles and teaching manuals written by Bryn Mawr faculty members. In an article on "Workers Education in the United States," Smith writes unequivocally that being unable "to sympathize with the problems and outlook of wage earners is to fail as a teacher" (196).

In getting to know their students, faculty were advised to draw on the growing literature of worker education: The Workers Education Bureau was established in 1921 and began publishing books and pamphlets on teaching soon after; various journals existed on workers education; the Affiliated Summer Schools for Women Workers published teaching materials; and several statistical studies complied by students and faculty themselves were available. To learn more specifically and individually about their Bryn Mawr students, faculty studied the lengthy application forms submitted by each student as well as students' academic and psychological test results. Furthermore, an autobiography assignment that was regularly given to every student very early in the term provided faculty with more valuable insights (see chapter 3).

Faculty were also counseled not to be afraid of controversial issues. Carter and Smith write that

> Those teachers who are afraid of controversial topics in the classroom cannot be considered qualified for this field of teaching. . . . To exclude from the class-

room questions of burning importance in our economic world means that those who are interested in them must forego the educational value of systematic analysis. (27)

Furthermore, these master teachers recommended that a broad range of opinion be expressed unhindered by any form of censorship. They also felt that students had a right to know their teachers' beliefs on all issues and, therefore, a teacher must "state fairly his own point of view, as one among others in the group" (27). Other constants in the Bryn Mawr pedagogy included the use of discussion instead of lecture for classroom instruction and the rejection of a "coverage" model of education. In its place was a thematic, interdisciplinary, and collaborative approach to the construction and transmission of knowledge. For example, if the subject of current working conditions came up in class discussion, and students expressed a desire for more information, other disciplinary perspectives might be brought in by the teacher in collaboration with a faculty member specialized in history, literature, or psychology; also students and teachers might conduct their own research through surveys or reading material, thus constructing knowledge themselves.

The first five years at the Summer School was a period of great curricular experimentation, and while a general framework eventually evolved, the curriculum was continually reviewed, critiqued, and amended. Initially determined to provide the women with fact-filled survey courses to "fill in" their knowledge of the liberal arts, faculty offered "content-driven" courses in separate disciplines. Students were taught five or six independent subjects, each by a different instructor and a tutor. Not surprisingly, the working women complained about the confusing array of conflicting, overlapping, and sometimes irrelevant bits of information presented to them. Each year for the first few years, the curriculum was changed, and what evolved in its place was a thematically based, interdisciplinary core of courses that centered around a problem or area of industrial life that was often chosen by the students themselves after much class discussion. Once a central topic or problem was determined, it would be examined from two main disciplinary perspectives with supplemental information from a third. For example, if students decided to study wage determination in textile mills, an economic analysis would reveal working women's role in generating profit; a historical study might show how wages had evolved in the industry. Simultaneously, the worker student might be assigned fiction about work in the mills. All the material was coordinated by three collaborating instructors: one in social science—typically economics; one in English (to teach reading, writing, speaking, and listening in terms of the topic under study); and one in either science, history, or psychology, each instructor teaching a separate class.

In accordance with the prevailing faith in empirical and psychological evaluation, the students were tested in reading and other academic skills and grouped according to ability into five "units" of about twenty students. This design thus became known as the "Unit Plan." In 1933, for example, it was reported that the "language handicapped unit" would study "current economic problems, drawing as far as possible on their own local experience" (Herrmann 2). Lillian Herstein, the instructor quoted earlier, was happy with her Summer School teaching experience because, for one thing, she had only about forty-five students, far fewer than in the Chicago high schools where she typically taught five classes of thirty students each. "At the Summer School I taught the way I never have been able to teach since" (22). Herstein explains how she worked with the "language handicaps," the immigrant girls, to find writing topics. Sitting with each woman and engaging her in conversation, she would exclaim, "Now that's something you should write about. . . . first days at Ellis Island, or the first accident on the job" (22). Expressing pride in her students, Herstein boasts that the "language handicaps" had the most articles in the end-of-session magazine because they wrote so well. The second group or unit of students in the 1933 summer session studied "government questions"; the third studied the labor movement; the fourth analyzed "social reorganization schemes" (Herrmann 2). The fifth unit, consisting of the most highly qualified students, would conduct a collaborative statistical study with economics professor Amy Hewes. The faculty also worked one-on-one with each student for a portion of the week, and undergraduate assistants tutored the students and assisted faculty in all activities.

## A NEW WAY TO TEACH: DEVELOPING A MATERIALIST PEDAGOGY

A characteristic that seems unusual compared to many of today's educational endeavors is the consistent use of activities with a "material" dimension. A transformation from text to extratextual context often occurred as immaterial classroom discourse became materialized through action in a wider academic, political, or cultural context. Ideas, information, and opinion were often given a physical presence or actually embodied through plays and "living newspapers." As faculty and students enacted it, the pedagogy often included a movement from the textual to the material realm of collective action in the public arena, such as union drives or strikes for better pay. Former Bryn Mawr teacher and labor educator Alice Hanson put it succinctly: "workers' education . . . trains for action" (114). Over the years, innovations in this materialist pedagogy became permanent parts of the curriculum. Dramatics, or the transformation of immaterial text into embodied form, played a growing role at the Summer School, as will be seen in a later chapter. Also, as I will illustrate, much of the writing curriculum could be considered "materialist" in its frequent "real world" representations and interventions, such as the creation of "scrapbooks," "workshops in print," laboratory notebooks, statistical reports, and visual aids. Since much of this work was done collaboratively, a collective materialization of conception and production ensued, requiring negotiation over content and other rhetorical features as students planned their work together. Silent and solitary acts of writing were largely replaced with physical manifestations of thought and desire, from the page, through the group.

Another innovative curricular feature with a material dimension was the "Social Sciences Workshop," actually a project room equipped with supplies and paraphernalia for constructing sets, costumes, visual aids, and other dramatic or academic props. Working independently or in consultation with each other in the workshop, the women created charts and graphs for their economics class, drawings and maps to advance ideas in history, and other illustrative materials to accompany book reviews in English class. Several curricular reports mention a "Science Museum" or "Laboratory" where exhibits and artifacts of a scientific nature were created or displayed (Herrmann 2). Carter and Smith write that the "workshop makes it possible for [students] to work with their hands on tangible material and, through this process, make an idea or a figure become alive and meaningful" (28). The benefits of the workshop pedagogy were twofold: It was an enjoyable and satisfying way for workers to work together acquiring information and, secondly, it offered them an effective way to represent knowledge and present it to others; "to take in and give out," as one enthusiastic student quoted in Carter and Smith explained (28). Accounts of workshop activity can be found in the appendix to chapter 2.

### APPENDIX: REFLECTIONS ON THE BRYN MAWR SUMMER SCHOOL AND WORKERS' EDUCATION

**"An Open Letter"**
**Zarie Arslanian**
***Shop and School,* 1937**

Dear Fellow Members of the Amalgamated:
Perhaps you would be interested in the very important things that are going on here at the Bryn Mawr Summer School. In the first place, I want

you all to be better informed as to why the college has this course for women workers in industry. We, a group of 60 girls, representing four countries, which are the United States, England, Sweden and Czechoslovakia, are brought together here to discuss our economic problems, and to try to understand the different systems of government throughout the world today. I hadn't realized how important such a study could be. These girls also represent nine big industries, such as steel, iron, glass, rubber, aluminum, clothing, textiles, garment and thread making. Beside these big industries, there are many small ones represented. I, for instance, am the only one from the cleaners' and dyers' establishment, so I have to speak for all of you, and that, believe me, is a very big job.

I have begun to realize how fortunate we are in having a newly organized union. Really, its possibilities are unlimited. Since I have heard some of the reports from other girls and their unions, I have realized how fortunate we are in having so many closed shops in Springfield. It is rare in many other industries.

Hence, I want to stress how important it is that everyone of you take an active interest in what is going on in the union. Still further, it is very important that we all, as the workers of America, keep ourselves well informed as to the economic and political conditions of the world today. It is important if we want to keep democracy in America.

To continue with the explanation of this course at Bryn Mawr, I thought you would like to know what we are studying. First, we have English. In this study we have included parliamentary procedure and also how to run efficient union meetings. We are also doing a great deal of reading concerning the workingman's problems, both past and present. By finding out what has and has not worked in the past and by studying what processes labor groups have used, we hope to gain a clearer idea of how to get favorable conditions for workers everywhere.

Closely connecting with English, we have a very interesting class in Economics. This subject covers the field of the working conditions in many major industries. Here we come into contact with each other's problems—in our places of work and in our unions. We also read up and discuss the labor laws which are supposed to benefit the workers.

Beside these two subjects we have also a course in science. This study includes discussions in astronomy, geology, biology, physiology, and psychology. We try to get a clear understanding of science as regards our everyday life in work and in homes.

We, here at Bryn Mawr, are very fortunate in having many well known leaders speak to us. We recently had a speaker who should be of particular interest to you. He was Mr. Potofsky, who is the assistant president of the Amalgamated Clothing Workers of America. He gave a very clear and precise explanation of the activities of the C.I.O. and also of our union. Another speaker was Tom Tippett, who, once a mine worker, is now a writer of labor literature and an active labor leader. He gave us a very vivid picture of the conditions of the mine workers in the South. Other well known speakers were Madam Perkins, the Secretary of Labor, and Bob Watt, who represented the United States in the International Labor Conference.

In conclusion, I want to say again that it is very important that we stand together, united, in our fight against capitalist tyranny. We must demand Industrial Democracy.

### "Six Weeks' Gleanings"
**Florence Baker**
*Echoes of Bryn Mawr*, 1927

On June 17 I left Philadelphia for the Summer School at Bryn Mawr, with my luggage in my hand. I was so enthusiastic over setting out that I could hardly bear the excitement, and I was equally enthusiastic upon my arrival. My impression was of a castle instead of a school. The lawns were green and the grey buildings were covered with vines.

Several days later we started our classes. In classrooms and on campus, discussions went on consistently. It took me by surprise to find that most of the students knew almost nothing of the question which interests me most: the Negro problem. I discovered that few of the girls were aware of the fact that the Negro plays a vital part in the economic and historical life of America. It is important that they should understand this, and also that they should learn the value of the prose, poetry, and music created by the Negro race in America.

In many other ways, also, I found out how much there was to be learned; it all seemed rather complicated. At the same time I recognized the subjects taught as beneficial and could see no reason why our ideas should not be made much broader. Of my courses, science, English, and economic history, English has been most useful to me. I have learned how to express my opinions without getting nervous. Public Speaking is responsible for that. As for science, I can see the necessity for learning about the heavenly bodies and also I find it amusing to see a star and know in what group it belongs.

How I hate the coming of August 13, when I must leave my fellow students and return to work!

### "Before and After I Came to Bryn Mawr"
### Lillian Dominick
### *Shop and School,* 1936

During the week of June 8th I was bubbling with enthusiasm, because my application blank had been accepted by the Bryn Mawr Committee to attend the Bryn Mawr Summer School. I had received a letter saying to be on the campus grounds by Saturday, June 13th. My leaving Pittsburgh, Friday, June 12th, made it possible for me to arrive at the appointed time. On my way to school, I was overjoyed, but it seemed to me as I came nearer and nearer to Bryn Mawr, I began to get nervous. Different questions popped into my mind, such as these: What is the school like? Will I like it? Will it fit with my interest? Maybe I should have made further investigations. Then I thought to myself, "Whatever it is like, I can adjust myself to the situation."

Then came the first week of school. I was greatly disappointed, because all I could hear was, "What union do you belong to? Are you organized."

To me my class seemed like a bunch of conspirators against their bosses. Although I do admit frankly that I wasn't labor conscious, I was completely ignorant about the Labor Movement.

My next thought was, "How am I going to connect my line of work with labor organization, when I am supremely interested in Social Service Work?" It had never occurred to me that in order to be a successful Social Worker one should know and understand the problems which confront the working class of people.

Along with organization, I heard politics being discussed. My questions were then, "What is their political party?" "How do they vote?" Without doubt it couldn't be the Republican or Democratic party. I discovered that these people had not a single party as I thought but a number of parties. Among them were one or two Republicans, a few Democrats, no Fascists, some Nonpartisans, and a majority of Communist and Socialist sympathizers.

Even though my first few weeks were discouraging, I feel as though I have learned a great deal, and do have something to offer to this great Labor Movement.

### "Editorial"
### Helen D. Meltzer
### *Echoes of Bryn Mawr,* 1927

Now that we have studied at Bryn Mawr for seven weeks we approach the question, What has Bryn Mawr done for us?

First of all, through the study of industrial problems we have gained a knowledge of difficult problems that economics deals with, and through that knowledge we have a better understanding of how we might cope with them in the future. We have gained rather than one set of ideas, a great many of which we can judge for ourselves and from which we can choose.

We all came with some prejudices and these were of two kinds; prejudices against ideas and prejudices against people. To how many of us, for instance, was economics a living term before we came to Bryn Mawr? Certain people as well as terms seemed hateful to us. It is only by association of people and exchange of ideas and opinions that these prejudices have been partially eradicated. Is not that a step toward our progress?

Studying economics, we have realized our position as industrial workers and as such we have begun to understand how we can best attain the ideals for which we are striving.

We hope the greatest influence of the Bryn Mawr Summer School will be felt when the students have gone back to tackle their industrial, home and civic problems, stimulated with purpose and persistency and with greater ardor for their fellow men and women, to strengthen their educational forces.

### "When Students Turn Teachers"
### Margaret Morton
### *Shop and School,* 1931

When students turn teachers at the Bryn Mawr Summer School, as they often do, they teach not only from books but from personal experience. You can see student-teachers all along the campus trying to talk to other students about a point of view that seems important to them. We have also had student speakers at assembly and at Sunday meetings. Programs have been arranged along a particular topic and students have been the main orators.

We had first-hand news about the textile strikes from students who took part in them. Grace Elliott, who was very active at Marion, spoke dramatically and sincerely of how the strike affected her, and her family and the community at large. Clemmie Handy, a Danville girl, told of her experiences there. She gave us a picture of the terrible living conditions that brought on the strike.

Estelle Dye, a Negro girl at the Bryn Mawr Summer School, talked to us in assembly about the Scottsboro Case. She told her story very well and without bias. Eight Negro boys have been sentenced to die from an alleged assault on two white girls. It has been proven that the boys are not guilty, but due to racial prejudices and mob action in the South, the verdict was

"Guilty." The day before the execution was set aside by various organizations for a world-wide protest demonstration. At the end of Estelle's talk a motion was made and carried that the students and faculty of the school should send a telegram asking for a pardon for the boys.

There have been other occasions when groups of students have been the teachers at meetings. The forum of unemployment of July 4th, discussed in another article, was perhaps the most interesting of them. But there was another important meeting in which the students from various workers' schools described these institutions to all of us.

We met on Sunday evening at dusk. First we sang workers' school songs, not only of Bryn Mawr but those from workers' schools of the world. Then the speeches followed. Ellen Elving, from Denmark, told of the schools in her country, and Eva Anderson, from Sweden, told of the ones in her land. Mille Sample, who was an English student at Bryn Mawr last summer, told of the English system. The American schools were described by those that knew them at first hand. Tillie Plebanek, who is at Bryn Mawr this summer, spoke of her experiences at Wisconsin last summer. Grace Elliott, Clemmie Handy and Mattie Bell Woods spoke of the Southern School. Freda Daum and Fannie Zinkoff told us about Bernard. Other students discussed the programs at workers' winter schools. Mary Koken, who now runs our cooperative store, discussed Brookwood; and Ellen Elving, the school at Vineyard Shore.

At the Women's Trade Union League conference, which was held on July 17th, the girls of Bryn Mawr told of what unemployment had meant to the workers. Mildred Miles, Estelle Dye, Sarah Greenspoon, Nora Quimatte, and Constance Hopkins spoke. All phases of unemployment and its effects were covered by the girls in the few moments of their talks. I doubt if our most expert economists could have done a better job in such a short time.

We expect at least two more students forums. The first on "The Need for Independent Political Action for Workers," and the second on "Looking Forward—What Can I Do When I Go Home?"

### "The Household Employees Come into Their Own or Household Employees Succeed at Bryn Mawr"
### Irene Rhones
### *Shop and School,* 1937

Now, for the first time, there is to be a National Committee of Household Workers. At the Bryn Mawr Summer School this year nine Household Employees were admitted as regular students as a result of recommendations passed by last year's students.

We were here on a trial basis to see if Household Employees had a place in this school along with industrial girls. Four afternoons a week we met in a group to discuss problems in Household Employment and devise plans for the possible solution of these problems. We discussed standards, legislation, education and organization from the standpoint of Household Employment, until we felt we had amassed sufficient information to act upon.

Now the problem was how to get started. Each girl told of groups or organizations in her city with which it might be possible to work. We all expressed the necessity of keeping in touch and informing one another of the success of our undertakings. Then just as naturally arose the idea of a National Committee for Household Employees. The idea sounded good to us, for we felt that before anything could be done, these employees themselves must be conscious enough of their needs to band together on a national scale and work for the improvement of their conditions.

We discussed at length what we should be called, where we would set the committee up and just what it would do. So that we wouldn't be confused with the National Committee on Household Employment, we decided to call ourselves the National Committee of Household Workers. Cincinnati seemed to be the most fertile ground for its beginning, and Fern Dunkin the best available and most capable to start it going. She is to be called Chairman of the committee. Each member of the Household Discussion Group will be a member of this National Committee. These members, scattered throughout the country, will send in all information pertaining to their local situation. From these reports, the National Committee will send out a monthly news letter of the latest developments in Household Employment all over the country and anything else of interest to workers. In this way, it will act as a coordinating body of Household Employment information this year with the end in view of increasing its influence and power as time goes on.

We feel that if this plan is successful, Household workers will have a medium through which to work more adequately for the attainment of their aims.

We feel, also, that after seven weeks at the Bryn Mawr School, the Household Workers have demonstrated how closely linked they are with industrial girls, and that they rightly have a place with them at the Summer School in the future.

**"Use It or Lose It"**
**Beatrice Van Duvall**
*Shop and School,* **1931**

Far upon the side of a mountain a stream of clear water ran riotously here and there until it finally reached the ocean. For thousands of years the water in the mountain stream was wasted. One day man had a vision; he saw the opportunity to use this water. Filters and conduits were built and now this water that was once wasted is piped and used by people in the valleys.

Man harnessed and checked this waste of water; so also, there is an opportunity for me to help the difficulties of the working people. I first realized the seriousness of the problem that faced the working people at the Sacramento Y.W.C.A. Convention. Often in our Industrial Girls' Club in Denver we would talk of our work, of how arduous it was, of how some of us received so little pay, although we worked harder than others who received good pay. We were told that white girls refused to work with Negro girls.

It was then that we started a real study of our work, keeping a record of everything we did in one week. The result was that some girls were working fourteen and fifteen hours a day, others working even longer. Other Y.W.C.A. Industrial Girls' Clubs were studying the same difficulties of household employees and presented their round table discussion of real facts. Here again I found out that the white girls in different areas were facing the same problems of hours, of wages, of living conditions, and of accidents and ill health while working. I then realized that here was an opportunity. Should I use it or lose it?

I see the need of organization especially of the Negro people. I feel the need of standardization of domestic work, the cooperation of all girls regardless of race.

I applied for a scholarship to Brookwood Labor College. The chairman of the faculty suggested that I attend Bryn Mawr Summer School before coming to Brookwood.

I hope through my contact with Bryn Mawr this summer and Brookwood this winter to be better fitted to use this great opportunity of trying to make people see the need of organization and especially the need of standardizing household employment. Here then is my opportunity. Shall I lose it as man lost the water for thousands of years? Or shall I, since I have caught the vision, use it?

### "The Heart and Soul of the People"
**Margaret Walsh**
*Bryn Mawr Echoes,* 1927

Bryn Mawr, you have fulfilled your promise to me. You have done your work and you have done it very well. You have given your all and have asked for nothing in return. Hope, you have again placed within me and in true modesty you say you would do more. Yes! You would do more; you would give as you have always given because—well, because you are Bryn Mawr.

To me you have given hope—a thing that for years lay dead within me. You have shown me a new road, one that in the past was covered with clouds of doubt; and you have given me the only thing that can break down barriers, send forth light, or bring true happiness—knowledge.

All this you have given to me. Why? Because you have a soul, a soul that is made of truth; a soul that sees the needs of others—and more; a soul that actually gives to others. You have a heart, the kind that beats with the hearts of us the workers, and you are—I know now—you are the workers. The workers' life, the workers' hope, the workers' chance of salvation. I know you now as a worker. You stand for us, within us; your hand is clasped with ours. Your end is our end; the end that will show us, the masses, how to see, how to listen, and—the finest thing of all—how to give. Through you we will give to others; we will give as never before, we will give without taking. Your soul has entered into us, your heart begins to beat within us and you have won. You have gained your end.

# Composition Instruction, Labor Education, and Bryn Mawr Materialist Writing Pedagogy

## 2

It has been argued that English composition would be of no use to the worker after leaving the school. We came here to study industrial problems and not to become writers. It is true we are here to study industrial problems but we have had industrial experiences which are an important contribution to the studying and to the solution of industrial problems. If, however, we do not know how to express ourselves and make known to others our experiences, they will be of no use. An economic textbook can explain the theory of the piece work system; but we who work in industry can make a valuable contribution to the theoretical discussion. Not all of us can get up before an audience and tell our experiences, but some people can write them a great deal better than tell about them.

Thus, we can see how the course in English composition does aid in carrying out the purpose of the Bryn Mawr Summer School by teaching us to express ourselves in writing which in turn helps us to think more clearly, and to speak more effectively.

—Ida Ritter, *Bryn Mawr Light*, 1925

Writing instruction at the Bryn Mawr Summer School presents a unique combination of pedagogical techniques and theories that were developing in the mainstream educational community of the times as well as in less conventional worker education projects. Histories of composition instruction have begun to show that many of the innovations attributed to the process approach over the last thirty years were actually "recycled" methodologies with a much longer history. It now appears that even though many of these techniques had disappeared from the central focus of composition instruction during the long reign of current-traditional rhetoric, they lived on in the repertoire of faculty at many institutions and were recorded mostly in sources other than textbooks, such as syllabi, lesson plans, journal articles, and professional books (Berlin; Connors; Holt; Kates; Russell, "Writing"; Varnum). Thus, at the Bryn Mawr Summer School of the 1920s and 1930s, we find numerous approaches that were later rediscovered as innovations of the "process movement": peer critique and collaboration, guided revision, assignments that link personal experience with work or academic disciplines, student publications, team teaching by faculty from diverse disciplines, and assignments that encourage students to see aspects of their experience as problems that can be resolved, similar to the "anti-banking" and "problem-posing" approach advocated by Paulo Freire.

What was different about the curriculum at the Summer School is how explicitly instructional materials related to students' lives; for example, almost all text used to teach writing was student-generated; writing topics came from students' work lives; and literature featured working people, their problems and successes. Other disciplines such as economics, psychology, and history were also treated from the worker's vantage point. This focus on material culture was to shape the entire educational project at the Summer School.

Jim Berlin's work presents a historical and theoretical context for understanding the Summer School project. In his chronicle of twentieth-century composition instruction in U.S. colleges and universities, Berlin maintains that current-traditional rhetoric prevailed in most writing classrooms, then as now (58). At the Summer School, however, this approach was largely, but not completely, rejected. Richard Young's six-part definition of current-traditional rhetoric provides useful criteria for evaluating Summer School writing pedagogy in this regard (31). Young maintains that current-traditional rhetoric places an "emphasis on the composed product rather than the composing process," and secondly, that it stresses "the classification of discourse into description, narration, exposition, and argument" (31). As will be seen below, students at the Summer School practiced a process approach to writing. They developed topics for writing in class discussions, they went over rough drafts with their instructor and tutors, and they collaborated with other women workers on writing projects. They also wrote a wide variety of genres, such as autobiographical essays, narratives of factory work, poetry, labor drama, and collaborative statistical reports. I found nothing to indicate that these genres were presented or discussed in terms of traditional modes. And while discourse may have been broken down for study by some Summer School instructors "into words, sentences and paragraphs," as Young ascribes to current-traditional rhetoric, this type of analysis almost always took place in the context of a student essay.

Young's fourth characteristic, a "strong concern with usage (syntax, spelling, punctuation)" (31) was solidly in place at the Summer School, although it did not predominate in writing instruction. Teachers and students alike believed that public writing demanded correctness, and students often voiced concern about their "English," worrying that their nonstandard grammar and spelling would ruin their chances of being taken seriously by a wider audience. To respond to this concern, standard written and spoken English became the goal for women workers, and English faculty taught mechanics and usage conventions through student writing. Even though the work of sociolinguists and descriptive grammarians done in the 1930s called for a contextual understanding of correctness issues rather than predetermined, fixed standards (Berlin 89), I uncovered no critique of standards by faculty or students. However, students were to master English through prose writing, not decontextualized grammar drills; I found no workbook-like materials nor any mention of punctuation drills in my review of curricular materials. Nor were students furnished with grammar handbooks, although a few such titles did appear on suggested reading lists given to students at the end of the summer sessions (see chapter 5 as well as the third note for that chapter).

As for Young's fifth characteristic, a strong "concern with style, economy, clarity, emphasis," I found only a focus on "clarity." The native-English-speaking women wrote in a straightforward style, characterized by "economy" and "emphasis." As for the nonnative speakers, their needs were more fundamental in terms of grammar and syntax, making clarity of primary importance. The main objective was that these women be understood and their ideas communicated in a way that would gain respect. Finally, faculty at the Summer School did teach Young's final current-traditional component, "the informal essay and research paper"; however, these papers were modified for Summer School students' needs. "Informal essays" became autobiographies or work narratives, and "research papers" became personal testimonies, student surveys, or collaborative statistical reports.

Indeed, Summer School teaching and writing went well beyond current-traditional rhetoric, and Berlin's overarching theoretical schema and history provide a useful framework for examining the wide scope of Summer School writing. In his catalogue of rhetorics that dominated the American scene over the twentieth century, the subjective/expressionistic and social/transactive rhetorics characterized the 1920s and 1930s. These rhetorics also shaped writing instruction at the Summer School. In Berlin's words,

> Although current-traditional rhetoric continued to be the most common approach in the college classroom, it was rivaled during the prosperous twenties by the appearance of a subjective rhetoric that celebrated the individual. This

rhetoric persisted through the thirties but was itself challenged by transactional
approaches that emphasized the social nature of human experience. (58)

This challenge came before the 1930s at the Summer School, where even at
its founding in 1921, a collective, social approach superseded the subjective,
individualist rhetoric that was a part of certain progressive educational agendas. The progressive philosophy of education held that human institutions
and character could be shaped in schools for the betterment of society as a
whole. Educational objectives were broad, aiming to improve democratic
government by teaching citizens to serve the common good while valuing
individual differences (Berlin 59). Progressive educators also put faith in the
findings of social scientists and frequently used empirical measurements of
aptitude, ability, and personality in an attempt to meet individual needs in
college courses. According to Berlin, progressive education was at once "psy-
chological/individualistic" and "social/communal," with the 1920s tending
toward the former and the 1930s the latter (60). Berlin points out that John
Dewey's work synthesized these two inclinations through an emphasis on
students' life experience—this synthesis undoubtedly influenced the student-centered curriculum during both decades at the Summer School (60).

Berlin credits another nationwide educational trend, the turn toward
expressionist rhetoric, for the tremendous growth in poetry and creative
writing courses in colleges and universities during the 1920s and 1930s (79).
Those expressionist educators with a more democratic bent assumed that
any student could write poetry, not only the literary genius. In mainstream
classrooms, the expressionist rhetoric encouraged students to find "truth"
in terms of their own individualistic vision and to express that truth in creative, original ways. As will be seen in chapters 5 and 6, the women workers
at the Summer School also had a passion for poetry, so much so that they
met with faculty after their regular classes to read and write verses, which
were published in their annual *Shop and School* magazines. But Summer
School poetry was not the introspective churnings of an individual consciousness expressing a unique vision. For the most part, the working
women's poetry voiced, in very specific and material terms, a collective desire for a better life.

Berlin's examples from the 1930s of freshman writing programs built on
rhetorics that address the "social problems caused by the country's economic failure" resemble the Summer School's focus on the material culture
of work and politics. These social rhetorics were described in *English Journal* articles by instructors at various colleges and universities across the
nation. Berlin cites one such instructor who had students find writing top-

ics from lively class discussions of current, controversial issues; another required students to write essays on "multiplying functions of government in the domain of economy, health, safety, education and cultural development" as these related to the students' local community (85). A similar wide-reaching course had students at Florida State College for Women write twelve essays over the semester critiquing their hometowns in social, political, and economic terms. To Berlin, the most significant example was Warren Taylor's freshman composition course at Wisconsin, which prepared students "to serve the political role of the individual in a democratic state" (86). Students were trained to critique arguments, find truth, and recommend actions that would solve social problems, creating a rhetoric of public discourse (86).

As will be seen, writing as taught at the Summer School included projects almost identical to the three cited above. What makes the Summer School pedagogy unique is its focus on working-class women. Also, the Summer School pedagogy goes further than any program described by Berlin in social/transactive dimensions. The working women used writing to remake their discursive selves, forging new and more powerful "real world" identities in the process. Their foray into public writing and publishing, as will be described below, was a powerful rhetorical move not often seen in higher education, even today. This recognition of the importance of writing in the public world of work and politics links the Summer School to another educational agenda. The effort to educate workers by nonacademic organizations such as unions, radical political groups, community groups, and religious groups anticipated the Summer School's transformative, materialist pedagogy.

### THE BRYN MAWR SUMMER SCHOOL AND
### THE WORKERS' EDUCATION MOVEMENT

The Summer School's practice corresponds to trends noted in the history of American worker education. Two main pedagogical tendencies can be observed in the effort to educate working people (Altenbaugh; Berlanger and Strom). One approach, characterized as practical, individualist, and vocational, teaches workers basic literacy skills, job-specific writing, or how to write and file a union grievance. The other educational approach advocates a broader, more comprehensive curriculum that introduces workers to the liberal arts, such as philosophy, literature, social sciences, and labor economics to provide them with a wide knowledge base from which to understand and critique their place in society. This approach also aspires to add an aesthetic dimension to workers' lives and often results in a radical curriculum, allied with leftist political ideology, sometimes even calling for a workers' state and culture.

A brief review of worker education in the nineteenth and twentieth centuries shows the ebb and flow of these tendencies. Kelly Berlanger and Linda Strom write that the earliest forms of worker education, the mechanics institutes of the 1820s and 1830s, were conservative and reinforced traditional American goals of "self-improvement and social mobility" (viii). Anne Ruggles Gere stresses that the working-class women's clubs of the late nineteenth and early twentieth centuries had similar aims but also used their publication, the *Club Worker,* to campaign for better living and working conditions (235). Continuing this shift towards a broader and more political curriculum, the 1920s and 1930s saw the development of residential and nonresidential colleges for workers, independent of mainstream educational institutions. The Bryn Mawr Summer School was one such institution, although its ties to Bryn Mawr College were apparent in terms of physical plant, indirect funding, administrative personel, and even its liberal arts curriculum. Regular Bryn Mawr faculty, however, were expressly prohibited from teaching at the Summer School. A return to vocationalism and utilitarian basic skills was to occur in the 1940s and 1950s, while contemporary education projects run by unions and university-based labor education programs have included both practical and critical approaches. Of course, conservative forces through the twentieth century have feared the second, more progressive tendency and preferred a more depoliticized education for workers. In 1937, such fear led the conservative leadership of the American Federation of Labor to turn its back on Brookwood College, the most radical of the labor colleges. Soon after, trustees at Bryn Mawr withdrew their support for the Summer School, dedicated as it was to the development of a working class that could speak, write, and think for itself at work and in the wider public arena.

## TEACHING WRITING AT THE BRYN MAWR SUMMER SCHOOL

As has been shown, many of the trends and tendencies shaping teaching and learning at the Bryn Mawr Summer School were located in the intellectual and political context of the age, including the thinking and practice in mainstream university pedagogy as well as the workers' education movement. Summer School faculty and students placed their particular stamp on these tendencies by creating a materialist pedagogy tailored to the needs of working-class women. However, practitioners of this pedagogy were careful to warn against merely copying techniques developed at the Summer School for use at other educational sites. Again and again, they caution against full scale adoption of lessons or curricula. They advise other workers' education programs to develop their own particular teaching techniques, adapting pedagogical activities to the specific working women and men involved, their industry, geographic location, and other characterizing factors.

Nevertheless, because the need for ideas and information on workers' education was great, several faculty did write books about the way women learned at the Summer School. Carter and Smith begin their suggestions for teaching writing to workers with recommendations that were commonplace among Summer School faculty: "It is wise in writing [instruction] to draw upon the workers' own background for subject matter or to correlate his writing for English class with what he is doing in other classes" (41). The authors emphasize the importance of a very thorough understanding of the worker students and their skills, interests, and needs. Typically, Carter and Smith point out, a group of workers will include a wide range of abilities. Some students will lack formal education; others may be fairly well educated but unable to speak English. Therefore, much elementary work will need to be done in "spelling, punctuation and sentence structure" while at the same time emphasizing effective communication in terms of influencing listeners and readers (41). Carter and Smith assert that traditional textbooks have little relevance for workers. Sometimes the material is classist as in the prompt that asks students to write about what they would do with $1,000; often times the tone and content is insultingly childish (31). The authors recommend that a class begin with a wide-ranging discussion of what "English" is, helping the students determine what they want to learn (38). Material for the course should be based on this discussion. Smith and Carter find that worker students want to be able to speak and write effectively about the social and economic conditions that influence their lives, but they also yearn to understand, appreciate, and even participate in more profound social and philosophical questioning as well as in the creation of art and literature (59).

In her 1929 account of Summer School writing, Smith notes that "Usually one paper is assigned to be written each week . . . , and many individual conferences are given" (*Women Workers* 83). She reports that some classes concentrate on the "study of the word with daily drills or tests on vocabulary and definitions, or word combinations" (83). In other classes, the "unity of the theme" has been a focus for writing or speaking. She mentions that student themes are mimeographed and distributed in class for study and that short themes are sometimes written in class. Repeatedly, she emphasizes that "life experience and the special interests of the students" are the best areas for finding subject matter for writing or speaking (83), and she provides a list of typical essays/speech topics:

Unemployment evils
Housing problems in New York City
Time work and piece work
Government ownership of coal mines
Married women in industry (84)

Examples of student essays can be found in the appendix to this chapter.

In her *Monograph on Methods of Teaching English to Workers' Classes,* written in 1931 and cited by many other educators of the time, Olga Law Plunder also emphasizes the importance of teaching from students' personal experience because of the added motivation it may bring: The student "wants to learn because his learning has brought him to a point where for him learning is the necessary and logical next step. And so his learning many not be separated from his experience" (3). Although Plunder also resists providing a plan for all workers classes, cautioning her readers to adapt her suggestions for their specific needs, she nevertheless provides a rough model for examining the writing process from whole to part then part to whole. She advises that "exercise material for the study of structure and of grammar can be taken from [students'] own writing" (5). By way of illustration, Plunder describes a class taught by an unnamed teacher at the Bryn Mawr Summer School who first instructs students to do a "free writing" (her term) on a choice of subjects including "A Critical Moment" and "A First Impression" (7). The teacher collects these paragraphs and begins the next class with a discussion of very basic questions: "How does one recognize a paragraph, and why is writing divided into units of this kind?" (7). Students are then asked to summarize in one sentence a paragraph about "The Shrinking Week and the Growing Wage." According to Plunder and other worker educators, students need practice in discussing and describing what they read to reinforce understanding. Again, based on their own sentences, students draw rhetorical conclusions about other standard features of paragraphs such as the use of topic sentences and methods of development (9). The fact that paragraphs are parts of a larger whole and must relate to this whole through transitions is pointed out; then Plunder has groups of students critique a number of successful and not so successful sentences taken from paragraphs written earlier. Plunder gives the following examples from student prose:

1. Progress is achievement, for the working class it would mean a better way of living and a better way of living would be to produce our requirement of food, shelter and clothing, and leave enough time that we may paint pictures or climb mountains or go to the movies or anything else that may please us in our non-economic hours.

2. But as yet these wonderful achievements are merely the result of some-one to commercialize some new invention. (10–11)

Next, a selection of topic sentences from previously written student para-graphs are read to the class. Here are Plunder's examples:

At first the noise terrified me.

I found my thoughts were working much faster than my machine.

On a beautiful June day I was out in quest of a new job.

A most important moment to me was the time I decided to come to Bryn Mawr Summer School.

The opening exercises gave new meaning and light to our responsibilities. (9)

After discussing the topic sentences and corresponding paragraphs, students participate in summarizing what they have learned. Later these summaries could be mimeographed for the students. Another interdisciplinary exercise that Plunder cites as helpful for worker students' involves their compiling a "master" outline for a course they are taking. For example, students might take notes in their economics class and then outline these notes in their En-glish class. In the following English class, these outlines are combined into a master outline which is mimeographed for each student. Other techniques recommended by Plunder have students outline essays they have written, discuss articles in class to gage comprehension, and define words commonly misused (11–12).

In another frequently cited book of the day, Jean Carter's *Mastering the Tools of the Trade: Suggestive Material for Experimental Use in the Teach-ing of English in Workers' Classes,* 1932, the tentativeness expressed in the title again reflects the reluctance to prescribe. The preface warns that the book is not to be considered a "standardized text" that will serve all classes equally well (3). "This is suggestive material—not *the* material" (3). The essential "tools" that Carter advocates are "the ability to understand others," which includes reading and listening, and "the ability to express oneself" which includes speaking and writing—recognizable goals of the "Communications movement," which Berlin has located in the 1940s (92–119). Chapters ex-plaining techniques for each of these "tools" are provided along with infor-mation on "Conducting a Meeting" and teaching with "Group Discussion."

Carter's last chapter is devoted to writing that she explains "can serve various purposes since some people only write to communicate, and others write to express their experiences and emotions in poems, plays or stories" (37). Carter begins with an emphasis on meaning and words, "as [words] are the fundamental tools" (37). She includes a study of precision in word usage followed by a discussion of connotation, using the word "radical" as an example. She too warns against studying arbitrary lists of words but advises students to create lists from their own mistakes. Next she turns to punctuation, stating simply that "it is necessary to use enough punctuation to make people understand what you mean" (38). Here is the example Carter uses to stress the importance of punctuation and its relationship to meaning; she has students compare the two poems:

> A working girl told this to me:
> "I joined the union unfortunately.
> I told the boss one day at three.
> The shop walked out at his decree.
> The scabs were brought by girls like me.
> The strike was won on bended knee . . ."

> A working girl told this to me:
> "I joined the union. Unfortunately
> I told the boss. One day at three
> The shop walked out. At his decree
> The scabs were brought. By girls like me
> The strike was won. On bended knee . . ." (39)

Other sections in her book are on taking notes, conducting a meeting using parliamentary procedure, and writing for the labor press, skills of much value to workers. She advises potential newspaper writers "to be brief, avoid drawing moral lessons for readers, put the biggest news in the first sentence following with details, and add a human interest" element (41). Carter's book includes several appendices: lists of reference books on writing and grammar, works of fiction, and an evaluation form asking for feedback from students and teachers. And like Plunder's book, Carter's is filled with examples of workers' beliefs and attitudes about the grammar and rhetoric she discusses. Carter tries to build self-confidence by showing workers what they actually know about writing or speaking and then teaching them how to find out what they do not know. An interview with Jean Carter written by a Summer School student is included in the appendix following this chapter.

### Cross-Curricular Writing Projects: Making "Scrapbooks"

A very successful and widely adopted pedagogical tool was begun by Gladys Palmer and her students in the "Trade Union Problems" unit of 1930. Again, as a way to give immaterial text a more material dimension and purpose, students compiled what Palmer called a "scrapbook," collecting and writing about their first-hand experiences at work: hardships on the factory floor, efforts at unionization, working to improve relationships with coworkers and supervisors. Twenty authors were included in the fifty-three page booklet, with articles averaging two single-spaced, typed pages each. The scrapbooks were mimeographed by the Affiliated Summer Schools, the umbrella organization of labor schools, and sold to labor groups for fifty cents. Each student also got a copy. In the foreword, Eleanor Coit, the Educational Secretary of the Affiliated Summer Schools, remarks that the booklet offered a method for other worker education groups as well as information that may be useful to others. Typically, however, she warns that the "value of the pamphlet lies partly in the information it contains. [But] It has greatest value in suggesting ways in which groups in many cities may analyze their *own* [italics mine] problems."

Palmer, an economist at the Wharton School, University of Pennsylvania, describes how the project got started in the introduction to the 1930 scrapbook. Each woman first orally shared with the class her own personal working experience, whether as a member of the International Ladies Garment Workers Union or as an unorganized woman from the textile trades. From these introductions, larger questions evolved leading to research about the history of the labor movement, its economic context, and different trade union philosophies and strategies. Since work was coordinated with the English class, reports on these topics were written for both the English and Economics instructors (1). "As far as possible, each student was assigned reports and special reading on the history of her own union or . . . trade" (1). This particular scrapbook focused on the textile and needle trades unions since these groups were well represented among the students, and these industries were "the most important women's trades" (1). The classes were supplemented by speakers from labor and industry as well as student speakers from the Brookwood Labor College. Many of these speeches were also included in the scrapbook along with a bibliography of pertinent readings. Palmer cautions, however, that the scrapbook is far from a complete representation of classwork. No class discussion was recorded, and space limitations only permitted printing one report from every student. Palmer concludes: "It is the hope of the editor that these [reports] may be found useful for other workers' classes interested in these problems, and that out of a series of similar projects there may be built a worker's text on the labor movement" (2).

This first *Scrapbook* was divided into three sections: "Typical Problems Facing Trade Unions Today," "The Background of the American Labor

Movement," and "How Unions Function." Selected essay titles read: "Women Workers in New England 1825–1860," "The Earliest Organization of Tailoresses and Seamstresses," "Origin of Collective Bargaining in the U.S.," and "The Problem of the Negro Worker 1860–1870."

A later scrapbook created in 1931 reflected different student needs and interests. Since students focused on workplace problems in their hometowns, the reports were organized by geographic region with each report placed in the historical context of the labor movement. This scrapbook contained six sections: "The South," "New England," "The Middle Eastern States," "The West," "The Rise of the Labor Movement," and a bibliography of recommended readings. Within the geographic sections were thirty-four articles from one to three pages long organized chronologically with the first article of each section providing the historical background for the labor situation in the area. Thus the articles move from "The West Virginia Coal Miner's Strike," "Early Factory Conditions in New England," and "The Full Fashioned Hosiery Industry in Philadelphia," to "The Great Pullman Strike," "The Colorado Coal Strikes," the "Origin of Collective Bargaining in the United States," and "The Rise of Left Wing Unionism in the United States."

Another scrapbook was produced in 1932 in the "Trade Union Problems Unit" taught by Bill Fincke, Tillie Lindsay, and Gladys Palmer. A full fifty-seven pages long, it was divided into four sections: "How a Union Works" (six articles), "Shop Conditions" (seven articles), "Group Action" (six articles), and "Individual Recollections" (five articles). The 1933 scrapbook was similarly arranged. Thirty-two pages long, the scrapbook contained three sections: "The Shop" (eight articles), "The Union" (six articles), and "Other Experiences of Workers" (six articles). An article from the 1932 scrapbook appears in the appendix that follows.

**Writing in the Disciplines: "Laboratory Notebooks"**

In her syllabus from 1922, we see that Amy Hewes, a well-known professor of economics at Mount Holyoke, helped her students compile statistical reports from data gathered by questioning and surveying each other. Hewes required that students use notebooks for recording information derived from the surveys and statistical research. She carefully describes how data was to be written down in the "loose-leaf notebooks" on 8½ x 11" paper. Her system sounds a bit like the more recent "double entry journaling" technique: "Descriptions, explanations, and analyses should be written on the right-hand page facing the tables or graphs entered on the left hand page" (1). Stressing the importance of visual components, she also gives advice on titles and other headings used with graphs or tables. They should be as short as possible, she advises, without sacrificing clarity; they should be in "Roman letters rather than script," and the importance of the material should correspond to the size of the lettering. Students should "leave abundant room for headings because cramped titles spoil the appearance of any table" (1). One of the projects her students worked on concerned their work life. They devised sampling questions regarding type and place of employment, length of time employed, periods of unemployment, and reasons for going to work (2). Answers to these questions were compiled into statistical reports.

### Writing in the Disciplines: Collaborative Statistical Studies

Information recorded in the laboratory notebooks was eventually used in the most impressive and far-reaching publishing project developed by Summer School faculty—the collaborative studies done by Hewes's "Advanced Unit." In compiling the reports, students learned writing and reporting skills as well as basic statistical and sampling techniques; they also made a contribution to the developing field of industrial research, and most importantly, provided the nation with a glimpse into the difficult lives of working women. Hewes's friendship with Frances Perkins, and others at the Department of Labor, may have led to these studies being issued as "Bulletins" by the Women's Bureau. Titles included *The First Job* (1922), *Women Workers and Family Support* (1925), *Changing Jobs* (1926), *Women Workers in the Third Year of the Depression* (1933), and *Women Workers and the N.R.A.* (1934). *The Savings of Women Workers* (1927), for example, began by a question raised in class: "Can young women in industry . . . save at a rate high enough to enable them to look forward to the years to come without harassing anxiety?" With this driving question, the women workers secured the cooperation of all 102 students in the school and conducted a statistical survey that concluded that "the future of women workers is one of great uncertainty" (7).

Returning to Smith's account of Summer School teaching, she provides only brief comments about writing assignments in classes besides English, although syllabi reveal that writing took place in them all. In describing how economics was taught by one instructor, Smith mentions "short papers written in class, blackboard summaries and outlines" (*Women Workers* 87). She adds that sometimes a class is divided into small groups to discuss a particularly difficult problem, each with a secretary to take notes and report back to the larger group. These reports are in turn discussed until a general consensus or solution is hammered out (87). In history sections, Smith remarks that the bulk of the course is taught through "lecture and discussion with occasional papers being assigned; very little reading is given," perhaps due to the heavy reading requirement in English classes (86).

## DIVERGENCE FROM CURRENT-TRADITIONAL RHETORIC

Turning again to the issues of composition history raised at the beginning of this chapter, it is clear that the techniques of guided revision, teaching grammar in the context of student discourse, and student-derived essay topics based on personal experience and interests, for example, have been long-standing practices. Furthermore, while none of these techniques would likely have been discovered from an examination of textbooks used at the Summer School, Robin Varnum's criticism (40) of the work of Jim Berlin and others is not supported here. Varnum objects to their characterization of "the first three decades of the twentieth century as a period during which current-traditional rhetoric went virtually unchallenged" (40). I do not believe that Summer School pedagogy refutes this claim. Indeed, it is readily apparent that the Summer School educators knew their pedagogy was unusual and went against the grain of the prevailing current-traditional wisdom. They published extensively to introduce others to their methods in worker education and carefully pointed out in these articles their differences with more traditional approaches. In the introduction to the Carter and Smith book for example, Eleanor Coit writes that "A specialized need was seen for a pamphlet such as this, which will interpret to the new group of educators interested in this workers' education field, the methods, techniques of teaching, and aims of the Workers Education Movement" (4). Plunder frames the situation this way: "The worker thus comes at studying with an equipment and an aim that is unlike that of other students" (2). Finally, in the preface to an issue on workers' education published as the "Fifth Yearbook of the John Dewey Society," Theodore Brameld declares that "workers' education . . . has arisen almost wholly outside, even unknownst to, most established institutions of learning" (vi). What took place at the Bryn Mawr Summer School was no doubt an extension of a progressive, democratic educational practice with complex roots, but its basic philosophy and design was at odds with the conventional writing instruction of the times. The extent of its divergence will be clear in the chapters that follow.

## A SUMMER SCHOOL LEGACY: MATERIALIST PEDAGOGY

Of the many ways Summer School teaching and writing may relate to our pedagogical thinking today, one of the most significant is in its materialist response to the post-process critique of decontextualized academic writing.

Indeed, nearly every aspect of Summer School pedagogy was imbued with a materialist specificity in traditional rhetorical terms of subject matter, purpose, writer, and audience. The "material world" loomed large in each area because the ultimate goal of faculty and students was to change it. They longed to transform the oppressive factory conditions that bent backs and strained eyes, to alter the social dynamic that erased working women from public discourse, to reshape the urban landscape, pock-marked by smoke stacks and gray industrial "parks." In almost every piece of text produced by the women workers, the material world provided the impetus for thinking, writing, criticism, and action. Summer School text materialized in empowering ways: in dramatic performances, in school-based and extracurricular political action, in publications for local and national distribution. Through a dialectic of self (re)presentation and action, students constructed new subjectivities in their writing and began to enact more powerful social roles. Thus, student writing acquired material dimensions as it led to change in the political world, and in turn the students' increased feelings of agency and empowerment led to more critical writing.

Much of their education at the Summer School was meant to launch students into the public sphere. They were encouraged to take part in progressive organizations, the labor movement, the pacifist movement, and the consumer movement, and to step into the public realm of political activity. As Susan Kates has written referring to a similar pedagogy practiced at Brookwood Labor College, "the instruction these teachers extended to students was often 'extracurricular'; that is to say, it reached beyond their respective institutions to students [and others] outside the academic institutions in which they were taught" (xiii). It was understood that the eight-week Summer School interlude was in preparation for more difficult work ahead. As we have seen, the women often wrote about the sadness and anger they felt at returning to the working world all too soon. The Summer School offered a self-consciously situated space, an energizing retreat, explicitly located historically and socially, where women workers could learn about their place in the monopoly capitalism of the age and plan a response to this oppressive system. Almost all text the women workers consumed and produced was critical of social relations and pointed to the time in which they would go back to their jobs and unions and work for social change.

In the protected space of the Summer School, women developed new textual identities through imagining and then writing themselves into more powerful social roles. They tried these stronger identities out at the Summer School. When worker students voiced their ambition to be a part of the curricular and administrative governing groups at the school, they were accorded half the representative power on these supervisory bodies. Students then pushed through many significant changes in courses taught, admissions policies, faculty selection, guest speakers, field trips, and more. Thus their transformation of the material began at the Summer School and, it was hoped, continued when they returned to work.

## POST-PROCESS CRITIQUE AND MATERIALIST PEDAGOGY

Since beginning my research on writing at the Bryn Mawr Summer School, the process approach, which has dominated composition teaching for decades, has been criticized by post-process theorists. What their critique calls for has much in common with the materialist pedagogy developed at the Bryn Mawr Summer School. The problem, as Sharon Crowley and others have pointed out, is that much process pedagogy posits a decontextualized student and ignores differences in terms of social class, economic background, race, home culture, and political environment among other important factors. "Composition scholarship and lore often proceeds as if the politics of class, status, and location were not operative in our classrooms" (Crowley, *Composition* 222). This ideologically tainted conception of an acontextual student mirrors the free-floating, ever-desiring consumer/agent of capitalist mythology. As Teresa Ebert has written,

> This is an agency necessary for the bourgeoisie—the consuming class pursuing the circuit of desire (consumption) in commodity capitalism. It is a notion of agency that entirely displaces the question of "need" as a revolutionary agency that is able to explain and transform the world. (804)

Furthermore, Crowley argues that the most commonly assigned genre of process pedagogy, the academic essay, is also an idealized form that "assumes that rhetorical situations are similar or the same across a certain range of possible settings" (*Composition* 233). In other words, academic essays are too often written in decontextualized classrooms, cut off from the way texts are produced and consumed in material culture.

Related to these post-process analyses are recent critiques of poststructuralism's "textual politics." John Trimbur has pointed out that "contemporary theorizing has entered pedagogy," and under this influence, pedagogy has taken a discursive turn (200). This discursive turn reinforces the acontextual process approach by arguing that textual critique offers a significant resistance to the unequal materiality of class. In response to this reductive discursivity, Trimbur ironically calls for a return to "vulgar marxism": "Vulgar marxism as I understand it is a necessary corrective to the tendency in postmodernist and postmarxist theorizing to see social experience as discursive and thereby to neglect the material conditions of life" (195). Similarly, Ebert criticizes many postmodern theories and pedagogies for promoting an intervention in discursive representation as a way to subvert these very representations. She instead calls for a critique that would explain the "social constructedness, historical causes, and political situationality of bodies," and that does not "erase the 'real' historical, material specificity of bodies: the materiality constituted *not* by an abstract, pure (ontological or textual) difference, but the historical struggles over the relations of production"(808). Ebert objects to the erasure of labor and class and to the focus on the local and antiglobal typical of discursive politics. She calls for a "red pedagogy," which, among other things, would teach students and workers of different nations about their common interests (810). She believes, as does Trimbur, that the critical discursive turn is itself characteristic of a relatively privileged first-world perspective, which, in line with its multinational capitalist context, favors the local, individual, free-floating signifier.

Trimbur and Crowley's post-process critique is also supported by poststructuralist feminists who point out that the notion of the discursivity of material reality leaves out important material dimensions of exploitation such as the body, working conditions, or a living wage. Dana L. Cloud, for example, critiques the "text centered approach that fails to locate a text in its ideological/cultural context for the purposes of critique" (150). She is wary of theorists who argue that "contexts are themselves intertextual, rather than material. So instead of discovering the economic or political interests motivating ideological discourses, the critic is reduced to describing patterns across cultural texts" (151). Cloud also objects to "the discursivity of the material," or the idea that reality is a discursive formation, to be improved or altered through discursive action. Under this manner of thinking, reality becomes in a sense unknowable because of the relative acceptability of varying interpretations of it, and revolutionary agency is thereby located in discourse and discursive acts.

One of the problems here as Cloud sees it is that although social discourses may come in fragmented forms, the oppressive social order is itself a totality that swallows up and disempowers resistant discourse (151). Thus cultural studies composition classes that critique dominant discourse do not necessarily challenge power structures. Critiques of "multiculturalism" have centered on this kind of approach where it is believed that just writing about "difference" will eradicate it. Both faculty and students at the Summer

School had faith in discursive reconstruction of materiality, but they were not what today might be called "textual determinists" who believe a mere critique of oppressive cultural texts in itself is sufficient for social change.

Sounding much like Summer School faculty and students in her focus on changing the extratextual world, Cloud writes that

> Radical textual readings of romance novels or *Star Trek* or of game shows, or Madonna, of biker culture or Oprah Winfrey or war do not undermine social relations unless those readings lead to some kind of concrete social oppositional action—a successful strike, a demonstration that builds a mass movement, or other collective and effective refusal of the prevailing social order. (151)

Cloud sees critique that is divorced from class-based collective activity as quite impotent. "We ought not to sacrifice the notions of practical truth, bodily reality, and material oppression to the tendency to render all of experience discursive, as if no one went hungry or died in war" (159). Or as Heidi Safia Mirza has written about black women, "For them power is not diffuse, localized and particular. Power is centralized and secure as it always has been, excluding, defining and self-legitimating" (20).

In its insistence on the material dimension of workers' exploitation, I think the Bryn Mawr Summer School project offers, if not a pedagogy for today, then useful ideas for creating one. As pointed out above, the Summer School pedagogy was in a continual state of evolution and revision, and included in its every textual manifestation a qualifier advising against the wholesale adoption of the described activity, approach, or theory. A review of its basic premises, however, can provide many serviceable ideas.

## ELEMENTS OF A MATERIALIST PEDAGOGY

The rhetoric that was taught at the Summer School was interventionist and meant to help women workers effect social change in material culture. To begin with, this rhetoric was inscribed in the types of writing women were assigned or chose to do. Students were not inclined or encouraged to write overly introspective or subjective texts without pragmatic aims. In their autobiographies, poetry, plays, labor journalism, statistical studies, and essays, the working women constructed counter hegemonic discourses that would help them see and dream beyond their socially prescribed roles. This was a pedagogy of production. As we have seen, a great many "material" artifacts were created by the students each session: their *Shop and School* magazines; the Department of Labor publications; the scrapbooks about working conditions and other work-related subjects; the "pictoral statistics," props, posters, and other items used to illustrate ideas, provide backdrops for plays, or make presentations about work.

When possible, the written products went beyond the classroom, into theaters, homes, labor unions, even the national discursive arena where they encountered living readers and became a component of other citizens' thought and action processes. The subject matter of much of the writing also had a material component since, as we have seen, women wrote about the material deprivations in their lives, the conditions of their work, their demands for improvement. Their multifaceted audience was also typically concrete and specific: their professors, the Bryn Mawr Summer School community, potential union or working-class peers, and on occasion, a government official, labor leader, politician, party strategist, or ordinary citizen who might pick up the U.S. Women's Bureau pamphlets by students at the Summer School.

Chapters to follow will focus on stylistic and thematic features, which also mark material or bodily states and transformations in much of the women's writing. In their autobiographies, for example, narrative subjectivity evolves from "I" to "we" as the working women go from individual agency to a collective one, exchanging the unitary bourgeois subjectivity for a working-class solidarity. In the Summer School poetry, a bodily motif frequently presents corporeal materiality pitted against machines. Bodies are at once sites of subjugation as well as resistance and liberation. Many times the women writers deconstruct androcentric dyads such as mind/body or culture/nature in favor of the more conventionally deprecated material factor.

Furthermore, women were encouraged to locate themselves and others in terms of their situated material subjectivity. Students examined the material context of their lives, politically, economically, culturally, technologically. Cultural texts of gender, race, class, ethnicity, religion, or geographic origin, to name a few, were brought to light and problematized, enabling the students to challenge stereotypes of "others" and themselves. The conflicts that this knowledge sometimes led to were not avoided but wrestled with, then lived with. Smith writes frequently in her accounts of the school how controversies such as whether or not to admit house workers to a Summer School for "industrial workers" were debated for days among the students both formally and informally until a vote of the student government resolved the issue (In this case, they were admitted.) (*Vistas* 145).

A general policy regarding overt faculty partisanship seems to have evolved after several years of discussion at faculty meetings. Instructors, mainly composed of leftists of various persuasions, wanted to be open about their strongly held political views. It was decided that teachers should reveal their own political, ethical, and moral values yet remain committed to presenting all sides of controversial issues to students. Again, political and cultural controversies were not avoided but brought into the classroom. Guest speakers, mostly, but not exclusively, of leftist and liberal bent often came to campus. And if the "outside" was brought "in," the students were also brought "out" to factories, grievance hearings, union meetings, election speeches, and plays, as well as to outdoor recreational facilities, going on several of these field trips a week. The analysis and interaction of material social processes going on inside and outside the Summer School was motivational in educational, occupational, and civic realms.

Finally, a materialist concept of class was "in the air" at Bryn Mawr and, probably, in much of the country in the 1920s and especially the 1930s. But the materiality of class was also overtly addressed in countless ways. There are many references in the texts written by both faculty and students of their working-class affiliation, both newly acquired and reaffirmed. The terms *workers* and *working class* were also frequently used in lesson materials. In addition, the Summer School was resolutely committed to the task of making knowledge material by building a working-class culture. At the same time, the idea was promoted that in spite of their differences, the commonality of oppression and exploitation united all workers, across gender and race.

Of course, such class homegeniety is not the case in many of our classrooms today, and using Summer School pedagogy with students from diverse class backgrounds would undoubtedly call for revisions and refashionings. But adopting the Summer School's focus on "material difference," not only in terms of class but also race, religion, politics, gender, geographic region, and industry, is undoubtedly an approach worth trying.

## APPENDIX: EXPOSITORY AND COLLABORATIVE WRITING

**"The Symbolic Jacket"**
**Anna Alpern**
*A Scrapbook of Industrial Workers' Experiences,* **"Individual Recollections"**
**section, 1932**

Whatever I know of styles in dressing was from an old fashioned book dated before the war, which I found in our small town dressmaker's workroom in Russia. The dresses we wore were made out of sack, old sheets, or tablecloths that did not need much style. It was not a question of style but of how to cover one's body in those days.

The leather jacket that came with the Revolution, was to me a symbol both of revolution and elegance that I could dream of. My admiration for the jacket I brought with me to America, and made sure to get one as soon as possible.

But my desired leather jacket brought me a lot of trouble after I had lost my first job and was looking for another one.

I answered an ad in the paper. It was a dressmaking shop. The man came to the door, who was short and stout, and had a big cigar in his mouth. With one glance at me, he burst out in a hoarse voice, "Can't use you," and slammed the door in front of my nose.

Next came a jewelry box factory. After waiting for one hour in the hall, I was admitted to an office where a tall handsome young man with a heavy cigar in his mouth (a sign of big business) was sitting behind a large mahogany desk with an air of dignity. He politely invited me to sit down and the questions began.

"What is a union shop?"

"I don't know what you mean[.]" (I had in fact belonged to a union for two years.)

"Don't you belong to a union?"

"No."

"You know I don't like it when someone else wants to run my business."

"Oh! I understand that."

"What is your name and address?"

I told him and he answered, "Come in tomorrow."

But tomorrow another man came out, I presume the foreman; he asked my name and disappeared. In a few minutes he came out again and the answer was, "I'm sorry Miss, the place is taken, come in some other time."

Then I applied as a learner in a millinery shop. The forelady who accepted the girls said to me, "I am sorry, Miss, we don't like Bolsheviks."

"What makes you think I am one?"

"Never mind, I can see it at once. These leather jackets and bushy hair, I know them well."

Later I got a job in a men's clothing shop. After I had worked there a few weeks, the boss showed a tendency to familiarity towards me. He promised to give me a lesson in behavior. For that he got the coat I had in my hands in his face and I quit the job. The reason for such behavior was again my leather jacket which made him think I was a Communist.

For a year I heard the words "I can't use you," "Not today," "Taken," "come some other time," etc., until I got sick and tired of it and decided to get rid of my jacket and become a lady. And sure enough, after I had dressed myself in the latest fashion, with lipstick in addition, although it was hard at first, I blushed, felt foolish, thought myself vulgar, but I got a job.

This occurred six years ago. Now there is no more danger in wearing a jacket. It does not signify radicalism, because the American student took to it.

**"The Social Science Workshop"**
**Margaret H. Collins**
*Shop and School,* **1938**

A large map, showing where all the students had come from, was made the first weekend we arrived. Everyone helped. Do you remember trying to find your name on the list, cutting it out, and pinning it up on the map? Soon a tangle of strings stretched from Kansas City in the west, Atlanta in the south, Toronto in the north, and far to the east — halfway across the room—three strings from England and Denmark. The Summer School at last had really opened.

During the first week urgent requests came in from various activities. The Cooperative Store, dramatics, and the library all wanted posters announcing their hours and place of business. The Recreation Committee sent in an s.o.s. for a map of the campus as students were getting lost trying to find the tennis courts and swimming pool.

Pictorial statistics next came into prominence. We decided to make a chart illustrating the different industries represented in the school. After a general plan for the chart was drawn up, the girls from each industry drew their own designs. Did you know before that there were twenty-six different industries represented—everything from automobiles to cosmetics? Unsuspected artists came to light. Mary Nero turned out to be a star in lettering. She has been in constant demand ever since. After the remarkable backdrop for the Wages and Hours Play, which Tzolouhi Ketchian painted, everyone knew that Tzolouhi was a born artist. But did you know that Helen Hart could draw a steel mill, Edna Horowitz a laundry mangle, or Sofie Fricke a pair of gloves?

Several students before giving reports in class came to the workshop to make pictorial statistics to help illustrate their main points. Jane Foster's talk in assembly on T.B. in which she showed some excellent professional pictorial statistics may have been responsible for arousing Julia Limric's interest. In any case Julia made a series of charts for her talk on medical care in the U.S. Did you see the chart Edith Yetka made for her talk on Cooperatives in Different Countries, or the one Mary Longley made on Employment in the Electrical Industry, or Tilly Franco's showing the trend in Union Membership since 1881?

Topics of general interest to the school were also illustrated in the workshop. Esther Perelson and Mary Nero with Edna's help made in record time two large charts on Income Distribution and the Cost of Living for the Wage-Hour Play. "Isms" were catching the attention of the school. Verva Moyer took the load in trying to work out a chart which would show the main differences in the various social philosophies. The work in Miss Hewes' unit inspired Helen Fausset and several others to work up a histomap of the labor movement. Helen has ambition of reducing the six-foot map to a few stencils which can be mimeographed for the whole school.

Another interest developed out of the nature walks. Mary Ann DeSalvo made posters to list the new birds, flowers and trees seen on each walk. Doris Pullman was our authority on astronomy and spatter prints. Did you see the sky maps Mary Longley and Tzolouhi made on large half domes of black paper? And did you know that Mary Ann and Mary Kisleiko were the artists for the spatter prints of leaves?

The week before the International Festival was a particularly lively one in the workshop. We thought it would be interesting to make a chart showing the different nationality backgrounds represented in the school. Celia Kurtz had the bright idea that, instead of using the symbol of a working woman for this chart, we should draw figures of girls in their native costumes. Mary Kisleiko followed up the idea by suggesting the illustrations in the National Geographic as excellent source material. A group of us collected data from the application blanks. Tzolouhi sketched the figures, Mary Nero drew a map of Europe and did the lettering, and each nationality group painted its own figures in their folk costumes. Did you see the Scottish Highlander in kilts whom Peg Richardson drew, or the pretty French peasant who Imelda Santerre to her surprise found she could paint? Did you know that a Turk and an Armenian discovered each other sitting side by side at Bryn Mawr? More than half the map of Europe was living peacefully together under one roof in a workers' school.

As Doris Prenner is frantically calling the deadline for late articles for the magazines, the workshop is just beginning its final (we hope!) school project. We can never be sure what new last minute demand may suddenly develop. Leslie may want another poster for the library. Peg Richardson's one on Calling All Books ought to bring results, but perhaps an addition to the poster—a little dynamite or a mad dog behind the silhouette of the girl running from Denbigh to the Library—will be needed to round up the last missing book. At the moment, however, we are not looking for new orders. Pressure from Anna Hall and various other shoppers at the Cooperative

Store has already pushed the workshop into the mass production scale. Pat, Dixie, Daisy and Tilly are the most active workers at the moment, but no doubt all of us will soon be called in to help for we are turning out stickers and banners for the whole school. A bright yellow sticker with a lantern and B.M.S.S. on it will cheer us on our way as we set off in a few days for different parts of the country.

The workshop at Bryn Mawr is only a beginning. Now that you know how to start, you can show others. Remember the equipment is not expensive: graph paper, plenty of pencils and rulers, some sheets of cardboard, India ink, and Speed Ball pens for lettering. These two pamphlets may be helpful: "Modern Lettering for Pen and Brush Poster Design" by Ross F. George (price $.50) and "Instructions for Chartmakers" published by Pictorial Statistics, Inc., 142 Lexington Ave., New York City (price $.30). Remember that pictorial statistics are not hard to make. In fact, the chart itself is comparatively easy. The hard work comes first: finding the facts you want to present, cutting out all non-essentials, and working out a play which will get across your idea in the shortest, clearest way. But it is fun. Go to it and good luck!

### "A Day on Strike"
### Edith Daum
### *Shop and School,* 1924

It was a large and gloomy hall where the strikers used to meet every day. A group of girls gathered in one corner were disputing whether to go out on the picket line or not, for it was very cold outside; the snow was deep, and the wind was unbearable so that one could hardly stand five minutes outside. "But we have to go; we must go," was heard from every corner of the hall. Everyone was excited and awaiting something unusual.

The door opened, and a figure, all covered with snow so that we could hardly see the face which was hidden in a scarf, pushed itself in and looked around. She opened her mouth and looked at everyone very much surprised and said: "A girl who was picketing one of the shops was beaten to blood by a policeman. And you are all here picketing the hall instead of the shops." And she ran out.

We all felt very much ashamed. It was not the beaten girl that made us feel so humiliated in that critical moment; it was not this at all, for we expected things like that. It was our weakness, the not believing in our own power which had started to appear in our minds and was now ruling us.

Within three weeks the great enthusiasm and belief in our own power with which we had gone out on strike disappeared. Phrases and words like "Worker's Power," "Our Existence," "Rule of Capitalism," were no more heard as often as in the beginning of our struggle. The atmosphere had become strained. Everyone was waiting for something extraordinary to happen. The situation had become unbearable, and we did not realize it until that very moment. The incident of the beaten girl was so impressive and unusual that we began to understand the situation thoroughly. We did not talk nor dispute among ourselves, but walked out with lowered heads, ashamed to look into each others' faces.

**"The Social Science Workshop and the Worker"**
**Sarah Lockstein**
*Shop and School*, 1932

Only a map or a chart, a picture or a clay model, and yet so much genuine benefit and pleasure is derived from just these things.

We create. To some of us the social science workshop is an answer to the continual longing to express something within us, which we have never been capable of bringing out in clear, concrete form. To many, it is the working with colors, to some, the modeling with clay, the shaping of an indefinite something into a quite definite and often beautiful something, and to some it is the planning and creating of charts and maps dealing with many different subjects.

This in itself—the opening of a gate to self-expression—is of tremendous importance. It is the beginning of a happier life for us.

Then, of course, there are more immediate and concrete results which we derive. It is easier for many of us to learn from pictures and charts than from reading texts. Making a chart or creating a map leaves a definite picture and impression on our minds.

Then too, since we work on the problems which are of interest to us, and which affect us most, we get a clearer understanding of those problems with which we are constantly faced, such as bank failures, immigration, concentration of industry, and so forth.

We also learn a great deal by watching with interest the work of our friends in the workshop, and by listening to the many opinions in reference to our work, which are often expressed.

I think, that by giving us a chance for self-expression, the workshop has given us an opportunity to further among others, that educational activity which we think so important in building a world of saner and happier living.

### "Right or Might?"
### Josephine Murawski
### *Shop and School,* 1934

We—forty five school boys and girls of all different shades of opinion—decided to parade on May thirtieth. We knew that wars were over markets—rich man's war and poor man's fight—and why should the poor man pay for it all? So with the one thought: "We're against war!" we tumbled into trucks and started off waving and shouting good-naturedly to passers-by and singing peace songs.

Suddenly the songs die down. Why the crowd? Who so many blue coats? Why the shining night sticks? Why the tear gas, and guns? Why do those firemen have their long snake-like hose connected to the hydrant? A crowd of at least three hundred ready to devour and wipe out forty-five youngsters ready to resist war.

White and shaky, we ride back home. Some of us had not even moved from our benches. No parade; plenty of violence; an unforgettable experience. Right has nothing to do with it; it's might.

### "Jean Carter—An Interview"
### Estelle Petelson
### *Shop and School,* 1937

"Miss Carter," I said, after she had graciously consented to be interviewed, "why are you doing this kind of work, namely, holding the office of Director of the Bryn Mawr Summer School?" "I believe that the hope for a new world is through education," was the reply.

Thus commenced the interview which will be indelible in my memory. Although I was in her office for almost all of two hours, I felt I had but read the introduction of a Great Classic. "What do you mean by a new world?" I queried. And Jean Carter sincerely and idealistically opened this Great Classic and let me read.

A new world would be a social order where all people could live an abundant life—that life consisting of the spirit as well as the body. Through workers' education may that new world be reached.

"Do you mean then, Miss Carter, that organizing the workers and teaching them the necessity of trade unionism will bring us the new world? Don't you think that that kind of education may tend to regiment the workers and narrow their views?" Again she opened the pages and I read as she spoke. She agreed that teaching only unionism would narrow our views as does the acceptance and dogmatic application of certain principles. To have an ideal concept is great, but how we attempt to plant it in others is a very delicate problem, unless we realize the sensitivities of human beings and the needs of others as our needs and so develop a feeling for each other. Although there are many ways leading to the new world, the education one is the most helpful. While it is true that most workers' education at present stresses unionism, it must ultimately become much broader. Trade unionism is of utmost importance in order to eliminate obstacles that keep us from developing. By bringing intelligent workers together from all parts of the country, we can study each others' problems and strive toward some solution. We can then continue in the field of organization and education and thus help others out of their long stagnation. All that the scientists, philosophers, literary men and artists have contributed to make life interesting as well as beautiful will be studied and enjoyed not only by the chosen few, but by all the people of the world. Thus through relating knowledge to human beings and applying it for the good of humanity will we reach the new world.

As Miss Carter spoke her face shone with hope and understanding and I knew that she was sincere. I became curious as to where she was born, and when I asked her she answered sweetly and with dignity.

Jean Carter was born in Rochester, New York, of class-conscious proletarian parents. After she graduated from the University of Rochester she taught in the public schools for thirteen years. She was not, however, caught in the clutches of the academic system. She taught workers' classes in the evenings because of her faith in attaining the desired goal. During summers she taught at workers' summer schools. Finally she gave up the security of teaching in the public schools and entered the precarious field of workers' education, because here all her efforts could be concentrated on the kind of education which will eventually bring the new world.

"May your ideal grow and spread, Miss Carter."

**"Unemployment as It Is Studied at Bryn Mawr"**
**Helen Taublieb**
*Shop and School,* **1931**

Since unemployment is a world wide problem at the present time, we are focusing our two months study on it at Bryn Mawr. The one hundred girls here are divided into five different units which discuss unemployment from various angles. We are exchanging experiences that some students have had both in this country and in foreign countries. With these experiences to build on, we go back into history and try to discover how unemployment came about. This study in the units gives a theoretical background for our future studies.

In our Trade Party the students from various trades in different industries dramatized the various causes of unemployment and showed how workers were deprived of their jobs. For instance, the textile industry showed the stretch-out system and technological unemployment; the needle trades brought out the speed-up system and changes in styles. In one scene we saw how the unemployed had to resort to the selling of apples, which is so popular on the sidewalks of New York City. Another group of students brought out the fact that the problem is international.

One day at assembly Mr. Ben Thomas told us about unemployment in Great Britain. It was quite evident that technology played a great part in creating this unemployment as well as Britain's dependence on export trade. English markets became limited as other countries became more industrialized and needed fewer exports.

One afternoon after tea Dr. Colston Warne spoke to us. He related some facts to us about the monopoly of markets, competition in prices and how means of production were being controlled by small groups. These questions have been studied in our units. After listening to Dr. Warne, one comes to the conclusion that unemployment cannot be looked upon as a one-country problem but rather as a world-wide one, and must be met as such.

As a means of solving the problem the students held a symposium on unemployment insurance. Olive McClung acted as chairman. Constance Hopkins told how this scheme is operated in England, how unemployment affected her, and how she secured some relief from the unemployment insurance. Ellen Elving from Denmark outlined for us the Danish and German plans and how they are operated. It is rather peculiar to see that in those three countries unemployment insurance is compulsory by government, whereas in the United States the only existing plans are some union and company plans. These were outlined for us by Aurelia Niehaus and Elsie Kramer. Nora Quimette explained the types of proposed bills. The American Association for Labor Legislation—Unemployment Reserve Law; the Conference for Progressive Labor Action—Unemployment Insurance Law; the Socialist Party—State Unemployment Insurance Law; and the Communist Party— National Unemployment Insurance Act. The Communist bill is the only federal law proposed.

"Unemployment insurance is a measure for immediate relief before society can be changed to do away with unemployment. If rightly set up, it may be the first step toward taking some income from the profiteers and using it to increase the purchasing power of the workers."

Summer School students studying in the Cloisters, M. Carey Thomas Library, Bryn Mawr College, 1928. Courtesy of Special Collections and University Libraries, Rutgers University Libraries.

Teresa Wolfson teaching her economics class in the Cloisters, M. Carey Thomas Library, Bryn Mawr College, 1929. Courtesy of Special Collections and University Libraries, Rutgers University Libraries.

An astronomy class, Bryn Mawr College. Courtesy of Special Collections and University Libraries, Rutgers University Libraries.

Ellen Kennan with her English class, Bryn Mawr College, 1931.
Courtesy of Special Collections and University Libraries, Rutgers
University Libraries.

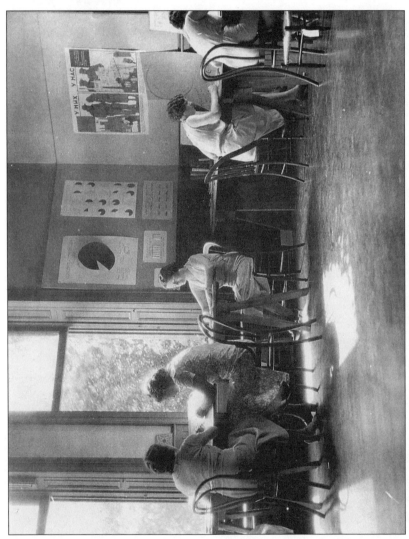

Summer School students in a social science workshop, Bryn Mawr College. Courtesy of Special Collections and University Libraries, Rutgers University Libraries.

Summer School students and faculty in the Mark Starr–Ture Unit around the Cloisters fountain, M. Carey Thomas Library, Bryn Mawr College, 1930. Courtesy of Special Collections and University Libraries, Rutgers University Libraries.

Dr. Colston Warne's economics discussion group, Bryn Mawr College, 1928. Courtesy of Special Collections and University Libraries, Rutgers University Libraries.

Meredith Giveus and unidentified instructor with economics class, the Cloisters, M. Carey Thomas Library, Bryn Mawr College, 1928. Courtesy of Special Collections and University Libraries, Rutgers University Libraries.

Mark Starr with economics class, Bryn Mawr College, 1929. Courtesy of Special Collections and University Libraries, Rutgers University Libraries.

Summer School students in science workshop, Bryn Mawr College. Courtesy of Special Collections and University Libraries, Rutgers University Libraries.

Poetry reading on the lawn in front of the M. Carey Thomas Library, Bryn Mawr College, 1928. Courtesy of Special Collections and University Libraries, Rutgers University Libraries.

Summer School students in the Cloisters, M. Carey Thomas Library, Bryn Mawr College, 1932. Courtesy of Special Collections and University Libraries, Rutgers University Libraries.

Summer School students reading, portico, M. Carey Thomas Library, Bryn Mawr College, 1929. Courtesy of Special Collections and University Libraries, Rutgers University Libraries.

Bryn Mawr Summer School outdoor dramatics, Bryn Mawr College. Courtesy of Special Collections and University Libraries, Rutgers University Libraries.

Summer School students in the science room, Bryn Mawr College, 1927. Courtesy of Special Collections and University Libraries, Rutgers University Libraries.

Summer School students in the library, Taylor Hall, Bryn Mawr College, 1933. Courtesy of Special Collections and University Libraries, Rutgers University Libraries.

### The Story of My Life

The first seventeen years of my life were spent on a small tobacco farm in Virginia. Mother and Daddy struggled hard for a mere existence for eight children. We did have enough to eat, such as it was: pork, potatoes and beans were our steady winter diet. We were happy together, though one need look but once to see the anxiety on our faces.

Poverty drove me to the shoe factory. When I was seventeen, I went to work expecting to help my family, but the first three months I was paid $8.00 a week for ten hours work a day. Then I was put on piece work and some weeks I couldn't make $8.00 because of the low prices they paid. Having to pay $6.00 of this for board and car fare, there was little left to buy clothes and to help my family.

Mother and Daddy lost their farm to the government for taxes after two years of dry weather in succession that caused a failure in the tobacco crop; they, too, moved to the city to look for work.

I was married when I was eighteen. My husband worked with carpenters laying foundations for houses. He seldom had enough work to pay the grocery bill and rent. After my baby was born, I had to go back to the factory to work and leave the baby with a maid. When the baby was ten months old, he died.

After fourteen years of work in the factory, all I have to show for my labor is a baby's grave in the cemetery and five operations. I had lost courage to carry on.

I was invited to the Y.W.C.A. Industrial club. Through the club I learned of Bryn Mawr Summer School, and was accepted as a student. Bryn Mawr has given me new life, and new hope, because it teaches the importance of organized labor, how to get laws passed that will benefit workers and what books are important for workers to read.

Now when I go home instead of thinking of things that happened in the past, I can try to organize workers and start a workers' class, though it is a slow, hard fight to get workers interested.

> Through Bryn Mawr I have learned not only how to play and enjoy
> life but I have also learned that other workers throughout the world are
> working with me for a better world for all workers. I'm sure my work will
> not be in vain!
>
> —Thelma Hunter, *Shop and School,* 1937

Since personal experience was to play such a key role in the course of instruction at the Summer School, it is not surprising that writing an autobiography was one of the first tasks the women were assigned in their English
composition class (Heller, "Blue Collars" 119). Indeed, a former instructor,
the late Alice Hansen Cook, emphasized the importance faculty gave to the
autobiography assignment and stressed that the assignment "was something
that we all did." The women wrote copiously at the urging of the predominantly female faculty, whose student-centered pedagogy helped transform
these women's untold dreams, desires, and fears into demands for social
justice. In their textual self-(re)presentations, these working women developed more critical and powerful voices by adapting the various discursive
formations culturally available to them for their own, often collective, ends.
My analysis of this discursive subjectivity, or self-re-creation through writing, will be informed by literary autobiographical criticism and linked to
composition research on gender and autobiography.

Today, some feminist and poststructuralist critics express a certain distrust
of autobiography, and, as I will discuss below, some scholars of composition
studies have also warned of the patriarchal cast of traditional autobiography
(see Rose; Flynn; Sirc; Linda H. Peterson). In *A Poetics of Women's Autobiography,* Sidonie Smith maintains that "During the past five hundred years,
autobiography has assumed a central position in the personal and literary
life of the West precisely because it serves as one of those generic contracts
that reproduces the patrilineage and its ideologies of gender" (44). Indeed,
autobiographical subjectivity is compromised by androcentric illusions of
a unified, autonomous self, which "valorizes individual integrity and sepa-
rateness and devalues personal and communal interdependency" (39).

Although faculty working at the Summer School in the 1920s and 1930s
would not have had expressed their understanding of subjectivity in contemporary poststructuralist terms, they were not uncritical of bourgeois
subjectivity. Judging from their assignments, faculty saw autobiography as
a way to represent the reconstruction of a subjectivity that was both self-criti-
cal and critical of the status quo. Perhaps because of their close association
with their working-class students, faculty came to understand the needs and
perspectives of these "others." In fact, the faculty also seemed aware of how

their own more privileged class backgrounds limited their ability to know their students. In her book on worker education, Hilda Worthington Smith wrote that

> The first concern of the teacher should be to discover the special interests and the occupational backgrounds of his students. . . . Without this background of detailed knowledge . . . , the teacher may plan instruction which is remote from any real significance in their daily lives. (*Opening* 25)

Smith and her faculty thus regarded the student autobiographies as a source of information crucial to classroom success. Another benefit of the autobiographical assignment, therefore, was helping the faculty understand whom they were teaching.

In her relevant essay on Victorian working-class autobiography, Regina Gagnier has shown the unfortunate results that can occur when working-class autobiographical subjects, both male and female, do not move beyond prevailing autobiographical conventions. Those working-class subjects who attempted to construct a subjectivity in terms of bourgeois norms including close family upbringing, lengthy schooling, romantic love, marriage, and a progressively successful career, often experienced narrative and psychological breakdown because of the disparity between what happened to them and what they believe should have happened according to bourgeois ideology. Gagnier finds that a happier outcome occurs when the working-class writer recognizes the difficulty, if not the impossibility of embourgeoisement and critiques the inequities of class structures, gaining strength through the representation of a collective subjectivity (114). For example, Gagnier cites Emma Smith's "Cornish Waif's Story," an autobiography in which Smith consistently denies her painful failures as a conventional wife and mother. Her autobiography ends with several mental breakdowns and two suicide attempts, which she tries to deemphasize with a platitudinous conclusion. Among Gagnier's examples of a more fulfilling working-class life story is Ellen Johnston's autobiography. Johnston, a power loom weaver, chronicles a tale of paternal abandonment, unrequited love, and illegitimate childbearing but also includes loving testimony to her public life in the factories through poems to factory men and women, their work, and international solidarity. Her narrative ends forcefully as she takes her foreman to court (111–14).

The Summer School approach to autobiography can be well illustrated through an example from one of the most popular and long-serving English composition instructors, Ellen Kennan. Teaching at the school from 1925 to 1938, she began all her classes with an autobiographical assignment, which was modified over the years to account for her students' life experiences and to produce increasingly more critical responses. The two versions of the assignment that follow reflect Kennan's growing awareness that workers' lives did not mirror the ideal bourgeois life pattern of familial nurturing, uninterrupted schooling, romantic love, and career development but instead likely involved truncated schooling and economically strained family relationships.

### Kennan's 1926 Autobiography Assignment

The first assignment is to write an essay about yourself.[1] The following questions are not designed as a kind of third degree. They are suggestions merely. Please answer as many of them as you will and add anything in your life which seems to you to have influenced you.

> What is your age?
> Where were you born?
> How far did you go in school?
> What studying have you done since you left school?
> What work do you do now?
> At what age did you begin?
> How did you happen to take up that kind of work?
> Do you like it?
> What work would you like to do if you had your choice and the training for it?
>    What would be your second choice?
> How did you happen to come to this school?
> What do you want to get from the school?
> Name the three books which you have read which you enjoyed the most
> What amusements are you fond of?
> What things in your training (either from your parents or teachers) are you
>    beginning to feel doubtful about?

Even in this early version of the assignment, Kennan clearly wanted her students to take a critical perspective on their lives. "Do you like it [your work]?" she prompts, and "What work would you like to do if you had your choice and the training for it?" With the final question on doubt, she avoids encouraging received opinions about how her students' lives should be unfolding.

### Kennan's 1934 Autobiography Assignment

First Composition:
  I. Family and Background
  II. Childhood:
      What is the first thing that you can remember?

What do you remember that you wish you could forget?

Did you have a grandmother?

What thing in your childhood are you glad about?

III. Education:

What schools did you go to?

What did you get outside of schools?

What did you fail to get?

What did you get that you later found untrue?

What friends did you have? Were they lasting ones?

IV. Work:

Did you choose it?

Do you like it?

What work would you do if you had your choice?

V. What do you do for fun?

Do you read, for example? What sort of books?

Do you go to plays?

Do you enjoy games, music, dancing?

Note: Don't take any of these questions as commands. Answer what you please. Tell everything about yourself that you will and can.

If you do not wish to write an autobiography, the following questions may suggest a different kind of composition:

I. What kind of life would you live if you could arrange your life just as you wished—if you could do as you wish and be what you wish.

II. What beliefs and ideas that you have grown up in [*sic*] are you beginning to question? What ones have you cast aside entirely? What first caused you to question accepted ideas? Do you now challenge some things that you formerly considered sacred?

III. If there is a particular subject that you have in mind and wish to write upon, you may do it, regardless of the other suggestions.

By 1934 Kennan has expanded the original assignment and divided it into five parts. Even though the categories may reflect bourgeois life patterns, questions asked encourage a critical examination of these patterns. Omitted from the 1934 assignment are the specific inquiries about age and birthplace, perhaps because this information was easily obtained from the lengthy application forms available on each student, or perhaps because such facts were not pertinent to the work ahead. We see that Kennan now invites her students to write on "Family and Background" as well as "Childhood." Perhaps she wanted to help students understand how these culturally derived constructs or discourses shaped the selves or subjectivities they were representing in their autobiographies. One can only speculate, but perhaps Kennan may have found that workers tended to neglect these categories if their experiences hadn't been as "happy" as prevailing ideology required. And true to her critical aims, Kennan also asks, "What do you remember [about your childhood] that you wish you could forget?" Similarly, Kennan wants a critical perspective on education. She prompts: "What did you get *outside* of schools?" "What did you *fail* to get?" "What did you get that you later found untrue?" [emphasis added]. Under "Childhood," the question about having a grandmother (as opposed to a grandfather) may reveal Kennan's hope for a more feminist investigation of family ancestry. Finally, Kennan exhibits a distrust of autobiographical subjectivity as she recommends that students tell "everything that you *will and can.*"[2]

## WOMEN WORKERS WRITING AUTOBIOGRAPHICAL NARRATIVES

The narratives below appeared in *Shop and School,* the student magazine published during every Summer School session. *Shop and School* contained prose, poetry, humor, and labor drama. I examined 163 narratives appearing in the last ten issues of *Shop and School* dating from 1928 to 1938,[3] the period when the students and faculty were organized in the successful interdisciplinary "unit system" described earlier. Because many teachers at the school assigned autobiographies, I have not been able to determine these students' English teachers. And while I cannot say for certain that the texts I examined were written for Kennan, the narratives fall readily into the categories set up by her assignment.[4]

By far the most popular topic among the students concerned their work lives. More than half of the pieces I examined were of this type. Titles include "Waste in My Shop," "My Start in Industry," "A Working Girl Speaks," "An Incident in My Shop," "Piece Work System," "The Long Arm of the Job," and "My First Experience as an Organizer." As the economic hardships and labor struggles of the 1930s increased, the titles begin to reflect more conflict as well as the resultant difficulties in workers' lives: "A Day Searching for a Job," "The New York Elevator Strike," "My First Arrest," "On the Picket Line," "The 1931 Hosiery Strike in Philadelphia," "An Experience with a Sweatshop Boss," "The Effect of Unemployment on One's Health." The next most popular topic was education. About 16 percent of the narratives dealt with this topic, whether stressing the value of the Bryn Mawr experience or the need for more workers' education projects, or offering a critique of earlier educational experiences. Another 15 percent of the pieces addressed family and background. Many of these narratives told how the economic conditions of the times led to extreme deprivations. Typical titles included "A Mining Village," "Motherless," "Homeless in Russia," or "My Childhood During the War." As the depression wore on, workers wrote less about their early childhood experiences and family background and more about their current economic difficulties in the context of the family: "The Pressure of High Rent," "The Effect of Unemployment on My Family."

The remaining narratives could be placed for the most part into Kennan's second group of topics. Some students wrote utopian descriptions of lives they dreamed of; others criticized forms of organized religion they had begun to doubt or wrote of a recently acquired sympathy for Southerners, Northerners, African Americans, Jews, or immigrant women met at the Summer School; others wrote about how they had begun to think of themselves as public speakers or activists. Still others described such things as the funeral of Nicola Sacco and Bartolomeo Vanzetti, a speech made to the Pennsylvania House of Representatives, a racist incident in a restaurant, or the Pennsylvania Amish. Incidentally, the "fun" category was hardly ever chosen. Hilda Smith comments that many workers had to be taught recreation while at the School, never having had the opportunity for it before (*Women Workers* 164).

### Narratives on Family and Childhood

The narratives on family, background, and childhood reveal a variety of subject positions that the writers often represented as evolving into collective narratives of desire and demands. Typically, an important shift in consciousness occurs, changing an isolated, powerless "I," who writes, into a more forceful "we," who acts. Beulah Parrish, a student at the Summer School in 1930, wrote this brief narrative about life in a southern mill town. A white student from Durham, North Carolina, Parrish revealed in her application that she was twenty-one years old when she attended the school. She had never voted and was not a union member but was a leader in her church and YWCA Industrial Club. She left school at age thirteen to work in a hosiery mill.

**Those Mill Villages**
**By Beulah Parrish, 1930**

For three years I lived in a southern mill village. I found it very unpleasant.

An employer may shout "Cheap Rent" all he wants to, but what do we get for our cheap rent?

The streets of the village are usually narrow and muddy. Sometimes they are poorly lighted. Most of the houses are small and have no bathtubs. In the village where I lived we were not allowed to have telephones. Our lights were turned off at certain hour every night. They were turned on again early in the morning, and then turned off at daylight. The lights were turned on for one day each week so that we could do our ironing.

It seems as though there were always more children in a mill village than anywhere else. Many of the mothers have to work in the mill. Their children, having no one to take care of them, roam about the streets wherever they please. People are inclined to look down on the people who live in a mill village.

The employer seems to think he more or less has control over the people. We workers do not want our employers to give us community houses and cheap rent, with lights and water free. We want wages that will enable us to live in better houses on better streets and to pay for our own amusements. We should feel much more independent—and that is how everybody wants to feel.

Notice how Parrish first represents her subjectivity: "'*I*' lived in a southern mill village. '*I*' found it very unpleasant." This first person singular narration is the conventional narrative device for autobiographies. Sidonie Smith argues that this "narrated I" typically presents a singular, unitary consciousness, the bourgeois subjectivity, which reflects on a painful past to be vanquished as the narrative progresses. As Parrish's example and others show, however, this pattern is not typical of the autobiographical narratives written at the Summer School. Parrish turns over her narrative to a narrating "we," a narrator of participation, a much stronger and more confident collective subject which, as noted earlier, Gagnier has found to be beneficial to working-class writers. "*We* workers do not want our employers to give us community houses and cheap rent," writes Parrish. "*We* want wages that will enable us to live in better houses on better streets. . . ." As is typical of this discursive move, the shift in person is often accompanied by a shift in tense. Thus, the exploited "I" is left in the past while the "we" becomes an active subject of the present or future and plays a public, adversarial role on behalf of all mill village workers. As is also typical, the "we" carries the more resistant stance of the narration. The narrated "I" is critical of her surroundings, but the narrated "we" offers solutions to the exploitation. While "I" generally belongs in the private sphere, "we" ventures into the "public domain." This shift in person, tense, and discursive domain occurred in three fourths of the narratives I examined, and there is no evidence that such shifts were prompted by material in the assignment. Thus another outcome of materialist pedagogy becomes apparent here, as a seemingly physical change has occurred, a reembodiment in the evolution from individual to collective agency.

As is typical of many of these working women, Parrish does not seem to have been exposed to a feminist critique of her work or home life, or if exposed to such a critique, she chose not to make it a part of her own discourse. She does not denounce the fact that the women workers she describes probably earned less than the men or that the women most likely returned from mill work to do a shift of housework. Although women's issues of home and family predominate in her narrative, they are presented in terms of prevailing cultural standards. For example, her use of the Victorian domestic discourse of woman as nurturer and homemaker legitimizes her struggle for "finer things" in culturally acceptable terms. In another discursive appropriation, she uses the androcentric discourse of worker empowerment to achieve a strengthened collective voice. This melding of discourses in her text, and in others that follow, offer examples of Mikhail Bakhtin's "heteroglossia," amalgams of various social discourses in dialogic interaction. That the women use and exploit various discourses for their own ends, incorporating them with personal discourses connected to their needs of work and family life, corresponds to the notion of "constructed knowledge." In *Women's Ways of Knowing,* Mary Field Belenky and her colleagues argue that women attain constructed knowledge when they welcome, rather than feel threatened by, the thoughts of others, integrating these thoughts into a personally meaningful set of beliefs.

The next narrative was written by an African American student.

### Looking Back
### By Eloise Fickland, 1933

If it were possible for me to turn and look back along the years of some six generations, I'd see my mother's maternal and paternal ancestors in this America.

My mother's mother was a slave. Four generations of these slaves had served four generations of one family. My mother is the result of the joining of the two families. We never knew my father's people. We never saw them and heard very little, for he died before we were old enough to be interested and to ask questions.

My maternal grandmother told many tales of the slave life, and The War. Some of these stories were very sad.

From the time I was able to sit on the floor and hold my sister I have had the responsibility of "the children." I was the one to whom each child came with all cares from a scratch to a fight; all secrets I kept, notes from teachers even; all kinds of trouble.

Well do I remember, once, when my next oldest sister and I had to act Santa. My father was away, and my mother was too ill to help. We had just finished trimming the tree, putting around the presents, and filling the stockings when we had to hide as my brother and next sister came down to take a look around. It was a narrow escape.

We were a happy group of youngsters. A group that was so sheltered that it has proven a handicap to some of us.

It is nearly nineteen years now since my father died. Ah! the awful change that death made. My oldest brother had just married. Yes, there was a little insurance. A methodist minister, how can he pay for a large policy with nine children to support?

Depression! The depression started nineteen years ago with us.

Eloise Fickland's autobiographical piece highlights many themes and emphases that scholars have identified with African American autobiography. Margo Culley writes that "For most black women, as for most black men, the foundational category [of being] is race" (8). Thus, Fickland begins her narrative by emphasizing her lengthy roots in this country and identifying herself as a descendant of slaves, an African American. She probably knew that few, if any, among her predominantly white schoolmates could claim to have had family in America for six generations, and this gave her a birthright and legitimacy that may have surprised them.

In an important critical essay, "In Search of the Black Female Self," Regina Blackburn locates three interrelated themes informing most black women's autobiographies: The first is defining the black self; the second is valuing that self; and the third is achieving an awareness of the double bind that being black and female imposes (136). True to the first of these points, Fickland defines herself matrilinealy, through her African American female ancestors, inheriting character and strength that her narrated "I" values greatly. Elizabeth Fox-Genovese has found that black female autobiographers make frequent reference to the love "felt for and felt from their female elders: mothers, aunts, grandmothers " (71). William L. Andrews has traced this tradition back to nineteenth-century female slave narratives. "In general, nineteenth-century black autobiographers single out their mothers, sisters and grandmothers for special praise," he writes (227). He continues, however, noting that because these autobiographers wanted "to reconcile an absolute moral standard for womanly virtue prescribed by white culture with the actual circumstances of a slave woman's complex lived experience," a certain ambivalence is found in their narratives (230). Perhaps a similar ambivalence motivated Fickland's rather oblique reference to her mother's conception as "the result of the joining of the two families."

Like Parrish, Fickland addresses concerns that are traditionally within women's domain: the home, mothering, children. Both use the conventions of Victorian domesticity to help register their points. Fickland appropriates this domestic discourse as she presents a self that others come to for solace and comfort. She was a mother with "children" before her time, and she derives a great deal of self-esteem and self-respect from this role. Fickland offers her experiences, and those of her forbearers, as evidence of her authenticity as a woman, again having to legitimize herself as Fox-Genovese notes, in terms of "bourgeois women's domestic discourse" (83). Neither Parrish nor Fickland explicitly critique this discourse of womanhood, but each uses it as a means to point out what they've been denied— material comfort, respect, and justice. Fickland, because she is black, must reassure her readers that she approximates the white feminine ideal. Parrish, because she is white, can, in this instance, take her gender for granted and directly protest the injustice of not having middle-class independence and comfort.

Fickland, however, has had to go well beyond the bounds of the white bourgeois or working-class mother and temporarily assume a role traditionally reserved for men. At Christmastime, she has played Santa, the mythical male provider, implying what others have stated more explicitly: that black women's status as women has not shielded them from "man's" work. Thus, Blackburn's third theme is present in an emergent form here. Not unlike the other African American woman autobiographers Blackburn studied, Fickland shows an awareness of the double oppression being both black and female imposes.

Her narration then slips into "we," but not the androcentric, narrating "we" of Parrish, which collectively confronts an oppressive situation in the present. Fickland's "we" is familial, woven in and out of her narrative, firmly connected to her past "I" by close ties of kinship. "We were a happy group of youngsters" she writes, perhaps too "sheltered" to successfully confront the racism of white culture. Suffering has long been a part of this family's collective experience—always present under the surface, it forces its way out in the narrative's bitter ending. Severe deprivation didn't begin with the Depression as it may have in the white culture. For her family, "the depression started nineteen years ago" with the death of her father and the "loss" of her older brother to marriage. In earnest, then, Fickland has permanently taken up the role of male provider for her family.

Perhaps Fickland does not use the collective, androcentric voice of worker empowerment because, as the daughter of a minister, she considered herself middle-class; or perhaps she had never been exposed to this rhetoric; perhaps she rejected it; or perhaps her purpose was to paint a familial portrait in African American terms. Since racial discrimination was the overriding historical factor contributing to Fickland's oppression, any discourse that did not give race prime consideration would not likely be adopted by her. Fox-Genovese argues that "the tension at the heart of black women's auto-biography derives in large part from the chasm between an autobiographer's intuitive sense of herself and her attitude toward her probable readers" (74). We feel this tension in Fickland's references to her mother's conception, her having to play Santa, her sheltered family, and her last overly controlled statement.

### Narratives of Work and Union

In her study of contemporary working-class women's writing, Janet Zandy finds that reference to historical events can trigger narrative response (*Calling Home* 11). She mentions that several contemporary women poets have written about the Triangle fire of 1911. Similarly, one of the women at Bryn Mawr wrote about experiencing the fire as a young woman working near the Manhattan factory.

**Sacrifice**

**By Rose Greenstein, 1930**

The most panic-stricken moment of my life was at the time of the Triangle fire in 1912 [*sic*], when I saw one hundred and fifty-four of my fellow-workers burned to death in a non-union dress shop. But it is not of my own sick horror that I want to tell you. It is of the revelation that that fire brought to all workers, everywhere.

The Triangle Waist and Dress Company was one of the largest of its kind at that time. The firm employed about three hundred people, mostly girls. During the historic strike of the Ladies Waist and Dressmakers' Union of 1909, we did not succeed in organizing that shop, though the workers put up one of the most heroic fights in the history of the trade. They were out on the streets twenty-six long and bitter weeks, and, finally, broken down by the brutality of the place, they gave up, but with an unbroken spirit. They decided to go back to work, but only to prepare themselves for a renewed struggle, in which they, and not the employers, should be victorious. To the sorrow of the working class, they did not live to see that day.

After the rest of the workers in the garment industry had won for themselves a fifty-hour week, and were working on Saturdays only until one o'clock, the Triangle factory still worked fifty-nine hours. And so it happened that one Saturday a crowd of us, going home at one o'clock from our shop across the street, called up to them a cheerful good-bye. It had become almost a tradition with us to cry out to them: "So long, until the victory is yours!"

But that Saturday was the last time we called. Nor did we ever see those glorious fighters again, for that very day, before five o'clock, they were smothered to death in a blaze that did barely any damage to the building or to the employers. Later, definite proof was brought forward that the doors had been bolted to keep out inspectors and interfering union members, and it was revealed that those who were not actually burned were found huddled together on the floor against locked doors. They had died of suffocation.

Since then, you are sure to find, on the third Sunday in March of every year, a group of workers from the Dressmakers' Union gathered around a grave in Brooklyn. They are honoring twenty-four unidentified victims, who fell in the workers' cause.

In his pioneering essay on working-class women's writing, Paul Lauter has pointed to the "instrumental" nature of much working-class women's writing, which unlike bourgeois autobiography, does not reflect on the path to success followed by an individual, but instead shows how a collectivity has struggled, and must continue to struggle, for a better life. Lauter also points out that a rich intertextuality links working-class women's narratives to other popular cultural forms and artifacts such as songs, workplace narratives, broadsides, political fables, union banners (18), and I might add, the Bible and political theory. "Sacrifice" is an example of such a richly intertextual and multivocal construction. Again, Bakhtin's notion of heteroglossia is helpful here as we notice the various discourses that assist the writer in telling her story.

From her first horrific statement concerning the burned women workers, Greenstein leaves the narrated "I," or "unitary subject" behind. She forcefully refuses to reflect on her "self" or on her unique response to this event: "It is not of my own sick horror that I want to tell you. It is of the revelation that that fire brought to all workers, everywhere." The author then records the history of a working-class struggle for fair wages from the inside, as one worker among many. Her first two paragraphs set the background for the tragedy in terms that reveal a familiarity with organizing tactics and collective, worker-centered interpretations of labor history. "During the historic strike of the Ladies Waist and Dressmakers' Union of 1909, we did not succeed in organizing that shop, though the workers put up one of the most heroic fights in the history of the trade." Greenstein's slightly unidiomatic "Until the victory is yours!" marks her as a recent immigrant, carrying the sociolinguistic strains of an experience steeped in European leftist ideology. Greenstein's phrasing also reveals her familiarity with left-wing rhetoric of worker empowerment: "all workers, everywhere," "to the sorrow of the working class," the "renewed struggle in which they . . . should be victorious." An allusion to messianic revelation and sacrifice is also found in the text. Greenstein says her narrative is about the "revelation that that fire brought to all workers, everywhere." "It was revealed that those who were not actually burned were found huddled together on the floor against the locked doors." Thus these young women workers died together as they worked together, collectively to the bitter end, giving their lives in the fight for workers' rights.

Greenstein shifts to a collective voice similar to Parrish's: "a crowd of us . . . called up to them a cheerful goodbye" and later, "Nor did we ever see those glorious fighters again." This is the narrative "we" of worker empowerment, a discourse the writer was familiar with through union and political work. The narrative inclusiveness continues with a direct address to the reader, "Since then, you are sure to find. . . ." And she ends with a tribute to the twenty-four unidentified victims, the "nameless" or "others" who fell for the still deferred "workers' cause." Again, it is the narrating "we" that participates in an example of active public resistance.

This next narrative offers one of the few critiques I found of sexism in unions, although it was undoubtedly present. According to her Summer School application, the writer, Sarah Gordon, was a Jewish immigrant with family in Russia and Poland. She was thirty-nine years old and had been in the United States for twenty years when she wrote this piece. She spoke Yiddish, Russian, and English. She worked as a hat trimmer and was a member of the Cap and Millinery Workers Union. She had already lost one job and been blacklisted after a very successful organizing drive among women workers in the glove trade. She had taken courses in literature and economics at the Rand School of Social Science and reports that she read "various daily papers" and "some magazines." Where she acquired her feminism is not evident, perhaps from her teacher at the Rand School. Or perhaps some feminism had been instilled in her union by organizers with ties to leftist political groups. For although rife with sexism themselves, these groups did at least address, the "Woman Question" (Coiner, "Literature" 164).

### A Typical Day in My Life
### By Sarah Gordon, 1929

What does a day in the life of a working girl mean? It seems so insignificant and yet it means so much. I have a habit of saying when I start out in the morning that I am going to war, for war it is for a worker, in an unorganized trade especially. We must always be on the defensive because we never can tell how our day will end; it depends on the mood of our employer. I will however try and describe one of the average days in my life.

I start the day wondering why the car company was allowed to raise the fare and was not made to add one or two cars so that the early morning passengers should at least have a seat. But I have found that there is an advantage in hanging on a strap shaking to and fro; it gives me an opportunity to observe my fellow passengers.

I love to observe people's faces; it is almost like reading books. I always wonder what is going on beyond their calm exteriors. I also like to observe what people are reading, for almost everybody is reading in the train. I have learned to classify people by their reading.

In the morning paper the average girl is reading the novel first, the young man the sports page, the middle-aged business man turns to the stock exchange news, and the elderly, tired-looking man tries to solve the crossword puzzle, probably as a means of relaxation, but very few people read the editorials, or the news of the day unless there is a big headline about a murder, a scandal, or a society wedding.

But I? I read all these people. Out of the train I come up to my shop, full of impressions. I would be glad if I were given work and were allowed to work my day through peacefully. But no!

Just one look at the boss who always wears a grouch on his face, another look at the boy who deals out the work, and at the girls who have come before me, and I instantly feel that there is trouble in the air. I do not question immediately but wait for developments.

In the meantime I have a feeling as though I were sitting on a slumbering volcano, I can never tell on which side the lava will break out. I do not have to wait very long before it comes. The boss cannot forgive the girls for making him pay three or five cents more on a hat. He begins picking at the work; he accuses them of unfairness, the girls defending themselves; there is general confusion.

A little later a heated argument among the girls about the unequal distribution of work, endless talk, some bitter words, general resentment, but who is to blame? The system, the struggle for existence.

Lunch hour—I eat my lunch in a hurry, and go out to the "corner" that is the "labor market" of the trade. There I meet the girls from other shops, also some union officials. We discuss conditions in the trade; we get some information as to what is happening in different places, but the most heated discussions are about the split in the organization. This is now the most vital question of the day.

I come back to work usually under the impression of the argument started on the street and am compelled to continue it, because half of the workers of our shop, that is, the men workers, belong to the opposition and are responsible for the break in our organization. These arguments take on very violent and in many cases dangerous forms. It is a very difficult life for us girls in these days; we have to fight our boss on one side, our union that should otherwise protect us on the other, and we are crushed between the two.

Under such physical and mental strain I finish my day's work.

And then the evening! That much desired evening! I straighten up my shoulders, walk out on the street, sniff some fresh air, and go to eat in a place where I can meet friends. We eat and talk about current events, and then we go to a lecture or a meeting or to see some good play, or to the Symphony Concert according to the day. This is the antitoxin which must counteract the poisonous effects of the day in the shop.

As in the other autobiographical narratives, Gordon makes use of a narrative "we" in the present tense and the public domain. But this time the "we" represents *women's* collective voice, not a masculinized workers' voice. "We have to fight our boss on one side, our union that should otherwise protect us on the other." Another salient characteristic of this piece is the frequent reference to physical violence with an emphasis on bodily harm. In Gordon's narrative, men are the source of this violence, and it is directed at women. She compares a working girl's life with "war." She sits on "slumbering lava" in fear of vitriolic eruptions from her boss as "he begins picking at their work and accus[ing] them of unfairness." Arguments with men in her union take on "violent" and "dangerous" forms. The women are "crushed" between their union and the boss. Sidonie Smith maintains that in bourgeois, androcentric autobiography—whether written by men or women—woman's sexuality, woman's body, her desire, is written out of the text, erased. When women autobiographers begin to address this lack, a new type of subjectivity may be created. In other words, this emphasis on the physicality of woman's experience in autobiography is a resistant, counterhegemonic move, a way to subvert the "metaphysical self" of disembodied, androcentric autobiography ("Resisting" 77), and again I would argue that such a move results from the materialist pedagogy practiced at the Summer School. Smith speculates that "With that new subjectivity may come a new system of values, a new kind of language and narrative form, perhaps even a new discourse, an alternative to the prevailing ideology of gender" (*A Poetics* 59). While we may have seen such a new discourse in the writing of French feminist critics and others, here we observe a much earlier attempt by an American working-class woman as she inserts a language of woman's desire into the previously male-centered discourse of worker collectivity. In her final comment, we sense the important regenerative power she experiences when meeting both physical and intellectual needs. Such a focus on the materiality of class experience results from a pedagogical emphasis on the world outside of texts.

**Narratives of Education: The Value of the Summer School Experience**

The last self-(re)presentation is by an African American woman whose experience at the Summer School seems to have changed her life quite substantially.

### It Set Me Thinking
### By Marion Jackson, 1937

When first I learned of Bryn Mawr's Summer School for Women Workers in Industry, immediately I decided I would like to attend. I never once took into consideration the true purpose of the school. I have always had a craving for knowledge, but I have never had time or money enough to complete my education; so, when at a YWCA conference I found out about this school, I thought, "Oh, how nice! Now, here's a chance for me to learn a little something. Who knows? Someday it may come in handy."

I have always felt one should learn all one can at every possible opportunity. I am terribly ashamed to say that I thought only of my own selfish gain. I was thinking of a possible chance of getting a better job, and I believe that foremost in my mind was money.

I am a piece-worker in a dress factory. My work is seasonal. It is not a very comfortable feeling when you realize that the end of the season is nigh, and soon your income will cease while your obligations will go on. For that reason I have always hoped for a steady job with steady pay, or, shall I say, secure employment.

I knew that this school was neither a trade nor a vocational one, but I believed that it gave one prestige to attend the school and meant much in one's favor when seeking employment. I therefore set out to gain admittance to Bryn Mawr.

On Monday, June 15, at the official opening exercises, I listened with profound interest to President Park. She related the origin of the school. It was a vision of former president M. Carey Thomas that led her to create a place where women working in industry might go to prepare themselves to meet any problems that might confront them in their field.

Dr. Susan Kingsbury in her address very clearly pointed out that any woman receiving this training should, when she has returned to her home, feel it her duty to render a service to fellow workers through leadership or individual service. There were many more interesting and important facts brought out through these and other speakers—far too numerous for me to mention.

This meeting to me was really an awakening! The true purpose of the school was unfolded.

It set me thinking. I have been asking myself, "What can I, in my small way, do to contribute to labor or humanity? I am only one little insignificant person among a multitude."

At such a time one has a feeling of inferiority, realizing the lack of training and experience; obviously one feels hopeless.

I come from the large and prosperous city of Philadelphia. There we have our trade unions, workers' education, adult education, peace conferences, youth congress groups, churches, and other civic organizations all seemingly well organized and fairly advanced in their movements, and so I still wondered what then could I do?

I was walking through the hall in Denbigh on Tuesday afternoon when the girl in room 13 called to me. She wanted to know what I could tell her about the Scottsboro case and about Angelo Herndon, the Negro organizer. I am a Negro; still I was forced to confess that there was very little I could tell her. Many of us feel that the Negro problem is a tremendous one and we feel so helpless in regard to it that we take the easiest way out and shut our eyes to much of the real suffering of our people. Of course, we know that this is the wrong way to look upon the matter; but then too we often feel that we are only one tenth of the population, and that is a very small minority. Then the girl in room 13 reminded me of the fact that nearly 90 percent of the Negro population were workers, and the workers are the masses. Therefore we need only to unite our forces and we will bring about a betterment of conditions for all. Through unity of forces we can break down race discrimination and class discrimination.

I am glad my sister student called me into her room that day. She set me thinking in an entirely different direction. I no longer think in terms of dollars and cents. I think in terms of what I can do for my class and my race. I feel that I too can do my part, be it ever so small. I feel that I will have accomplished a great deal if I am able to convince other Negroes that we as a race must stop sitting down and taking it on the chin, so to speak.

We must stop looking for the path of easiness, for we must face facts and learn truths, —know the cause in order to find a cure.

I intend therefore on returning home to connect myself with the National Negro Congress and to learn Negro history, since what education I do have I have received in the public schools and any favorable facts pertaining to the Negro were very intentionally omitted.

I have then to thank Bryn Mawr for putting me on the right track.

I have Bryn Mawr to thank for making me race and class conscious.

Similar to Fickland, Jackson concentrates on the tasks of defining and assigning value to a black self in her narrative. Details of the interactions between the writer, college administrators, and a student illustrate Jackson's awakening and growth from self-interested individualism to racial pride and working-class solidarity. Although Jackson mentions no ties to left-wing political organizations, this type of "working-class success story" Mary Jo Maynes points out, was common among European socialist autobiographers in the early 1900's ("Gender and Narrative" 110). Jackson admits that her first reason for coming to Bryn Mawr was the desire to complete her education for "selfish gain." Motivated by bourgeois values, Jackson's narrated "I" understood "that it gave one prestige to attend the school and meant much in one's favor when seeking employment." It wasn't until the opening exercises that she learned from President Park the true purpose of the school: "to render service to fellow workers through leadership or individual service." Park and other speakers motivated the narrated "I" to a certain extent, and Jackson came away committed to seeking change for "labor [and] humanity." At that point, she still felt, however, that "I am only one little insignificant person among a multitude." This feeling of unimportance has been commonly voiced by white working-class writers, male and female. In Gagnier's study of the ways white Victorian working-class autobiographies differed from those written by members of the white middle class, she describes the "social atom" phenomenon, in which, for a variety of reasons, the narrative begins with a "statement of the author's ordinariness." Such is not the case for the conventional bourgeois autobiographer who frequently starts with family lineage or a birth date (103).

Continuing to describe her past subjectivity, Jackson creates a narrated "we," which begins to identify with many of the Philadelphia movements for civic and worker improvement. "There we have our trade unions, workers' education, adult education, peace conferences. . . ." But this collective "we" is not an empowered one. Jackson "still wonder[s] what then could I do?" Up to this point in the narrative, Jackson has not yet dealt with her blackness. Perhaps the source of her powerlessness lies in the fact that her "we" is still racially unaware. Blackburn has written that

> most African-American female autobiographers confess to one incident in their early years that awakened them to their color; this recognition scene evoke[s] an awareness of their blackness and of its significance, and it had a lasting influence on their lives. (134)

The incident involving the "girl in room 13" serves this purpose for Jackson. Although the girl subsumes the black cause within the larger struggle, she "reminds" Jackson "of the fact that nearly 90 percent of the Negro population were workers," and "the workers are the masses," powerful in their numbers. For Jackson, there is no assimilating the black cause in the white one. She separates the issues of race and class. Although she is willing to join forces with white workers, she keeps racial equality a separate and distinct goal. Like Fickland, Jackson's subjectivity slips back and forth between "I" and "we." On returning home, "I" intends to joint the "National Negro Congress and to learn Negro history." Thus, with consciousness raised, Jackson seems motivated to act only when she does so as an African American in a larger workers' movement. Similar to most of her counterparts in the School, Jackson does not discuss her problems from a gendered perspective.

In the context of the Bryn Mawr Summer School, the autobiographical assignment was often successful in encouraging the women workers to represent empowered, collective subject positions through their narratives and occasionally to take up "social feminist" or "industrial feminist" positions. In their autobiographies, the working women were offered the opportunity to represent newly acquired versions of more powerful selves. Although these ideas of empowered selfhood were usually derived from androcentric configurations offered to workers in their Bryn Mawr classroom as well as in institutions of working-class culture, the women often used this rhetoric to win better working conditions and more respect on the job. Follow-up studies of alumnae also attest to the fact that many went back to their communities and became civic, church, and union leaders (Heller, "Blue" 122–23). These accomplishments were remarkable indeed.

## WOMEN AND AUTOBIOGRAPHY:
### WORKERS AND STUDENTS, PAST AND PRESENT

Important implications for writing instructors can be drawn from comparisons among the Bryn Mawr autobiographers, literary autobiographers, and studies of student autobiographers. The research on autobiography by literary critics and composition theorists alike has revealed that many women focus on human relationships in their writing to a greater extent than men. This finding tends to hold true across race and class—at least in the United States. For example, in her groundbreaking study of women autobiographers, Estelle C. Jelinek found that these writers concentrate on "personal lives—domestic details, family difficulties, close friends, and especially people who influenced them" (8). Elizabeth Flynn reports that the narratives of her female college students are "stories of interaction, of connection, or of frustrated connection" (428). Similarly, Linda H. Peterson notes that "the topics that women students choose are almost always 'relational'—i.e., they focus on the relationship of the writer with some other person or group" (173). The same focus on relationships is present in the Bryn Mawr narratives by both black and white women and in Zandy's anthology of contempo-

rary working-class women writers. In explaining women's greater concern
with human interactions, researchers in both scholarly groups tend to rely
on social constructivist readings of Nancy Chodorow's theories or Carol
Gilligan's extension of them or both. (See Sidonie Smith; Susan Stanford
Friedman; Shirley K. Rose; Flynn; Peterson; and Geoffrey Sirc). Friedman
asserts that applying Chodorow's theories of selfhood (as well as those of
Sheila Rowbotham) "to women's autobiographical texts—particularly those
by women who also belong to racial, ethnic, sexual and religious minorities"
helps expand the autobiographical canon by deemphasizing the androcentric or conventional focus on the individual self (35). Quoting Chodorow,
Friedman asserts that "we can anticipate finding in women's texts a consciousness of self in which 'the individual does not oppose herself to all others,' nor 'feel herself to exist outside of others, but very much with others in
an interdependent existence'" (41). Since many women have been found to
write in this manner, their focus on relationship and their deemphasis of the
individual ego need not, indeed, must not be devalued in academic writing.
As Peterson cautions, "evaluation of personal essays should not privilege certain gender-specific modes of self-representation, nor penalize others" (175).

Another point shared by both compositionists writing about autobiography and literary critics of autobiography is their emphasis on the poststructuralist notion of a discursive or textual construction of subjectivity.
They argue that gender is a social construct shaped by cultural beliefs, values, and attitudes—all "texts" in their language-constitutive nature. These
texts motivate the behaviors marking gender. For example, Sidonie Smith
writes that the tropes an autobiographer uses in self-(re)presentation "are
always cast in language and are always motivated by cultural expectations,
habits and systems of interpretation pressing on her at the scene of writing"
(*A Poetics* 47). Similarly, Geoffrey Sirc argues that "any occasion for the actual production of written discourse is going to reflect the way that the writer
(as well as the text) has been inscribed into the forms of gender's discourse"
(4). Since in our culture, conventional discourses of gender, race, and class
are not equal in the opportunities they provide individuals, the activity of
reconstructing subjectivity through autobiography for more powerful self-
(re)presentation is a valuable assignment in a writing class whose aim is,
among other things, to build self-confidence and social equality. Feminist
poststructuralist Chris Weedon writes:

> As individuals we are not the mere objects of language but the sites of discursive
> struggle, a struggle which takes place in the consciousness of the individual. . . .
> The individual who has a memory and an already discursively constituted sense

of identity may resist particular interpellations or produce new versions of meaning from the conflicts and contradictions between existing discourses. Knowledge of more than one discourse and the recognition that meaning is plural allows for a measure of choice on the part of the individual and even where choice is not available, resistance is still possible. (106)

It seems clear from the current research by compositionists and from the evidence provided by the Summer School autobiographies that certain textual and extratextual conditions for autobiographical writing produce more empowered subjectivities than others. Sirc's assignment, to "recreate for me in words a single incident in which you were involved or which you witnessed," provides a good example of disempowering textual conditions (5). This topic did not result, for the most part, in self-(re)presentations of strength for his women students. Sirc reports that most of their written responses did indeed include scenarios of nurturing or of providing care (7); however, he also found that the women students "were more likely to picture themselves as confused and out of control" than the male writers (8). When women's traditional focus on others is accompanied by an autobiographical subjectivity that is devalued, subservient, or exploited, instructors who are teaching for the empowerment of women need to reevaluate their assignments and provide textual contexts (readings, assignments, discussions) that are conducive to personal growth. As Sidonie Smith maintains,

> to write an autobiography from that speaking posture [oppressed], does not . . . liberate woman from the fictions that bind her; indeed, it may embed her even more deeply in them since it promotes identification with the very essentialist ideology that renders woman's story a story of silence, powerlessness, self-effacement. (*A Poetics* 53)

Sirc (8), Flynn (434), and Peterson (173) voice similar concerns. That the texts written by the women workers are so strikingly different from Sirc's further underscores this point. There were almost no voices of confusion or disorientation among the Bryn Mawr narratives I examined, and I maintain that one reason for their strength lies in the textual context for writing encountered at the Bryn Mawr Summer School, as well as in the unions, the YWCA, and progressive churches where these women came into contact with empowering discourses. Also, as we have seen, the Kennan assignment asked for a critical appraisal of the workers' life situations. Thus, the Bryn Mawr project teaches the importance of exposing students to an array of empowering voices so that they are better able to meld those voices with their own. Several feminist scholars support this contention. Weedon argues that to reconstruct more appropriate subjectivities for themselves "women need access to the different subject positions offered in imaginative alternatives to the present, in humorous critiques and even by positive heroines" (172). Linda Peterson recommends that "the readings suggested as models for the [autobiographical] assignment should include examples by and about both masculine and feminine subjects" (175). And Patricia Bizzell has advocated a pedagogy for the composition class that will "generate egalitarian social power relations" (55). She urges composition teachers to offer readings "that are not simply pluralistic, but politically engaged in a variety of ways; and . . . to try to get students into these texts even if they initially seem very un-congenial" (67). Of course, as Bizzell implies, our focus should not solely be on women. Members of the working class and minorities also need to read discourse about collective strength and control.

The use of a collective subjectivity ("we") marks the most significant difference between the student autobiographical writing reported on by compositionists and that of the Bryn Mawr writers. The crucial factor that produced this striking stylistic feature was likely the extratextual context in which the working women were writing and yet determined to change. In "Literary Theory, Teaching Composition, and Feminist Response," I argued for the importance of the wider social, economic, and political context in producing critical literacy. Both text and subjectivity have a dialectical relationship with material conditions, such as the economy in which they occur, and both respond to and influence these conditions in the culture at large. As Weedon writes, "discursive practices are embedded in material power relations which also require transformation for change to be realized," yet these "material power relations constitute and inhere within discursive practices" (106). When people believe that better lives are possible through writing, their writing will reflect this expectation. The theories and practices of worker empowerment offered at Bryn Mawr and in other collective movements of the time may have led the women workers to believe that their lives could be improved through school and writing, organizing and protesting. Such worker "texts" did in turn influence the social, economic, and political context of the period. The shift in the Bryn Mawr narratives from the private "I" to the more public "we" likely arose from this more public and material arena for the students' collective writing and actions.

Thus, for working women in the early 1900s, Gagnier concludes that "Contrary to the claims on behalf of a room of one's own, workers' autobiographies suggest that writing women were those whose work took them out of the home" (100). This supports findings by social historians that "the process of self-discovery and emergence of a group consciousness for early-twentieth-century women depended on employment outside the home" (Eisenstein 9). This group consciousness is indeed very crucial to women's empowerment, but I would add that history also shows that unless women and other oppressed groups are provided with the discourse of collective experience, protest, and power, they will likely remain in a weakened, individualist state. In the manner of the Bryn Mawr educators, I think we need to study our students through their autobiographies and other means and strive to create textual and even extratextual contexts that lead them to greater confidence in themselves and as a group. Occasionally, requiring students to write in a collective voice might change their perceptions of themselves as isolated individuals with disparate problems to a powerful collectivity with legitimate rights and demands. If students learn to write as "we," instructors may find them better able to appreciate the benefits of collective endeavor. We may even reencounter the raised consciousness and liberating discourse that characterized the students at the Bryn Mawr Summer School back in the 1920s and 1930s.

## APPENDIX: AUTOBIOGRAPHICAL WRITINGS
## BY BRYN MAWR SUMMER SCHOOL STUDENTS

**"This America"**
**Thelma Brown**
*Shop and School,* **1936**

I went walking one day. Everywhere I look, I thought, "What a beautiful place this America is!" But when I peered more closely, I saw the strangest thing. Here was a dream of a home sitting away among the tall trees. Empty! "A summer home," someone said.

And as I walked along, I saw a little one-room cabin. It was running over with life, with little barefoot, sun-baked children playing in the yard. No green grass in this yard; only hard-packed dirt.

Then I passed a beautiful meadow. It was green and smooth. There was a horse and pony grazing. But as I was wondering how I would climb the steep hill in the distance, I saw a farmer and his son plowing on this steep, rocky hillside. "How can they make things grow there?" I thought. The farmer, the son, and the horse, they didn't look as if they had ever had a full meal.

Then I began to think abut the empty dream house,
The one-room cabin with all the children,
The big, green meadow with only animals in it,

The farmer with a hill full of rocks and red dirt to wrench a living out of. Then I got mad.

### "The Funeral of Sacco and Vanzetti"
### Frieda Daun
### *Shop and School*, 1937

That rainy and weary Sunday, a hot August day, will never leave my thoughts. It was the last day of a horrible, painful, seven year old story, known in every corner of the world. It was the last day of life for two innocent men who had been locked up in the jails of Massachusetts, for seven years; the last day of hearing their voices lifted in appeal in our courts, and addressing the workers of the world, in protest against this terrible injustice that was being visited upon them. Protests from all over the world came pouring into Boston. The appeals and protests failed. The ruling class would not listen. They answered, "We must do away with the two damnable anarchists." Three prominent men of Boston, governor Fuller, Judge Thayer and President Lowell of Harvard University, were chosen to decide whether Sacco and Vanzetti had had a fair trial. Their reply was, "Yes." So the two men were electrocuted.

I have no words to describe the painful feeling in my heart, when I read in the papers the following morning, "Sacco and Vanzetti were executed this morning. Funeral will take place Sunday."

Sunday morning I rushed quickly to the big square in the Italian section of Boston, where the funeral procession was to begin. People were constantly coming in, despite the rain that lasted the whole day. The crowd was getting bigger and bigger. Machines with banners and flowers coming in from all sides. A huge banner read, "Workers of the World, remember the death of our two martyrs." Another one read, "Massachusetts' Justice Crucified." Many small banners carrying similar mottos were distributed to the people who marched. Hundreds of bouquets and baskets of flowers were sent from all kinds of unions and labor organizations from all over the country. The trucks and machines, which were loaded with flowers, moved slowly. Huge masses of people marched behind them with banners in their hands, or pinned to their sleeves. These read, "Remember August 22, 1927." The trucks and flowers stretched out in a long procession.

We started from the square to the heart of the city. Hundreds of mounted police walked after us. They did not allow us to march in large groups nor to stop. "Keep on marching", they yelled. My brother was hit by one of them, for talking to bystanders, and asking them to join the protest. As we marched by the Common, people looked at us curiously. Many laughed, joked, or shouted, "Look at the anarchists marching!" We moved on to Beacon Street. A group of ladies were standing near a rich apartment house and I heard one say, "Aren't those people perfectly stupid making so much fuss over two ignorant Italians." Another voice, "Look at the 'wops' marching!" We marched on to the city hall. The crowd was getting still bigger, as we marched on towards the cemetery which was quite a distance from the place from which we started. The rain came down slowly, continuously, but it did not stop the marchers. With umbrellas and raincoats people marched on in a last protest. I felt that even the clouds protested against the cruel decision, and sent the rain upon the earth. The whole atmosphere, the very air, was tense; a heavy strain was felt by everybody that Sunday.

### "My Last Job"
### Wilma Gerhart
### *A Scrapbook of Industrial Workers Experiences*, 1932

In January I started to work in a drapery shop. It was a new shop started by two brothers. Four skimpy windows facing a narrow alley were the only ventilation. The sewing machines were against an ice-cold wall, so that we had to wear our coats nearly all the day. Mr. A—— did not like this as it hindered us in our work, and the work was not going out so fast. If he said anything we told him to give us more heat, or we would walk out on him. We were not allowed to talk but we did just the same, for half the time he wasn't around. The floor lady was only a young kid and she didn't know anything about the work. We kept working quite steady for about four months when suddenly the place went bankrupt. The landlord was not paid, the girls were not paid, and Mr. A—— was not home when we called him on the telephone.

We girls then got together and marched up to the county clerk, to ask him to help us get our pay. He talked to us for a while and then called up Mr. B——, but the secretary said he was at court. The county clerk thought about ten minutes, and then said, "I can't help you girls, you'll have to go to the District Court Attorney." We asked why he couldn't help us, when the laws printed on a cardboard notice on the wall said to go to the county clerk for compensation. And he said, "I told you before I could not help you." As much as to say, get out. Just before we left the office, one of the girls asked, "Do you know Mr. B—— very well?" He said, "Yes, why?" "Oh! Graft works better with graft. Good day." We left right after that without giving him time to say anything, then marched to the District Court Attorney. People turned out to stare at us for we looked like we were on parade.

The District Court Attorney sat in his chair, as comfortable as any political person could look. Feet high on the desk, smoking a cigar that looked a little better than a five or ten cent cigar, and gazing at cars slowly passing up and down the business street. He looked at us and asked what we wanted, without even taking his feet off the desk. We explained to him the same details, as we had to the county clerk. He again turned away and looked at the traffic. Suddenly he came to life, so that we all jumped at the suddenness of it. He said he would call Mr. B——. His secretary connected them. They conversed for about ten minutes. He then said to us, "Mr. Potts had no money and can't pay you, so I can't do anything more." We left him without further remarks, but we all had decided to write to the Department of Labor. One woman hired a lawyer, who immediately got in touch with the Department. He took down our names, and how much money we all were to receive. I've heard no more since then for I had to leave for Bryn Mawr.

### "Sold Out"
**Agnes de Nicholas**
*Shop and School,* 1936

It was August of 1934. In Pawtucket, Rhode Island, and the heart of the textile industry, a storm was brewing. Workers were dissatisfied, they worked hard in their respective plants. Conditions were bad, people were hungry, men, women and children were tired of being exploited. There were mass meetings with various union officials. Everyone had agreed that something must be done to alleviate some of the unnecessary misery.

Morning papers with three inch headlines announced a general strike. Newsboys screamed out these headlines, "Francis Gorman declares a general strike! Textile workers be prepared to go out on the picket line!"

The word spread rapidly. Everyone was saying, "Strike! We must strike!"

The Saylesville plant of Pawtucket was one of the first to answer this call. Workers mobilized their forces. Picket lines were formed. Long files of explicated wage earners were picketing, two abreast, smiles on their faces, songs on their lips. Such orderly ranks, even those who were not strike sympathizers had to grant that they were conducting themselves in gentlemanly fashion.

This of course was not the opinion of those who had shares in the plant. One of those personages being Theodore Green, governor of the state of Rhode Island. He must protect his property at all cost even though there wasn't the slightest sign of violence. Governor Green ordered out the militia. Miles of barbed wire were raised on the factory. Uniformed soldiers with their bayonets patrolled the grounds day and night.

The workers were infuriated. They had done nothing to cause this barricade to be put up. An old gentleman of about fifty, with a shock of silvery gray hair, who had been on the picket line all day stopped for a drink of water.

The soldiers on guard misinterpreting this pause fired a shot into the crowd.

The war was on. Strikers picked up sticks, stones, broken pieces of glass and fought back. The mass moved forward, hundreds of maddened picketers into a nearby cemetery. There was a sacred ground behind tombstones where was fought one of the most horrible battles known to the New England textile center.

For three days and nights this warfare went on. Tear gas bombs were thrown into the crowd to blind them and force them back. Unaimed shots were fired injuring old men and women who were not strike participants. Brothers fighting one another, one sworn to his country, the other sworn to the picket line. Girls and wives whose sweethearts and husbands had to force them back with the sharp points of their bayonets. For miles around the smell of tear gas and the sound of breaking glass filled the countryside.

Four days later the papers once more issued the proclamation that all strikers should return to their looms and machines.

The strikers were sold out. Nothing had been gained. Union officials were powerless. There were insufficient funds to keep the strike going, or that at least was the explanation given.

Must the workers be continually sold out due to corruptness in the union itself? No, I don't think so. Men must be made to realize the power of mass organization; they are the producers of production. When a strike is called they should march as one—not one plant but all textile industries paralyzing the whole field. Manufacturers will have to meet their demands if they want to remain in business. May general organized labor be ours in the near future!

### "On The Job"
### Nida Panglo
### *Bryn Mawr Light*, 1925

When I was offered my job as Business Agent [for a labor union] some years ago, I took it with great reluctance. I had joined the waitresses' union, while working in a restaurant in a department store, and had got fired for doing so. I was out of work, but I hesitated before taking a job with such responsibility.

I started on my job, as Business Agent of the Waitresses' union with many misgivings. On Monday morning I started on my duties assured by the Business Agent of an affiliated men's union, of his help and advice. With this hope, I entered his office.

"Well, I see you are on the job," he said "what do you think you should do first?"

"I came here," I replied timidly, "supposing you would tell me a little of what my duties would be."

"You will visit the various restaurants," he said as he busied himself with the mail before him, "talk to the waitresses and try to get them to come into the union."

"Well, what shall I say to them, what argument may I use?" I asked.

"Use your own argument," he answered, as he turned to answer the telephone, "You'll have to learn by hard knocks how to get them in."

I started out on my journey, filled with mixed emotions. I wondered where I would go first. I had an impulse to run away because I felt that with no more definite ideas, I simply could not go and talk to girls. I went into a restaurant, approached a girl and asked her to join the union. She looked at me and said, "Aw! What d' I want t' join the union fer? Hain't no good." And walked away.

I felt like going through the floor, my heart sank. How little I knew! Tears came to my eyes, and I hurried out, to walk along the street talking to myself. After many similar attempts, I finally learned how to talk to girls, how to persuade them to join the union for their own good. After many experiences, disappointments and discouragements, I saw our union grow.

After about six months, came the question of a raise in wages, betterment of conditions and reduction of working hours. The union members had to agree upon what increase they would ask, and after days of arguments, the agreement was ready to be presented to the employer.

We found a man who refused to give the raise, though he had stated that he had made a profit, and that his business was a paying institution. Every effort having failed to bring about a settlement, the inevitable strike came.

I shall never forget the bitterness and suffering of that, my first strike! I had to be on the picket line to encourage, and oversee the others. As we walked up and down, men and women would go into the restaurant, and as they passed us, they offered insult after insult until we wanted to scream and strike some one, but we always had to be careful, for there was the law, to protect the employer and the public. A woman started into the restaurant; she stopped, look at me contemptuously and said "You ought to be home, washing clothes, instead of here hurting this poor man, you nasty thing." I couldn't stand it any longer; so I answered her back. Then the long arm of the law reached me, stuck me into the patrol wagon, and then into jail. After weeks of struggle this employer agreed to settle and everyone went back to work, and I had to go on to the next task.

The tasks of a Business Agent are many and varied. In the course of a day she is called upon to meet many different situations. A girl comes to me crying. Her baby is sick, but she can't quit work for baby needs food, and medicine. I have to help her, find care for the baby, encourage her to keep up her spirit. Then some girl has a grievance against her employer, and I must iron it out. A girl quits her job, and I must find her another if possible, and fill the place she left.

I have the union books to keep, the dues to collect, the treasury to watch and social affairs to manage. I must keep my union on the map by telling every other union that we are organized, and by reminding them to eat in union restaurants.

I close my desk at the end of the day and wend my way homeward to my family, feeling happy that I shall have a few hours rest that night. I got myself all comfortable, when the telephone rings, and someone says, "Jennie Smith was badly scalded in the kitchen and we have sent her to the hospital." I wearily dress, and then hurry to Jennie, see her cared for and then fill the place she has just left. I drag myself home again, wondering, "What next?"

### "My Great Grandmother"
### Annie Thompson
### *Shop and School,* 1937

My great grandmother, Mollie Clay, was born May 28, 1850, in Auto River, Virginia. At the age of fourteen, she was sold as a slave to Mrs. Goodman. Mrs. Goodman was very mean to her. Every morning she would have to get up at four o'clock and cook breakfast. After breakfast she washed dishes and cleaned the house. If the work wasn't done well Mrs. Goodman whipped Grandmother.

At the age of eighteen Grandmother married John Clay and moved to Evington, Virginia. She was the mother of fourteen children, seven girls and seven boys. Grandmother was very happy with all of these children. She would always sit down and sing to them. Her favorite songs were "I'm Going Down to the River of Jordan" and "Everyday Will Be Sunday." At the age of eighty Grandmother's health wasn't good, so her daughter in New Jersey went after her. Grandmother stayed in New Jersey three years. She died at the age of eighty-five.

**"Childhood Recollections"**
**Wanda Wosnak**
*A Scrapbook of Industrial Worker's Experiences,* **"Individual Recollections"**
**section, 1932**

When we were living in Massachusetts, mother had a boarding house in which she made a livelihood for the family. Dad was a weaver, but seldom worked, and if he did work, he never contributed to the family upkeep. He thought since mother had the children it was her duty to support us. Although he never interfered with our upbringing or what religious denomination mother wanted us to belong to; that was a woman's affair—the home and the children.

Of course my home life was very interesting as I was the youngest in the family—my two sisters and brothers were already wage earners. We had men of all walks of life boarding with us, some were religious or anti-religious, some were socialists, progressives, and democrats. There were always discussions or arguments at the dinner table and sometime it would last the whole evening. I formed my ideas and opinions about the labor movement very early, although I didn't know the history of it.

One of the socialists, who later became my brother-in-law, had a great influence on our outlook on life. He had all kinds of labor newspapers, pamphlets and magazines come to the house. I remember reading in the "Appeal To Reason" (I believe it was a socialist paper) about the Colorado Coal Strike, and how the State Militia mowed down the striking miners, their wives and children. They also shot into the miner's homes. I was horrified and read the article and translated it to my mother. She saw how upset I was about it so she asked me not to read the "Appeal to Reason" any more. However, I never kept her wish.

One year, when we were having a presidential election there was much discussion at home about the election. Some of them were saying, "Its about time the working class would wake up and stop voting the Republican and Democratic ticket which protects big business. But vote the Socialist Party ticket which is the working class party which fights for the rights of labor."

So the day before the Presidential election our teacher at school gave us a treat and let us vote, too. So she wrote the name on the blackboard: W. H. Taft on the Republican ticket, W. Wilson on the Democratic ticket and T. Roosevelt on the Progressive ticket, but no name for the Socialist Party ticket. Of course, she didn't expect any of us to vote differently. Before she had time to hand us the ballots to vote on, up went my hand. When she called on me I said, "I wanted to vote for the Socialist Party Ticket!" "Well," she said, "who is running for president on the Socialist ticket?" By this time with the rest of the children all listening and staring at me, I got so confused and embarrassed I really forgot who it was. But somehow we managed to find out and I voted the Socialist ticket that day!

# Material Texts: Labor Drama at the Bryn Mawr Summer School

## 4

It is surprising how little difficulty the students have writing their own plays. They use the newspapers and magazine accounts of current events as a source of material. These provide plenty of material on labor problems, such as the wage and hour bill, strikes, unemployment, and numerous other important matters. One excellent example was the play, *The Wage and Hour Bill* written and produced by the students this summer. It was presented in the form of a "Living Newspaper." These subjects are so vital to the working people that the students not only act their parts, but actually live them. Some of the lines were improvised as they went on the stage which was very effective, because it was so realistic. Another good example was the skit, *You've Got Something There* which brought out clearly the advantage of collective bargaining.... The technique that students develop remains in their minds and that helps them to carry on dramatics education in their own communities and unions.
—Anne D. Baden, *Shop and School,* 1938

As revealed in the words of this student, labor drama played a very important role in the educational agenda of the Bryn Mawr Summer School for Women Workers. Several extensive productions and numerous skits were performed during every summer session. The Summer School's academic and aesthetic agendas evolved out of a focus on the experiences of the working women and a desire to help them improve their lives in terms they themselves articulated. The creation of a workers' theater offered a number of benefits along these lines. Labor drama, in its essence a public and collective endeavor, provided discourse for the transformative social project envisioned at the Summer School. Because creating plays and skits calls for synthesizing experience into a performative mode, workers conceptualized, evaluated, and critiqued their lives, often forcefully (re)writing themselves personally and collectively into current events and public discourse. Furthermore, in researching and writing plays, the students encountered academic discourse and the discourses of public policy and journalism. Since these discourses had to be "translated" into appropriate registers for plays performed for the Summer School, union, community, church, or YWCA, the women gained a great deal of rhetorical sophistication. And again, the focus here is on the material culture, with transformative text achieving a material dimension in its theatrical embodiment (which in the case of Summer School dramatics included both actors and audience) and, perhaps, also achieving a higher degree of material reality as these more progressive social texts became accepted in the culture at large. The Summer School women found the dramatic unity of ideas and action satisfying because it mirrored a unity of mind and body, a state of being longed for in much of their textual production (see chapter 5).

Another benefit of dramatic activity was that it linked the working women to the important working-class cultural aesthetic of the time, with its roots in the more distant tradition of folk performance. The richly varied discursive context of the Summer School again calls to mind Bakhtin's concept of "heteroglossia," which Diane Price Herndl has defined as "multiple voices expressing multiple ideologies from different strata of language-in-use" (9). As will be seen in the excerpts and commentary to follow, the working women brought their own marginalized voices to the Summer School, where they encountered other discursive forms, forging more powerful voices in the process. Their strengthened discursive subjectivities countered the bourgeois hegemonic discourse that textually oppressed and even erased them. Indeed, of all the Summer School's literacy practices, labor drama was likely the most transformative, enabling the women to grow intellectually, politically, and aesthetically. Dramatic productions, from complicated pageants to improvised skits, became an increasingly important activity over the years. For example, more than thirty-five theatrical pieces were produced during the summer of 1936 alone (Esther Peterson, *Dramatics*). Two goals predominate in accounts of the school's dramatic activity: to help the working women reconstruct more powerful subjectivities and, ultimately, build an egalitarian working-class culture that reflected their interests, needs, and desires.

## WORKERS' CULTURE: BUILDING ON THE PAST

In examining the Summer School's theatrical arts program, it is important to understand that it occurred in the context of a larger workers' theater movement, which had its own history, harking back to European folk performances. A more recent precursor, however, was the participatory pageant performed in the United States in the 1910s and 1920s by civic associations, churches, unions, immigrant groups, and even corporations to involve cast and audience in a morale building spectacle. These pageants combined song, dance, mass chants, and often spectacular costumes, scenery, and orchestration to make their dramatic point. *The Paterson Strike Pageant* of 1913 offers an influential example. It was organized by the Industrial Workers of the World (Wobblies) and directed by John Reed, left-wing journalist and activist who was to write *Ten Days That Shook the World*, an eye-witness account of the Russian Revolution. Performed in Madison Square Garden with a cast of fifteen hundred striking immigrant silk workers before a crowd of fifteen thousand, *The Paterson Strike Pageant* publicized the oppressive conditions that led to a three-month strike at a local mill (Nochlin 87).

A continent away, participatory pageants were being used to build support for the Russian Revolution, but the need for a more mobile and adaptable stage led to the development of an extensive *agitprop* theater by the Moscow Blue Blouses, a revolutionary acting troop that inspired the early Soviet workers. The agitprop (agitation and propaganda) theater spread with the communist movement to other working-class organizations of Europe. Drama historian Daniel Friedman credits a German immigrant workers' theater called the *Prolet-Buehne* with introducing this type of labor drama to American workers in the New York area (114). Most of the Bryn Mawr plays can be characterized as such.

In the United States, workers' theater groups formed in unions, political groups, the Ys, and churches, wherever workers' concerns predominated and energy was available for combining educational, organizing, and aesthetic endeavors into plays or skits. At the height of the workers' theater movement "hundreds of troupes and tens of thousands of workers . . . wrote, directed, performed and attended their own theatrical pieces" (D. Friedman 111). In 1935, a national organization called the League of Workers' Theatres reported a membership of four hundred theater groups in twenty-eight cities across the United States. The League published a monthly journal, *New Theater,* which, at its height, had a circulation of eighteen thousand (114).

## WORKERS' THEATER: GENRES FROM THE WORKING CLASS

Productions developed at the Bryn Mawr Summer School fit easily into the dramatic styles common to the workers' theater movement of the 1930s. The most popular theatrical form was the "mass recitation" adapted from the early participatory pageants (D. Friedman 114). Often combined with group movement and musical or rhythmic accompaniment, the mass recitations were typically performed by a worker's chorus reciting verse in a dramatic context that pitted workers against a capitalist boss. The point, usually political, was simple and direct. The acting style stressed clarity of voice and gesture (McDermott 126). The agitprop skit, which typically included mass chants, was the other very popular form of the day. Daniel Friedman writes that it involved radical political content, an extremely physical acting style, and a montage plot structure based on political concepts, rather than linear development of character and plot (111). Many agitprop skits combined short, scenic episodes into longer plays, in the manner of *Waiting for Lefty,* the workers' theater hit of the 1930s written by Clifford Odets. This form is seen frequently in the Summer School repertoire. Another popular workers' theater style used at the Summer School was the "election script." In these skits, various political parties, Democrat, Republican, Communist, Socialist, or Fascist, were poked fun at or praised, depending upon the political tendency of the theatrical group (McDermott 128). Another genre of Russian origin also frequently produced at the Summer School was the "living newspaper" or dramatized news story. Made famous in the United States by the Federal Theater Project under the direction of Hallie Flanagan, these productions portrayed important current events, emphasizing their effects on the working class (Goldstein and McDermott 84). Other well-liked forms included "cabaret-style revues, vaudeville-like comedy routines, political circuses, . . . and pantomimes" (D. Friedman 115). Music and percussion instruments were often used in all genres to energize the audience, and spectators and actors together often sang a spirited rendition of "L'Internationale" at the end of a production (McConachie and Friedman 14). Humor and satire were staples in this theater, and as with other forms of working-class art, "contents and forms [were drawn] from folk and popular tradition" (12). Thus, the Summer School students used melodies from popular songs and nursery rhymes in their productions, rewriting the words to suit their purposes.

In characterizing theater for working-class audiences, Bruce A. McConachie and Daniel Friedman argue that what most separated the workers' stage from the mainstream theater of the day was the blurred distinction between actors and spectators (14). Summer School student Victoria Grala wrote an account of this phenomenon in the 1937 issue of *Shop and School.*

> A unique and somewhat startling technique which was used over and over again in our drama this summer, was that of actors speaking from different parts of the audience. . . . We discovered that an emotional feeling of unity resulted from such drama, because we were sympathetic with these audience actors and felt in our own hearts what they themselves were speaking in the play. Then again, it broke the sharp line which is usually found between actors and audience as we were as one with the players. (34)

McConachie and Friedman point out that unlike the more mainstream drama of the 1930s, workers' theater did not delve into the psychological make up of its characters, choosing instead to stress themes of social morality (12). McConachie and Friedman also emphasize the strong emotional effect of many working-class dramatic productions, designed for the most part to build class consciousness and underscore the need for social change from the workers' perspective.

### Goal: A Workers' Culture

According to Daniel Friedman, the ultimate goal of the workers' theater was to "create a distinct working class culture which . . . would reflect and inspire . . . workers in their economic and political struggles" (111). The words of an anonymous Summer School student echo this intention. Her unusual use of the feminine possessive pronoun indicates her belief that this culture will include working-class women's perspectives also:

> real labor drama is only now beginning to be written and produced. Its unestablished place in the field of the arts means that anyone and everyone can contribute her [*sic*] own experiences and feelings to the experimental performance which will in the end build a firm Workers' Art. ("Experiments" 1)

Hilda Smith also mentions this goal in her characteristically visionary style. She commends this "new and living drama of the people, drawn from the deep sources of daily living, with potential power to recreate new life for the workers themselves and for others" (*Women Workers* 167).

### Goal: Reconstructing Subjectivities Through Drama

As pointed out in chapter 3, poststructuralist feminists and compositionists have argued that access to a variety of powerful discursive subjectivities is crucial for producing empowered subject positions in women. In assigning drama a central pedagogical role and in recognizing its catalytic function in the reconstruction of subjectivities, Bryn Mawr Summer School was at the forefront of the worker education and organizing movements of the age. As I have previously pointed out, many Summer School faculty and administrators were leaders in the field of worker education, and their views on labor drama and other issues were frequently published in leading scholarly journals. In 1935, for example, the *Journal of Adult Education* published a symposium of articles on "Creative Expression" in which Jean Carter, instructor and later a director of the Summer School, published a piece entitled "Labor Drama." Arguing from a philosophical as well as pedagogical perspective, she discusses the benefits of using drama in the classroom. In making drama out of their fragmented life and work experiences, she explains, workers "find a medium for reconstruction and expression . . . which thereby creates a unity between life and art—a higher mode of living than is normally open to the worker" (179). In another article, Carter praises schools [such as Bryn Mawr] whose dramatic productions have as their "primary aim, the education and the re-creation of the workers taking part in the play rather than the converting of a prospective audience." ( "Labor Drama" [introduction] 1)

In the same issue of the *Journal of Adult Education,* Ester Peterson, the talented and energetic Director of Dramatics and Recreation who was later to serve in several presidential administrations, describes how she used the enthusiasm and experience of working women to help them develop skits and dances from their own lives. She also explains how material studied in the "academic" subjects found its way into the students' productions, achieving a unity of mind and body typically denied to workers. In a more recent interview, Peterson recalled another innovative dramatic technique: the Summer School's use of role-playing to boost the women workers' morale and self-confidence. "We started that back in the 20's and 30's long before there was anything else like it" she recalls (Goldfarb 335). In the role-playing exercise she describes below, the women practiced standing up to and appropriating a hostile and powerful patriarchal discourse:

> They [the workers] said that they would never dare to stand up in union meetings . . . in front of all the men. But we developed them. We'd put on plays. They'd take parts; they played that they were men. They experienced the kind of heckling they would get. They took the parts of the boss, the citizens. (330)

Again, student Victoria Grala praises dramatic activity for other reasons that underscore its transformative potential. She points out that group planning produces a feeling of solidarity and unity among those putting together a play, and the process usually requires research which "forces" the workers "to face problems and to think clearly in an attempt to solve them" (34). Thus, in learning how to best portray their own difficult working conditions, students began to use the discourses of economics and the social sciences to call for a better life for themselves.

The process used to develop the skits, plays, recitations, songs, and dances performed at the Summer School was paramount in students' experience of self-representation and reconstruction. The actual writing down of a play was the last step in a long procedure or may never have occurred at all. Indeed, references to the benefits of improvisation are frequent—one such mention was made in Baden's remarks that prefaced this chapter. If dialogue was not written down, of course, it could be personalized and tailored to fit different individuals and situations.

The importance accorded the dramatic activity is best revealed by the fact that as director, Smith was herself primarily in charge of it during the first ten years of the school's existence. In her autobiography, she describes a way of organizing a series of spontaneous skits, encouraging workers to find the dramatic in their own daily experience. The "girls" were divided into groups—perhaps according to industry—to prepare for the "Trade Party," an annual event in which the various trades represented by the students at the Summer School were presented in skits. For ten minutes they worked on developing scenes. Then "without stage, scenery or curtain," the brief scenes were acted (*Opening* 138). Afterwards, the audience discussed their merits and pointed out shortcomings.

In their publications, faculty repeatedly emphasize the importance of the reconstructive experience for students as they acted in their productions. Calling the work "experimental" ("Labor Drama" [introduction] 4), Carter describes how a group of students critiqued and improved their skits. After viewing a skit together, she asked students what they liked. Responses such as "I could hardly wait to see how it was coming out" or "People don't act like that in a real shop" led to discussions about "climax, suspense, economy of words, and the effectiveness of expressing ideas through a movement, a gesture, or a look" (3). After this discussion, the actors might continue to polish a piece. Eventually, writes Carter, "in the course of several weeks something may be produced that seems worthy of being written down and presented to a larger audience" (3). She points out that the instructor eventually discovers that presenting a play has become less and less important to the students as the interest in making the play has developed, and that the real satisfaction is in the *reconstruction* [emphasis mine] of students' own experiences (3).

In her 1936 report to faculty and administration, "Dramatics and Recreation," Peterson explains how the play *America You Called Us* was developed by the dramatics group from a poem written in the creative writing group (5). She remarks that the students seemed to have "a real feeling" for the material. This was probably because the content was discussed so widely before it was written by a smaller group.

> Miss Lockwood and Mr. Cummins [English and economics instructors] gave excellent assistance in building in the student body a vivid understanding of the dramatic quality of those periods of American history. This plus the general [an-

tipathy] toward war, made the performance mark a stage in the thinking of the students rather than a dramatic production. (5)

Such consolidation of the dramatics and academic program was one way dramatics evolved over the years. A related trend was the increasing importance dramatics assumed in the overall curriculum: At first an extracurricular, evening project, it eventually became a central activity with a director, an assistant director, and a place in the morning academic schedule. Another trend was that subject matter for the skits and plays came increasingly from the students' life experiences mediated by material they were studying in classes.

## THE DEVELOPMENT OF A DRAMATICS CURRICULUM

The evolution of the dramatics curriculum is well documented in the internal memos, project reports, and Curriculum Committee minutes, which record the important insights and struggles of the students and faculty who pushed for more theatrical activities. Writing in 1929 about the significance of dramatics at the school, Smith comments that on numerous occasions, the faculty argued about how much time to allot to drama and other "recreational" activities. Smith asserts that in spite of the concern with the time taken away from "more serious" academic subjects, both faculty and students alike seemed to want to stick to the large festivals and performances. She comments that an effort was made to include all students in the programs, so as not to divide the audience into actors and spectators (*Women Workers* 167). By 1932, the minutes of an Instruction Committee meeting recommend that three elective projects be set up for the following summer session: a science project, a history project, and a project in dramatics ("Minutes" 1). The minutes stressed the benefits gained by students of former years through putting their ideas into dramatic form. It seemed important, again, that a small group have a fairly intensive interest in this project throughout the summer and that this group do some writing. A larger group would take part in the eventual productions (3).

It was also pointed out that the students would find the knowledge of methods of producing labor drama invaluable in their local communities. In this regard, a faculty member suggested that help in staging the Summer School productions might be obtained from the Group Theater. Smith, however, objected, reporting that she would prefer to work with a senior from Vassar College "who had a great interest in labor drama and wanted to be of assistance" ("Minutes" 3). Thus Smith underscores her desire to forge links between students from the women's colleges and the working women.

In the 1936 summer session, recreation, music, and dramatics were put under the dynamic direction of Ester Peterson. She remarks in her yearly report that combining these three activities was very effective, although the staff was still too small ("Dramatics" 1). She reports that the year's dramatics work grew out of the "experiences of the students as these were given significance through the class work" (1). Peterson laments the fact that the dramatics staff did not spend as much time with the "unit instructors" (of English and economics) as they would have liked. She was pleased that many of the women workers could pick out dramatic situations from their own experience and use the dramatic method to express ideas (3). She reports that faculty tried to give the students enough experience developing original material that they would be able to put together their own dramatic presentations when they returned to their homes. Peterson goes on to list over thirty-five short plays, skits, and mass recitations, many including song, interpretive dancing, and folk dancing, that the students participated in over the summer (3).

By 1937, Smith was intensely involved in the Teacher Education Project of the WPA, and Jean Carter, former Summer School teacher, had become the school's director. Nineteen thirty-seven seems to have been the crowning year for Summer School dramatics. In her "Report to Faculty" of May 1937, Carter notes that in addition to the regular division of the student body into units concentrating on English and economics, instructors for science, dramatics, recreation, and "workshop" would cut across the units to work with the entire school. She announces that morning periods would be scheduled for dramatics so that the dramatics instructor could count on some regular time for meeting all students in small groups (2). In her report for this year, Peterson praises this new system, saying it was now possible for her to develop a greater degree of continuity in the program by seeing students regularly and getting to know their classwork. She could also visit economics classes "to help students and faculty see opportunities for relating the dramatics and economics class programs" (1). She also mentions the great benefit of learning about "newer stage techniques for expressing important ideas" that students acquired by seeing a production of *An American Tragedy* by the Hedgerow Theater (2).

## DRAMATIC PRODUCTION AT THE SUMMER SCHOOL: MAKING POLITICAL MATERIAL

Although largely ignored in histories of the workers' theater movement, "some of the earliest regular work in labor drama in America was done in connection with the resident labor colleges and summer schools for workers" (Ransdell 3). Even though the height of the workers' theater movement was around 1934, the Bryn Mawr Summer School, for example, had put on labor dramas since the early 1920s. In my research among student publications and reports on the dramatic activity, I encountered over fifty-two labor dramas written at the Summer School. Certainly there were numerous others not preserved in writing.

A brief chronological account of the dramatic activities recorded in issues of *Shop and School,* curricular reports, and memos reveals how the plays and skits evolved over the years in terms of style and content. In 1922, Haroldine Humphreys, Director of Dramatics, reports on the workers' dramatic activities in the *Bryn Mawr Alumnae Bulletin.* In praising two of the performances that were to become annual events at the Summer School, the International Peace Festival and the closing Lantern Ceremony, Humphreys keys in on characteristics that continued to be important over the years. "Here was drama 'of the people' freed from stage tradition and as pure as Greek ritual," she writes. "The same principle of disregarding the spectator and emphasizing the ceremonial significance" was observed (17). The "Calendar" of the 1924 *Bryn Mawr Daisy* records that the students from the advanced economics class staged a mock arbitration case based on an actual happening between an employer who had broken his contract with a union. "The discussion was quite spirited besides being educational, and the debate was enjoyed by both audience and actors."

In her chronicle of the daily events published in the 1928 *Echo,* student Ruthella Stambaugh mentions that her favorite skit was by the laundry workers who humorously acted out the tortuous path of a sheet in its journey through a laundry. She also reports on plays attended by students at the Hedgerow Theater: Susan Glaspell's *The Inheritors,* Shaw's *Arms and the Man,* and Ibsen's *Pillar's of Society* (39–43). The 1929 *Outcrop* reports that a class studying American civilization put on a skit during which workers, dressed in colonial costumes, read the *Declaration of Independence* amid much applause. A "page" distributed copies to every table so that all could follow along. The reading was followed by everyone singing *The Internationale* and *The Star Spangled Banner* (19).

Instructor Florence M. Pharo used dramatics in the speaking component of her English course in 1930. She and her students worked up a series of short sketches about Bryn Mawr. "Four girls, wearing hats and carrying suitcases, pretended that they were traveling back to New York from Bryn Mawr. In the train they discussed Bryn Mawr naturally and informally" (4). Another skit from her class showed southern girls organizing a "club" (probably a YWCA). The southern girls sang a duet, which one of them had composed (4). In their calendar report for 1930, students Ruth Epstein and Margaret Sofia mention dramatizing different kinds of union activities. The students in these skits showed how meetings were conducted and important matters were settled (53).

In a report entitled "Experiments in Labor Dramatics . . ." written in 1932 by workers and an unnamed undergraduate "Dramatics Assistant," the following "Animated Press" (living newspaper) appeared in outline form:

Characters:

> Editor-in-Chief
>
> Foreign Editor
>
> Domestic News Editor
>
> Fashion Editor
>
> Society Editor

News of the Day:

> Domestic:
>
> > 1. Dies Bill[1]
> >
> > 2. Political Campaign Speeches
> >
> > 3. Stamp Tax
>
> Foreign:
>
> > 1. Lausanne Conference
> >
> > 2. Great Britain vs. Ireland
> >
> > 3. Recognition of Russia needed
> >
> > 4. Tragedies of recent Kings—a song
>
> Society:
>
> > 1. An extravagant society wedding
>
> Fashions:
>
> > 1. Show of dresses and hats from the Co-Operative Store (run by the workers at the School)
>
> Amusements:
>
> > 1. Modern version of *Alice in Wonderland*
> >
> > 2. Music by Edith Berkowitz
> >
> > 3. Newsboys on the street selling "Extras."

In *Labor Dramatics,* the scrapbook of the Dramatics Project Group 1933, it is reported that students in the Palmer-Finck Unit attended a hearing on sweatshop conditions in Norristown, Pennsylvania. When they returned, the students acted out what they had seen for the rest of the Summer School. They portrayed a judge, a representative from the Central Labor Council, and several witnesses. The hearing concerned a complaint waged against the Pioneer Coat Company, where the employer kept the employees' drinking water in dirty barrels. Even though previously prosecuted, the employer refused to improve worksite conditions. The wages were also very low. Girls doing piece work for a full week received from one to three dollars. One handsewer, aged nineteen, received only one dollar for a full week's work. The students also acted out another complaint against the Reading Clothing Company, where a sixteen-year-old girl worked in unsanitary conditions with no restroom facilities for two and a half cents an hour. *Labor Dramatics* contained the following "Mother Goose Depression Pantomime" by student Jennie Previti, first published in the 1933 issue of *Shop and School.*

Stage Directions: *The characters assemble backstage. Mother Goose comes forward and reads the opening verses:*
Mother Goose Land is unhappy these days
Her children have brought her despair
They have nothing to eat
No clothes and no heat
There's misery everywhere.
*The sheriff swaggers in, examines everything in sight, and walks off with a large market basket. Mother Hubbard appears with her dog under her arm, looks in her cupboard, and sits down and weeps.*
Old Mother Hubbard went to the cupboard
To fetch her doggie a bone
When she got here
She found the house bare
The sheriff had come and was gone.
*Jack Horner runs in with an empty pie plate and curls up dejectedly on the floor. He sticks his thumb into the empty pie plate with great disgust.*
Little Jack Horner sat in a corner
Without his Christmas pie
The next time I hope
For Labor we'll vote
His unemployed father did sigh.

Peterson's 1936 report to the director describes in detail how the year's Trade Party was produced. As the students were looking for a unifying theme, someone complained that the Supreme Court had worsened the plight of the workers in almost every trade by declaring various parts of the National Industrial Recovery Act unconstitutional. "So 'Unconstitutional' became the cry and theme of the Trade Party" ("Dramatics" 2). The theme song was written to the tune of "Are You Sleeping, Brother John":

> Null and void, null and void
> Unconstitutional, unconstitutional
> We cannot enforce it,
> We cannot enforce it,
> Null and void, null and void.

(2)

Off stage, a chorus of workers read from the Declaration of Independence and the Constitution while a group of judges in stylized robes and masks quoted from the balcony parts of famous decisions that declared certain legislative acts "null and void." Against this setting, more than thirteen groups presented their trades. "In 'Push Press,' the papermaker, through work motions and sounds, typified the rhythm and monotony of the press" (2). In "Buttons," a worker sat at her machine sorting buttons: large, small, plain, fancy. Her thoughts were revealed through a poem she had written. The most humorous part of the year's Trade Party, according to Peterson, was the skit given by the service workers, called "Tarts and Flours": "It had a freshness that was delightful for the students acted so naturally. New lines and incidents appeared in the production which were never heard in the rehearsals" (2). The Trade Party continued with "Lies from Above," as the jewelry workers revealed the need for regulated working conditions in their shops. The skit showed "the plight of the sympathetic forelady who has to enforce unfair rules to keep her job" (2). When she exclaims: "It was so much better under the N.R.A.," the Supreme Court becomes lighted, rises, and says "Unconstitutional!" (2). In "Shop Talk," radio makers portrayed work on the conveyor belt. "The noise, smoke, and rackety rhythm of the equipment, the tension and speed of the workers to keep up production leads to exhaustion when the bell rings" (2). While the tired workers are trying to keep up the pace, a radio broadcast comes on announcing that the Supreme Court had declared the minimum wage law "unconstitutional."

In addition to the skits and sketches developed and improvised by the students, Peterson also mentions that they put on "Free Tom Mooney," a mass recitation obtained from the Brookwood (labor college) Players as well as a skit originally produced by the professional Theater Guild. Peterson concludes that throughout the summer, "the students learned that the most effective dramatic productions are possible without even memorizing parts, and without all the paraphernalia of production" (6).

In her director's report for 1937, Carter praised Peterson's work with the students in dramatics. "It offered opportunity for expression of both experiences of individuals and activities of the classroom" ("Report" 2). She remarks that "in addition to a large number of original skits worked out by individuals and groups, two long plays of real significance were developed" (2). The first play, *Who Are the Workers,* grew out of an attempt in an economics class to define the term "workers." It was a kind of pageant that involved the whole school. Each trade group worked out the dramatization of its industry, and the foreign students introduced the idea of the "interrelation of workers of the world" (2). The other play, *Packing! Packing! Packing!* was the result of an intensive study in one class of the Supreme Court issue. In the form of a "Living Newspaper," the forty-seven-page play presented the entire history of the Court from 1790 to the present day, exposing the continuing political nature of its composition and concluding with some indication of how it might be pressured to evolve in a more worker-friendly fashion in the future. Carter again writes that the dramatics instructor and all others concerned considered the process and not the product of primary importance. The analysis and research that went into the preparation of the material and the planning of the presentation had immediate educational value, for knowledge and understanding were subjected to the test of expression (2).

Judging by the commentary in *Shop and School,* 1937 was the year of the most dramatic activity. The "Calendar of Events" lists an impromptu skit, *The Workers' Spirit,* along with six other productions: *The Whistle Blows, May Day, Who Are the Workers, The Pied Piper, War Drums* and *Packing, Packing, Packing.* In addition, the workers attended *The [sic] American Tragedy* and *Aria da Capo* by the Hedgerow Theater. In the 1938 issue of *Shop and School,* the last to be published on the Bryn Mawr campus, student Anne Baden made the remarks that began this chapter (46). Also in that issue, Sally Russian records the summer's events and lists the following student productions: *You've Got Something There, Wages and Hours, Stop Those War Drums* and *We Tomorrow.* She also mentions attending *A Moral Entertainment* by the Federal Theater Project and the Hedgerow Theater production of *The Frodi* (47). As we have seen, students were often taken to see socially relevant plays staged by professional and workers' theatrical groups, or they watched plays staged on campus by such groups.[2] The plays watched and read added to the rich discursive context that the workers drew upon to create their own productions.

What follows is an analysis of the prelude to *It's Unconstitutional.* This introductory skit well illustrates the rich intertextuality typical of Summer School dramatics. (The full text of the prelude can be found in the appendix that follows this chapter.) Feminist dialogics, a gendered interpretation of Bakhtinian concepts such as "heteroglossia" and the "carnivalesque," is helpful in understanding how this skit resisted hegemonic discourse and generated empowered discursive subjectivities for the women workers. As will be illustrated below, there is a gendered dimension to many of the dialogic interactions in the prelude. These interactions include those between "official" and "unofficial discourses," languages of black and white workers, and the working class and bourgeoisie. Elements of the carnivalesque can also be found in the prelude. Indeed, the discursive appropriations and parody, textual embodiments, costuming (masquerade), music, and humor of the workers' stage mirror the potentially subversive activities of the carnival.[3]

The characters in the prelude present a colorful gallery of the silenced. They portray women who are even today rarely accorded a public forum: miners' and farmers' wives, high school and college students, a waitress, an office worker, and elderly woman, an African American "girl," and a "laundress." All are, as well, unemployed, adding economic insult to social injury. Providing these marginalized women a public, discursive voice remains a noteworthy accomplishment in itself. More importantly though, in the context of the skit, the juxtaposition of their unofficial discourse of colloquial yet substantive and meaningful complaint with the more official, officious, and hegemonic language of government and its various representatives acts to relativize both discourses and thus enhance the status of the discourse of the unemployed. The official discourse was at the same time demystified by the workers as they began to understand and use it through the research, writing, and production of the play. To craft a dramatic scenario with its own internal momentum, many of the more legalistic and unfamiliar pronouncements of "official discourse,"—discourse that, according to Bakhtin, reflects the monologic desires of hegemonic power relations—had to be explained and reinterpreted by the working women to hold the audience's interest. The demystification took place in dialogic fashion, with much of the discourse in the play pairing legal terminology with the language of the working class. Such juxtapositions ironically render the pompous language of government and law ever more distant and hypocritical. For example, the play opens with the Preamble to the Constitution, which contains idealistic phrases such as "form a more perfect union, establish justice," and "promote the general welfare." Next a "Male Voice" pronounces that "The judicial power of the United States shall be vested in one Supreme Court. The judicial power shall extend to all cases, in law and equity arising under the Constitution." Voices of the "Judges" then speak their designated duty in unison: "When an Act of Congress conflicts with the superior law, the Supreme Court cannot enforce it, but must declare it null and void." Key phrases from the Declaration of Independence follow. All this "official discourse" is countered and exposed as untruth in the scene that unfolds. A cast of working-class characters representing typical Depression era perspectives in terms of gender, race, class, age, and occupation recount their lived experiences, which contradict the avowed ideals of our nation's founding discourse. In the familiar cadences of the waitress and office worker, the characters' relate their unfortunately typical experiences of economic injustice, and the audience undoubtedly recognizes the truth in what they are saying. Time after time, the workers voice a complaint and refer to a bill enacted in Congress that might remedy their plight only to meet with the same refrain from the justices: "It's unconstitutional."

While for the most part Summer School student discourse presents the voice of worker protest and desire as male, the prelude does express concerns of importance to women. The farmer's wife complains about the living conditions of her children, "they'd be better dead / Than grow up in a sty." The waitress expresses sisterly sympathy with these complaints. Gender is not designated for many of the roles in this script, and since few men were involved with the Summer School, women more than likely played almost all parts. The variety of roles offered them an expanded array of subject positions as well as a greater awareness of the problems of different kinds of workers. Through these roles, the actors often strengthened the voices of the oppressed, and when acting as judges and Supreme Court justices, they also spoke the powerful discourse of androcentric hegemony. Significantly, a "Male Voice" is called for in the stage directions to speak the masterful discourse of constitutional law. In terms of Bakhtinian theory, the centripetal discursive force of this conservative voice offsets the centrifugal refrain of the collective, feminine "Voices Off Stage" who appropriate the words of the Constitution and the Declaration of Independence (Bakhtin, *Dialogic* 272). As the "Voices" proclaim the urgency of the country's most neglected ideals, "justice, tranquility" and "blessings of liberty," the feminized recitation acquires an ironic and humorous tone, while testimony from the unemployed reveals how hollow these hallowed words have become, perhaps especially to women. By the end of the skit and after hearing from the previously marginalized, the very meaning of the Declaration of Independence has been transformed, and the words "duty of the people, to alter, abolish it" chanted by the "Voices" justifies even revolutionary action.

Audience and actors alike were probably pleasantly surprised to find themselves ridiculing powerful government figures in this skit. In both becoming and mocking Republicans, Democrats, politicians, and judges, spectators and actors begin to see these groups from a more familiarized yet paradoxically critical (estranged) perspective, which domesticates previously sanctified discourse and power structures. This dual experience of familiarization and estrangement felt by both the actors and audience is again "carnivalesque" in nature *(Rabelais)*. Wearing costumes of the "other," the rich and the powerful, is a defiant, if not empowering, aspect of traditional carnival, and adorning the robe of a justice in the prelude has the same effect.

The complex interplay of race, class, and gender in the short sequence containing the "negro girl" presents a more problematic discursive maneuver. The passage begins with references to the bodily oppression experienced by members of the working class, both black and white, male and female. The "old woman" complains of the heat; the "negro" inquires about aching feet. The one protests that she is "too old to work," the other that she is "too black." Both are trapped in bodies that the prevailing powers deem unacceptable. The "waitress" reveals a triple blindness to class, race, and gender in her declaration to the African American that "You've got the same right as ANYONE else. Why don't you raise hell about it?" Ironically, as a white working-class woman, the waitress herself doesn't have the same rights as her male counterpart and certainly not as the male bourgeois "ANYONE" she seems to be referring to. She is also blind to the racist social structures and laws that oppress African Americans. Her ignorance is partially allayed by the "negro girl's" revelation about what can happen to African Americans when they protest. She cites ways the white racist majority has denied blacks their constitutional rights, through the "chain gang, or lynching or Herndon."[4] As is typically the case with Summer School discourse, the class perspective is privileged over that of gender and race. Differences among workers are ignored for the purpose of joining the centripetal, white, androcentric voice of working-class protest. Or perhaps it is the unifying experience of bodily oppression endured by all workers and referred to at the beginning of this sequence rather than the power of androcentric rhetoric that led working women to privilege class in this way.

The skit quite successfully defuses a common bourgeois strategy for controlling the working class, pitting worker against worker for an ever decreasing wage. For example, the WPA worker complains that the meager "six dollars a month" given to the high school student "should have been ours." Then the laundress exclaims, "I'm one up," since she is making "Six bucks a week"—a sharp decline, however, from her previous twelve. This anti-worker discourse, which mirrors the competitive, individualist rhetoric of the patriarchal bourgeoisie, is subverted in several ways. For one thing, the WPA worker also informs his listeners that plenty of money "went / To the great War Powers!" and not to the Americans who needed it, thus directing workers' anger away from each other. At this point the unemployed begin to voice together a series of worker demands: the N.R.A., a Child Labor Amendment, a minimum wage, antilynching legislation. By the end of the skit, these individual complaints are subsumed in the collective demands of the "unemployed," a voice stronger and united.

## WORKERS AND LITERARY CRITICISM: ENTERING THE CONVERSATION

Although providing an analysis of a play in contemporary critical terms may yield insights of interest to today's scholars, in terms of historiography, it is also important to see how the creators of this piece may have evaluated it or may have been responding to critical voices of the age in producing it. In its heyday, workers's theater was rife with debates over aesthetic and political issues such as its ultimate purpose or the most useful theatrical style, expressivist or socialist realist. Students at the Summer School debated these same issues. Here is the way student Nina Lamousen framed critical questions for her worker classmates in the 1934 issue of *Shop and School.*

### What Do You Think

What do we expect from a workers' theater? Should it be a wailing wall where they go over their sufferings and misery in a dramatic, highly intensified form? What is the psychological effect of it?

Should a worker be shown the jerky movements of machines? But is it not the mechanization that he dreads, his whole body being tense in protest? Jerky movements of impressionistic dances—convulsions of decadence—do they appeal to him who stepped not so long ago out of the realm of folklore and round dances?

Or would a worker better enjoy rhythmic movements and music that flows in harmonious cadence, which straightens out the furrows of the brow, untangles and eases the nerves strung and overtaxed in mechanical speed-up?

The very name "workers' theater" suggests a certain kind of play, suggests propaganda to propagate ideas, to spread them. What is the chance to attract the general public? Interested workers will come, but they already know this side of life. What of the general public that should be there?

How should we attract them? Should we present our ideas in a crude, though true-to-life picture, or should we select the elegant setting of black and pink and lavender a la *Aria da Capo* even if *Tragikos* is there, ever present?

Or is the satire better? It gives us a feeling of superiority, but gives to the audience a chance to laugh, though they are laughing at their own faults. Laughter takes out the sting of antagonism. Would the general public accept it?

What is the better way? What do you think?

The replies the women workers may have given to Lamousen's questions are suggested in their Summer School productions. There is no doubt that the workers wanted to be entertained at the theater, especially to laugh. Their pieces were also very rhetorical and aimed at prompting the spectators—in the case of the Summer School theater, these were mainly students and faculty—to participate in the workers' cause by joining unions and becoming active in governmental reform efforts and protest groups; the pieces were also educational in that they presented information crucial to workers' understanding of political and economic issues. Finally, the pieces were oppositional in that they presented a workers' discourse to counter conservative ideology. The Summer School theater was not generally a "wailing wall," although grievances and hardships were certainly voiced. The resulting psychological effect was energizing, not despairing. The scenic devices were simple and adaptable; their descriptions do not suggest crudeness on the one hand, nor elegance on the other, but basic, minimal use of available materials to create a strong scenic image. Satire and parody were preferred modes of discourse, again giving both the workers and any bourgeois members of the audience a chance to laugh, though in the case of the bourgeoisie, "they [would be] laughing at their own faults," while the workers would experience "a feeling of superiority." This high level of emotional satisfaction was also an important requirement of Summer School theater and indicates its function as a discourse of desire for the women workers.

## THE LEGACY OF DRAMATIC DISCOURSE

Students and faculty at the Bryn Mawr Summer School thus built a heteroglossic drama program that included a great variety of discursive experiences promoting student development and social change. In fact, they seemed to have practiced sixty years ago what Clar Doyle argues for in a book aimed at current drama educators. Sounding remarkably like faculty and students at the Summer School in his recognition of dramatics as a tool for social justice, he writes that

A critical drama should help students examine their own life experiences through the reflective analysis of role playing and improvisation. . . . Drama must become, in the process of schooling, a movement toward a consciousness of what might be. In doing so, drama can aid in bringing about needed social changes that through critical consciousness could result in a freer human development. (80)

## APPENDIX: THE PRELUDE TO *IT'S UNCONSTITUTIONAL*

*Voices Off Stage:* We the people of the United States in order to form a more perfect union, establish justice, insure domestic tranquility, provide for the common defense, promote the general welfare, and secure the blessings of liberty to ourselves and our posterity, do ordain and establish *the Constitution of the United States of America.*

*Male Voice:* The judicial power of the United States shall be vested in one Supreme Court. The judicial power shall extend to all cases, in law and equity, arising under the Constitution.

*Judges:* The Constitution is the Supreme Law of the Land.
  The Supreme Court has taken an oath to uphold the Constitution.
  When an Act of Congress conflicts with the superior law, the Supreme Court cannot enforce it, but must declare it null and void.

*Voices Off Stage:* . . . all men are created equal . . . life . . . liberty . . . happiness. Whenever any form of government becomes destructive of these ends, it is the right of the people to alter or abolish it and institute new government, laying its foundations on such principles and organizing its powers in such form as to them shall seem most likely to effect their safety and happiness . . . justice, tranquility . . . blessings of liberty.

*Judges: (Woven in with above speech of voices off stage.)* When an Act of Congress conflicts with the superior law, the Supreme Court cannot enforce it, but must declare it null and void.

*(Clatter of Girl's Heels Walking to Work.)*

*Girl's Voice:* Come on, Mamie, I can't wait all day.
*Mamie:* I'm not going in.
*Voice:* What's the matter, laid off?
*Mamie:* Tough luck. See you later.

### The Unemployed

*Scene: An employment office—one or two benches. Waitress enters and sits on bench. Office worker enters and sits opposite waitress.*

*Waitress:* What's your racket?

*Office Worker:* Aw, just another of the unemployed. Office work,—in a bank I used to be. Yes, *used* to be. And then we merged with another bank. They had no place for me, so—*(with a shrug)—*

*Waitress:* Tough luck kid.
    I wrecked myself
    Waiting on tables
    For a dozen years
    Luggin' a tray
    Just couldn't take it
    Ten hours a day.
*Office Worker:* But the N.R.A.?
*Democrats:* We, the Democrats, made the N.R.A.
*G.O.P.:* We, the Republicans, are here to say:
    Boondoggling, waste.
*Supreme Court:* It's Unconstitutional!
*Waitress:* Yeah, the N.R.A.

(Negro girl enters and sits down. Old woman enters shortly after and sits
    down beside her.)

*Old woman:* How hot it is!
*Negro:* Do your feet ache?
*Waitress:* I'll bet they ache!
*Old Woman:* Can't get back! Too old to work!
*Negro:* And I'm too black!
*Waitress:* Aw, don't take it—You've got the same right as ANYONE else. Why
    don't you raise hell about it?
*Negro:* Have you heard of the chain gang, or lynching, or Herndon? We united
    in protest but they used an old, old, law on him,—insurrection they called
    it, My Lord! My Lord!
*Supreme Court:* The conviction stands.
*Old Woman:* I've worked for years, seven dollars a week. Can't save a cent.
*Democrats:* But we've taken care of social security.
*Republicans:* Boondoggling, Waste!
*Old Woman:* That's not for me
    There is a law that could help, you see
    But that would be
*Supreme Court:* Most unconstitutional.

*(Farmer's wife enters and sits.)*
*(High school student also enters.)*

*Farmer's Wife:* Will we have to wait long?
    I have children at home
    If you can call it home.

*Waitress:* Kids, oh?
    I like kids.
*Farmer's Wife:* But they'd better be dead
    Than grow in a sty.
    We did have a farm
    They could see the sky
    And speak to the sun
    And the earth was warm
    And the hay smelled nice
    Now their playmates are
    Cockroaches and lice.
*Waitress:* Kids
    Cockroaches
    Lice!
    My God! I feel sick!
*High School Student:* But what about the A.A.A. [Agricultural Adjustment
    Administration]?
*Democrats:* 'Twas an awful wrench
    But after a while
    Came the A.A.A.
    And the sunshine of our smile
*Republicans:* Boondoggling, Waste
*Supreme Court:* It's unconstitutional.

*(College student enters with diploma in hand.)*

*College Student (to Waitress):* Move over, sister.

*(W.P.A. Worker Enters.)*

*Democrats:* We love our youth
    We see their rights.
*Youth:* Six dollars a month
    To sit home nights.
*W.P.A. Worker:* Six dollars a month
    That should have been ours;
    But there's plenty that went
    To the great War Powers!

*(Laundress enters as the youth says "Six")*

*Laundress:* O, I'm one up

Six bucks a week;
I did get twelve
I could get by.

*Waitress:* That's what you'd call
A fifty-fifty cut.

*Youth:* But what about the minimum?

*Laundress:* A minimum, Huh!
We'd scrub and sing
For the minimum.
A minimum, Huh!
There's no such thing!
Or haven't you heard
Like everything else

*Supreme Court:* It's unconstitutional!

*(Coal miner's wife enters on the "unconstitutional.")*

*Wife:* Unconstitutional?
Guffey Act,[5] eh?
My husband works, did work
In a mine, but its unconstitutional
Work, employment, coal to burn
That is if you steal it
It's unconstitutional
What does it mean?

*Supreme Court:* When an Act of Congress conflicts with the superior law, the Supreme Count cannot enforce it but must declare it null and void.

*Unemployed:* We want so little, the N.R.A.

*Politicians:* Interference with American rights.

*Supreme Court:* Unconstitutional.

*Unemployed:* Insurance, Child Labor Amendment

*Politicians:* Shsshh! That's dangerous *(aside)*
Interference with American rights.

*Supreme Court:* Unconstitutional.

*Unemployed:* Minimum Wage Protection, Anti-Lynching, Youth Act, Housing

*Supreme Court:* Unconstitutional

*Politicians:* The natural forces of recovery will re-absorb them into industry . . .
will absorb . . . will absorb

*(Voices Off Stage):* In order to form a more perfect union . . . justice, tranquility, blessings of liberty . . .

*Supreme Court:* Null and void . . . unconstitutional.

*Voices:* . . . government becomes destructive of these ends . . . right of people . . .
nay . . . duty of people, to alter, abolish it.

*Unemployed:* Let the corpses lie!
New millions risen
From school and shop
From mine and soil
Together reach
Together toil.
Let the corpses lie!
Here, take my hand
And in our grip
There shall be power
There shall be power
To sense rebirth
To know the hour.

# Women Workers and Literary Discourse: Transgressive Reading and Writing

## 5

## A New Dawn

Did workers create these odes and poems
That so charmed a listening throng?
How come you know such descriptive phrases?
Telling of life in its sorrow and song.

Did suffering bring those truths to light,
Make tongue speak what heart could not tell.
Such fine spirits just can't be crushed.
What unseen powers made you rebel?

Whatever it is that has unearthed these rhymes,
Their truths should obtain us better times,
Let's take them with us, near and far,
And call them, if you like, the
Spirit of Bryn Mawr.
—Marjorie Moss, *Shop and School,* 1936

The "odes and poems" written by women belt makers, hat band stitchers, and cigar packers at the Summer School were indeed an extension of their "spirit," a working-class spirit and voice that grew more powerful, resistant, and "transgressive," using bell hooks's term, after their eight-week Bryn Mawr experience. Enabled by scholarships, these young women welcomed the respite from exhausting factory work and reveled in their return to academics. Inspired and encouraged by a dedicated faculty of scholars and teachers, the women developed a well-informed militancy as evidenced in *Shop and School.* In their poetry and prose, the worker writers denounced the injustices they experienced in the factories and demanded better working conditions. But beyond these practical assertions, they also showed a proclivity for philosophical musings on such abstract topics as the purpose of labor, the social function of art, and the role of nature in daily life. Most significantly, the Bryn Mawr Summer School students created a unique working-class literary discourse, a discourse rare to this day as the aesthetic and intellectual production of working-class women continues to be erased.

A useful approach to the study of this discourse is the poststructuralist notion that empowered agency and subjectivity can be constructed by appropriating discursive formations available to individuals at a particular cultural moment. In their literary production, the women workers chose to use much of the empowering rhetoric they encountered in the public debates of the 1920s, and especially the 1930s, when working-class demands became public policy. But the Summer School added to its students' rich array of progressive discourse through the literary texts offered to students as well as the democratic discourse employed in administrative and classroom affairs. Also, faculty helped the women transgress limiting social boundaries in encouraging the reconstruction of their students' textual subjectivities through fiction and nonfiction reading and writing. This investigation into the impressive accomplishments of Summer School students responds to the question raised in Moss's poem: Just how did the Summer School experience help working women find "descriptive phrases" for essays, write rebellious poetry demanding "better times," or search for the "truths" of literature and philosophy? In other words, what discursive contexts motivated and inspired these women to begin a journey into both the consumption and production of an activist literature? The answer to these questions will provide long-overdue recognition for this singular institution dedicated to meeting the educational and creative needs of working women. Also, recovery of the students' creative writing will add to a developing body of literary production: working-class women's fiction and poetry.[1] Finally, this study will provide valuable insights for today's educators grappling with gendered and classed pedagogies, liberatory teaching, and issues of authority and agency in the classroom. As Susan Wells has ably demonstrated, it is up to teachers, administrators, and students to construct the space within which public writing can emerge from cloistered classrooms (328). As will be seen, such a space was constructed at the Summer School.

In the pages that follow, faculty and especially student voices are central to a four-part analysis of the Summer School literary achievement. The chapter opens with faculty views on the classroom practice of including workers in the appreciation as well as creation of literature; this is followed by the materialist pedagogy that ensued, then students' views about reading and writing literature, and, finally, a selection and interpretation of student poetry. As will be seen, the working women's poetry took them out of the silence imposed on women and the working class and into the public discursive arena, where they made assertions in a strengthened voice on matters previously denied them. A selection of the working women's poetry is included in the appendix that follows this chapter.

### LITERARY DISCOURSE FOR WOMEN WORKERS: AN EMPOWERING CLASSROOM TEXT

Although institutions of higher learning have introduced their students to vernacular literature since the late nineteenth century, it has been much less commonly offered to the working class. Perhaps the first major commitment to do so began with the worker colleges of the 1920s and 1930s. (In addition to Bryn Mawr, these colleges were Brookwood Labor College, Barnard Summer School, Southern Summer School, University of Wisconsin Summer School, Vineyard Shore School for Women Workers, and the Summer School for Office Workers.) These schools advocated the study of literature from a more utilitarian and democratic perspective than their mainstream counterparts, and Bryn Mawr Summer School, where directors, faculty, and students were firmly convinced of the value of literature in a curriculum for workers, was a leader in this approach. Hilda Smith comments in her book on the Summer School that

> literature should not be regarded only as a means of relaxation, and therefore, a luxury. It is a necessity for the intelligent understanding of life, and for that reason is fundamental in carrying out the purpose of a workers' school. (*Women Workers* 73)

Even more surprising is the fact that Smith did not divorce the study of literature from literary production. Indeed, she saw a necessary relationship and aspired to have the women workers emerge as creative writers: "From the joy and illumination the industrial worker finds in literature, one may foreshadow what her creative expression might be, once released from the monotony and fatigue of the long day in the factory" (*Women Workers* 142).

Helen Lockwood, influential Summer School instructor and Vassar College colleague of Gertrude Buck and Laura Wylie, also argues strongly that workers should study literature in her book on the writing of French and English working men of 1830–1848; she too refuses to divorce the act of reading literature from writing it. Foreshadowing contemporary poststructuralists, she explores the role literary discourse plays in the social construction of subjectivities and institutions by explaining how worker writers of the nineteenth century benefited from their typically brief study of the classics. Through literature she writes, workers, found their way to a large world beyond their own narrow horizon. Their imaginations were released. They saw their work in relation to the whole of humanity. They learned to *speak* [emphasis mine] of its glory or of its contrasts, between their destiny as toilers and that of the people making profits at their expense. (230)

Thus, Lockwood argues that through the study of literature, workers are inspired to become writers as well as readers of their own world. She also affirms a faith in the power of workers' literature to remold social institutions in ways more democratic and less oppressive to workers (9).

The Summer School faculty's continual search for the best way to teach literature and other subjects to workers is well documented. Always hopeful of finding just the right curricular mix, faculty offered literature as a separate subject, in conjunction with history and art, and combined with composition, never settling for any one approach (H. Smith, *Women Workers* 87). Course syllabi also reveal that a wide range of literary works were covered over the years. In early sessions, students were subjected to a very comprehensive survey approach in an attempt to compensate for their sparse literary backgrounds. Laura Wylie's syllabus of 1926, for example, placed literature in the context of world civilization and included extensive outlines of historical and literary events. Centering her course around dramatic texts, Wylie assigned several Shakespearian plays along with John Galsworthy's *The Mob* and Susan Glaspell's *The Inheritors*. She notes in her syllabus that the class will "spend much time . . . finding and understanding such contemporary ideas and social situations and problems as are reflected in the books read" (30). This tendency became more pronounced over the years as diverse approaches were united by a faculty commitment to make course material relevant to workers' lives. Thus classes might focus on nineteenth-century American fiction or British Romantics; others might begin with Old English literature and end with contemporary labor drama; still others charted the development of American literature. But all literary study was to provide context and perspectives for understanding issues of vital concern to workers of the day. In fact, for some faculty, literature was to be studied not so much for its own sake, but to illustrate the effect in human terms of economic contexts. In an article entitled "The Place of Literature in Workers' Education," William Fincke, Christian pacifist and cofounder (along with his wife, Helen) of the Brookwood Labor College, explains what this approach might mean in terms of a specific piece of literature. Since interactive discussion was the goal at the Summer School and in worker education classes in general, teachers wanted students to connect course content to their own experience. Fincke offers these sample questions to stimulate class discussion of *Inheritance,* a novel by Phyllis Bentley.

> What were the British textile workers in the story fighting for in the early eighteen hundreds? Is there any good logic behind the prevention of the introduction of machinery—when not? Is the progressive remoteness of the owners in the story typical? If so, what does it mean we have to cope with in modern times? Could we get anywhere by the cooperation dreamed of by young David? In what American industry has labor worked along a scheme of this sort? What successes has organized labor's cooperation [led to]? What weaknesses? (12)

Another example of the faculty mind-set comes from the work of Jean Carter, whose syllabus and course notes grew into an egalitarian, non-elitist study of American literature, which she continually revised on the basis of class reading and discussion (title page). Ultimately published by the Affiliated Schools for Women Workers in 1933 as *This America: A Study of Literature Interpreting the Development of American Civilization,* it was distributed to other worker classes with the proviso that each adapt the material to "discussions of those economic problems in which their members are most vitally concerned" (Coit 3). The thirty-five-page document proceeds geographically with chapters entitled "Our Roots," "New England," "The South," "Some of the Middle Eastern States," and "The Westward Movement," each chapter showing how the social and industrial development of the country is reflected in literature, and including much folk literature and what later became known as "people's literature." The bibliographies at the end of each chapter are replete with works of socially conscious fiction and nonfiction as well as many works by women writers. In her assertion that American "cultural and economic life . . . have been and are interdependent," Carter articulates what is today called a social constructionist tendency in literary study (*This America* 2).

Possibly in response to the economic and political crises confronting the United States in the 1930s, syllabi from the final years of the Summer School show faculty much less concerned with filling gaps in student knowledge than helping them analyze the contemporary economic and political scene through literature of social criticism and leftist critique. In their report to the director in 1937, Mount Holyoke economist Amy Hewes and her colleague in English Isabel Cerney refer to a method of literary study adapted from the European Folk High Schools, in which literature was read aloud in class and then discussed in smaller groups (Smith, *Women Workers* 119). Students were thus helped in their basic reading skills, in reading comprehension, and in their ability to relate their reading to their own and others' lives. Hewes and Cerney comment on the results of this process:

> A few short stories and sketches read to the class provoked discussion of content rather than form. This was partly dictated by the socio-economic content of the selections read, partly by the insistent avidity of the class for general information and understanding. (5)

Hewes and Cerney also report that the class as a whole read or heard individual reports on *Mill Shadows* ("A play about textile workers in the South") by Tom Tippett,[2] *Strike* by Mary Heaton Vorse, *To Make My Bread* ("When the southern mountaineer becomes an industrial worker") by Grace Lumpkin, *Days of Wrath* by Andre Malraux, *Waiting for Lefty* by Clifford Odets, *We, the People* ("Depression drama on the ruin of two families") by Elmer Rice, *Call Home the Heart* ("A story in which the Gastonia strike comes to life") by Fielding Burke, *The Shadow Before* ("A cross section of a New England textile town torn by a strike") by William Rollins Jr., *Fontamara* ("Italian peasants tell their own story of life under fascism") by Ignazio Silone, *Inheritance* ("A panoramic story of an English textile family") by Phyllis Bentley, *The People, Yes* by Carl Sandburg, and *A Footnote to Folly* ("Autobiography of a newspaper woman who has covered the chief labor strikes in recent American history") by Vorse (6). Besides the reading lists that appeared in individual faculty syllabi distributed to the students, others were compiled for wider worker audiences. These lists give further insight into the kind of literary discourse students were encountering at the Summer School.[3]

Smith reports that "'More poetry' was a constant cry during the summer," and that "instructors and tutors do their best to satisfy this desire" (*Women Workers* 119). A great number of the best-known poets through the ages were assigned, but as with literature, poetry celebrating the common people and their right to justice and a better life predominated. Not surprisingly, the "high modernists," T. S. Eliot and Ezra Pound, with their themes of pessimism, futility, apathy, and degradation, were not valued at the Summer School. On the other hand, Walt Whitman's *Leaves of Grass* was a very common item on syllabi and reading lists along with Carl Sandburg's *Chicago Poems* and *The People, Yes*. Also frequently recommended were Archibald Macleish's *Land of the Free*, Stephen Vincent Benet's *John Brown's Body*, Upton Sinclair's *The Cry for Justice*, and Marguerite Wilkinson's anthology *New Voices*.[4] African American poetry recommended included that of Langston Hughes, Countee Cullen's anthology of black poetry, and Stirling Brown's *Southern Roads*. From this list, it is clear that the working women were provided with fiction and poetry celebrating the working class and its daily experience, offering empowered textual subjectivities, and often calling for worker empowerment.

## WOMEN WORKERS ON STUDYING LITERATURE AND POETRY

Who were the women workers as readers and writers, what kind of literary background did they bring to the Summer School, and what did they think of the literary education they were receiving? The Summer School aimed to recruit workers who had the potential to become leaders in the worker's movement. All came to the Summer School with a great variety of discursive social, economic, and political texts in their cultural backgrounds. In some cases they had read a good deal of "highbrow" literature. This was particularly true of the immigrant Jewish women, who often included lengthy lists of books read on their application forms. On the other hand, the educational and literary background of the native-born American students, whether white or black, wasn't nearly so strong even though their ability with English was, of course, often far superior to the foreign-born workers.

Thus, an examination of the application forms of forty-eight randomly selected students revealed in some cases a rather sophisticated range of books read—the same in some cases as those to be later assigned by faculty. Among those books most frequently listed were Tolstoy's *Anna Karenina* and *War and Peace,* Dostoyevsky's *Crime and Punishment,* Knute Hansum's *Growth of the Soil* ("Norwegian peasants battle the earth"), Paul Eric Remarque's *All Quiet on the Western Front,* Jack London's *The Iron Heel* ("A prediction of an inevitable social revolution in the United States"), H. G. Wells's *Men Like Gods,* Martin Anderson Nero's *Pelle the Conqueror* ("Life of a Danish boy . . . his apprenticeship, union activities and continual rebellion against the social conditions in which he finds himself"), and Vorse's *Strike.* Also mentioned is fiction by Upton Sinclair and Sinclair Lewis, as well as plays by Eugene O'Neill.

The newspapers and journals cited most regularly by the women workers include the *Nation* (the most frequently named publication), *New York Times, Daily Worker, Labor Age, Reader's Digest, Saturday Evening Post, Ladies' Home Journal, McCall's,* and *Literary Digest.* Several African American women cited the *Crisis* (journal of the National Association for the Advancement of Colored People); one student listed the *Afro-American* and the *Black Man.*

The value of reading was the subject of several impressive commentaries written by students and published in *Shop and School.* In an article entitled "What Literature Means to Me," Jeanne Paul, the editor-in-chief of the 1926 issue, writes that she found in novels "things which my heart had often felt but could never have spoken. . . . something in me had been satisfied. My possessing this magic key somewhat made up for my dull world." Twenty-eight-year-old Rose Kruger, a cigar factory worker of German descent from St. Paul, Minnesota, examines with pride her newly acquired understanding of literature's historical and sociological underpinnings. As we have seen, these discursive contexts were emphasized in the social constructionist approach of her classes. "Our studies have now brought us to the point where we realize that great literature is inseparable from the political and social changes of the period in which it was produced." Kruger, who was also editor of the student magazine in 1924, stresses that work by "sculptors, painters and architects" as well as "men of science" is influenced by political events and the economy. Lucretia Gregorio, a twenty-seven-year-old Italian garment worker from New York, brings these interrelations to the fore in her article, "What Carl Sandburg Means to Me" published in a "Special Poetry Number" of the student magazine also in 1924. Perhaps a classmate of Kruger's, Gregorio confesses to previously associating poetry with "dreamers and thinkers of fine, delicate thoughts" until reading about Sandburg's "Stormy, husky, brawling / City of the Big Shoulders" in his poetic tribute to Chicago.. Through this poem, Gregorio has begun to understand how, in poststructuralist terms, varying cultural texts can compliment, construct, or transgress their own or other discursive boundaries. She explains how Sandburg, a great favorite of both faculty and students, expands poetic discourse to include a "vivid, vigorous, living picture of Chicago" and the "economics" of the working class who built it. Presumably in class discussion, Chicago has been associated with the economics of productive labor and a masculinized working class. Sandburg "makes economics a brutal and savage thing;" but Gregorio is "glad he makes it brag and laugh and fight instead of submitting dull and dispirited to fate." Thus, as a member of the working class—even as a female member—Gregorio has begun to see herself as part of the economic engine destined to improve society, and furthermore, through the poem, discursive abstractions of worker empowerment become embodied in a discursive subjectivity that transgresses its conventional modesty: "Life is hard and life is cruel, but isn't it better to fight it than fear it. This is how Sandburg makes me feel, and to think of him is to lift my head."

Indeed, transgression in both the discursive and the material realms of cultural practice is typical for students at the Summer School. Twenty-seven-year-old Ruby Clodfelter, a white "utility girl" at the Hanes Knitting Company of North Carolina, enters and extends several discursive domains usually off-limits to southern working women. Managing editor of the *Bryn Mawr Light* of 1925, Clodfelter proudly proclaims that as a second-year student, she has acquired three "New Viewpoints" at the Summer School: She now finds herself supporting equality for the "negro"; she accepts the idea of evolution; and she supports the organized labor movement. Evidence of her new attitudes had appeared in the 1924 *Daisy* in "Negro Literature and Art." (This article was published 2 years before African Americans were admitted to the Summer School.) In arguing to improve the "place of the negro" in American society, Clodfelter advocates, albeit in a slightly patronizing tone, expanding conventional canonical discourse to include more African American literature. All that is required, she writes, is that we examine the many works of literature and music that prove African American talent and creativity. Her knowledgeable account begins with the "Uncle Remus" stories, the "Negro spirituals," and ragtime. Turning to literary accomplishments, she points out that there have been "at least thirty writers who showed marked ability" between the poet Phyllis Wheatley and the writer Paul Lawrence Dunbar. Illustrating a sophisticated awareness of discursive propriety, she praises Dunbar's use of black dialect and compares him to Robert Burns, who glorified the dialect of Scottish peasants. She also points out that Dunbar has written verse in "literary English" and is the author of four novels and several volumes of short stories. She goes on to cite other artists and their work: William Stanley Braithwaite, W. E. B. Dubois, Benjamin Brawley, Claude McKay, Fenton Johnson, and John W. Holloway. She pays special attention to George M. Horton, whose poems express "a bitter complaint against bondage and a great desire for freedom." Turning to African American women writers, she mentions Jessie Fauset, Georgia Douglas Johnson, and Anne Spencer. Ironically, many of Clodfelter's artists are still waiting to join the literary canon today.

In 1936, the student body made its most radical recommendations concerning the English curriculum to the Joint Administrative Committee ("Recommendations" 12).[5] Among other things, the women proposed that "Supervised study [hall] should be abolished and two periods of economic history and two of proletarian literature be substituted instead" (13). Student Gay McNamara provides a spirited definition and defense of "Proletarian Literature" in the 1936 issue of *Shop and School*. She writes that "Proletarian literature [is] that kind of composition which deals with working class problems and conveys the ideals of needed changes in the social system."

She addresses several theoretical issues, revealing a sophisticated under-standing of the leftist literary controversies of the day. Yes, she argues, work-ing-class literature could be considered "propaganda, but most literature, directly or indirectly, is also propaganda" in that it "teaches a moral" or "in-fluences the minds of readers." She criticizes Upton Sinclair for the crudeness of his work; later proletarian novelists such as Andre Malraux will undoubt-edly produce literature that will take "its place as art, as good literature," she declares. McNamara prefers that workers do their own writing, but since most lack the time or inclination, "those who can deal with working class problems sympathetically and progressively should be included among the creators of the new literature." McNamara calls for uplifting novels, plays, and poetry to "be written in the language of the workers. . . . simple . . . and yet so interesting and well-written that [they] can reach the . . . majority of the people." Finally, she proclaims that this literature

> is the effort to be heard of millions of challenging voices. Crush it and it will spring up again, for it is the expression of our present day, the only true literature of the workers of our time.

McNamara lends her voice to this working-class chorus through numerous pieces she writes for the Summer School student publication. Her article on "Proletarian Literature" can be read in the appendix to this chapter. Her poems are on the web site connected to this book.

## A MATERIALIST PEDAGOGY FOR WORKING WOMEN WRITERS

As we have seen, both faculty and students looked for a focus on material culture in literature; they wanted to read and write content that was relevant to the lived experience of people in the world. They approached the study of literature from the non-elitist assumption that workers should produce their own works of art. Faculty articulated this view in books, articles, and syllabi. In *Education and the Worker Student,* authors Carter and Smith give two reasons for the emphasis on creative writing at the Summer School. Writing may provide an "emotional outlet" for the woman worker, allowing for the expression of needs and demands as well as relieving her of tensions encountered at work and other areas of life (59). Writing is also important because it may give others a glimpse into the life of an industrial worker from an uncommon, firsthand perspective (59–60). In her own book on teaching, Carter urges workers to write, implying that it is their duty to express them-selves through poetry or fiction. Carter explains that "Industrial workers have an unusually rich and unexploited field so far as novels, plays and po-ems are concerned" (*This America* 39).

Carter and Smith stress that students should draw on their own lives for material, but teachers may have to convince students that their experiences will interest others. They advise students that "Your experiences may seem dull and uninteresting to you because you are so close to them, but they may be something new and even startling to somebody else" (60). The first chapter of Carter's guide to American literature previously mentioned, "Our Roots," also argues that worker experience is an appropriate subject matter for literature. In examining American folklore, Carter legitimizes it and praises it as an "expression growing out of the needs and emotions, manners and customs, hopes and aspirations, of a people, and closely associated with their mode of living and means of earning a livelihood." Similarly, Carter asks workers to look at their own writing as literature to cherish (3).

Summer School faculty and students also seemed to have been influenced by the broader leftist project of building a working-class culture in the United States. In "Symposium on Creative Expression" published in a 1935 issue of the *Journal of Adult Education,* English faculty member William Fincke asserts that

> It would seem logical that the experiences of industrial workers in writing groups established throughout the country might have a significant effect upon our national literature. . . . In the beginnings of articulateness among those more close to the borderline of survival and those who participate firsthand in processes productive of life's necessities, we have the promise of a vastly greater literary perspective. (185)

Recognizing the constitutive role of discourse in shaping lives and social institutions, Fincke adds that "writing metamorphoses . . . into a socializing force" when presented to a receptive audience (185).

As was the case with dramatic production, creative writing was a group activity, but unlike the study of literature and eventually dramatics, creative writing never secured a regular slot in the daytime course schedule. Although a few faculty such as Ellen Kennan and Grace Hawk assigned poetry or narratives in their composition or literature class, in most instances, the creative writers were a self-selected group who met with a faculty sponsor in the evenings once or twice a week to exchange and critique poems and stories.

Sounding remarkably like more recent teachers of composition and creative writing, Carter and Smith promote what amounts to a workshop/process approach. They recommend small writing groups of no more than ten to twelve students to facilitate discussion and sharing of work (61). They emphasize that the teacher should establish a friendly and trusting atmosphere so that students will feel comfortable sharing drafts and critiquing each other's writing. In addition to group work, Carter and Smith stress that "there must also be individual conferences" to focus on unique problems and to help students develop ideas they may be reluctant to share with the whole class (61). To further motivate student writers, the authors suggest distributing mimeographed editions of their work as well as encouraging students to submit their writing to labor or other interested small presses (62). Sounding even more like today's teachers of writing, the authors stress that "a fine craftsman is never completely satisfied," and "though ideas may come in a flash which we call inspiration, they usually require hours of work before they are beautifully or effectively expressed" (62). In other words, revision can improve writing.

Finally, in the syllabus of a team-taught class, we find yet another recommendation that resembles current composition pedagogy:

> Don't be afraid of blank white paper. Put down your story as you see it, and let the grammar and form take care of itself while you are writing it for the first time. It can be smoothed over later if necessary to make it clear. The aim is not perfect English, but rather enough words and enough sense of grammar to make yourself clear and alive in your writing. . . . (Berman, Herrmann, and Shepherd 3)

This remarkable excerpt recommending what today is known as "free writing" was written well over seventy years ago. These same faculty advise their students to "write about things you know and have experienced" (Berman, Herrmann, and Shepherd 3). This repeated call for experiential writing makes it difficult to find unequivocally fictional prose examples among the women workers' published writing. Indeed, given Barbara Foley's documentation of the American left's enthusiasm at the time for the "sketch," a first-person, nonfictional text much promoted by Soviet critics and writers (66), my sense is that for the most part, the Summer School narratives are nonfictional; thus this analysis of creative writing is focused on the workers' poetry rather than longer prose pieces, which might not in fact be fiction. Examples of sketches and other apparently nonfiction prose pieces appear in the appendix to chapter 1.

## LITERARY DISCOURSE BY WOMEN WORKERS:
## A POETIC SENSIBILITY

Judging by the amount of poetry they published over the years, the working women shared the faculty's enthusiasm for the literary arts—especially poetry. From the very first summer session in 1921, poetry was included in *Shop and School,* although there were only two poems in that issue. The high point for poetry was the 1934 issue, in which nearly half of the forty-five pieces were poems. An examination of the poetry published in the student publications from 1924 to 1938, a total of 185 poems, revealed that slightly more than half of the poems are rhyming, and verse is typically free or iambic. Stylistically, the lyric mode predominates. Like much of the poetry they were reading at the Summer School, the student poetry generally fits into what David Perkins has termed the first "modern" phase of American poetry (296). Written in reaction to the Romantic influence and genteel tradition of the Victorian lyric, this early-twentieth-century poetry is "direct and accessible," speakers are attractive, and the tone is affirmative or stoically pessimistic (298). The subject matter is broad and experiential. Many poems have social or political themes and celebrate American democracy. Style is frequently colloquial, the dialect American; verse is often free (306–10). The women worker's poetic taste departed from the mainstream on at least one account, however. According to Perkins, in American high schools, colleges, and reading clubs of the 1930s, the notion of contemporary poetry was likely to mean the "short, free-verse poems of tender impressionism" such as Sandburg's "Fog" or "Cool Tombs" (297). As we have seen, what workers liked were Sandburg's more political poems and his forceful, action-packed impressions of ordinary American life.

The style and themes of the workers' verse remained quite consistent over the years. Their poems are short, averaging just twenty-one lines. Topics are approached from a "subjective" or personal perspective. Only slightly more than a third of the poems are actually written in first person, however, with about a third of these directly addressing a "you" interlocutor. Fewer still (less than 15 percent) are written from a collective "we" perspective. The remaining half are written in third person as a commentary, observation, or declaration. The poetry is rhetorical, provoking its audience through stylistic devices such as repetition, sound imagery, machine rhythms, questions, dialogue, narration, exclamation, and direct address.

While none of the poetry is confined to the narrow thematic realm of emotive confessionalism, much of it takes on a reflective, contemplative tone through philosophical inquiry, expressions of hope and desire, advice, warnings, exhortations, and opinions. At least three-fourths of the poetry could be characterized as "lyrical protest poetry," written to right a wrong, reveal an inequality, or demand justice. The greatest number of poems, about a third, are about work life. Over half of these concern work with machines, and many contain a bodily emphasis.[6] Another major topic is nature, its gifts and revitalizing powers, followed by poems on political or social issues, such as those praising the Soviet Union, poems critical of the rich, poems protesting unemployment and child labor, poems calling for working-class unity. The value of education is another prominent theme, typically put forward in an ode of praise to Bryn Mawr. The remainder of the poems can be divided among a wide variety of subjects: six on the injustice of racism, three on challenges confronting "youth," two individual character sketches, three prayers for peace and racial harmony, and two desolate descriptions of urban landscapes. No poems explore family relationships, the writer's personal background, union issues, or strikes, all areas dealt with quite extensively in the women's autobiographies. Romantic relationships are very rarely voiced, and sexual encounters are not broached in any of the workers' published writing.

### Poems on Work Life and Machines

#### My Job

Weary, monotonous
is everyday toil!
Happy when the time passes by.
No love for the work do I feel,
Just mechanically pushing the wheel.

(Helen Roseman, 1931 *Shop and School* 30)

Perhaps it should not be surprising to find the machine predominant in working women's poetry, vexed as they were by mechanical devices every day. Furthermore, they lived at a time when mechanization was ever present in discursive contexts. Warren Susman writes that Americans of the 1920s and 1930s "were conscious of living in the machine age" (188); another scholar asserts that "In the 1920's and 1930's a machine aesthetic dominated virtually all modern styles and movements" (Sayre 314). However, the American response to machines and the industrial era they ushered in has been mixed mainly because the improvements in communications, sanitation, and material wellbeing brought about by the Industrial Revolution were unevenly distributed. Also, many gains were offset by painful disruptions in social and ecological relationships and cherished ways of life; reactions to these circumstances were also mediated by gender, race, class, and other cultural circumstances.

Those reactions given the loudest cultural voice were, of course, white, male, and generally bourgeois. Lords of industry such as Henry Ford and other members of the Taylorist ruling class extolled the advantages of industrial capitalism. These powerful voices sold the ensuing material culture to Americans largely through the new commercialized discourses of advertising and marketing (Susman 128). Karl Marx also offered a widely circulated validation of the machine, but not without a critique of industrialism. Viewing technology as a neutral tool with emancipatory potential for the working class (495), Marx nevertheless argued that the large-scale use of machines in capitalist industrial production resulted in alienating the worker from labor and the product of labor (503–8). There is ample evidence that this Marxist view was familiar to the women workers at the Summer School. Elizabeth Perlman, writing in the 1932 issue of *Shop and School,* remarks that

> While machinery is detrimental to American workers, it helps the Russian workers to obtain more leisure and to better their conditions, because the machines there are used for the workers' interest instead of private profit.

Perlman's defense of the Soviet Union also suggests familiarity with discourses of the American left, which may have emphasized the benefits of Soviet style industrialism.

The literature the women workers read at the Summer School no doubt reinforced their own experiential hostility towards machines. Kathleen Woodward writes that the "American literary imagination of the 20th century [and before] . . . . adopted an anti-technological stance" (47). And as we have seen, many Bryn Mawr classes read Bentley's *Inheritance,* which chronicles the Luddites' losing battle against the power loom in the British textile mills. Several other works appearing in the Affiliated Schools for Workers "Suggested Reading List" were equally "anti-machine."[7]

Unlike the mainstream bourgeois discourse, the working-class response to "technological progress" has been largely negative through the ages, and the antipathy cuts across race and gender, although as in bourgeois culture, the loudest voice has been white and male. Male workers have objected foremost to the loss of jobs that typically results from the introduction of machinery or automation, but also to the deskilling involved, to the loss of autonomy in the workplace, and to the surveillance techniques used to regulate the pace of factory production (Montgomery 9–27). Women workers echo these complaints when given the chance. Roseman's poem cited above illustrates the high degree of workplace alienation and dissatisfaction experienced by women factory workers.

### Working Class vs. Gender and Race

Indeed, manifestations of class-based solidarity seem to prevail over resistant feminisms or racial affirmations in an analysis of the working women's poetry. For example, an overriding working-class identity is displayed in this poem from the 1930 *Shop and School* by Mary Montgomery, a twenty-year-old African American "maid" at the Philadelphia Electric Company.

### A Change in the Universe

I have a vision of the days of forestry
When the valleys were cold and gray,
And of the barren desert with a burning heat
With the air and the water a mystery;
I no longer can say that now,
For science has controlled them all.
Work, toil, labor, unemployment and industry,
These too help people to comprise the world.
Assiduous persons hurry to and fro.
What has caused these changes in the universe?
Inventions, machinery; they have revolutionized the world—
So we now work hand and hand in industry,
A mass trying hard to control machinery.

(10)

Her poem may reflect newly acquired vocabulary and appreciation for empirical science and its mastery over the environment, yet her vision undercuts these accomplishments with its reference to the tyranny of technology. Montgomery imparts agency to "inventions, machinery; they have revolutionized the world." Her Summer School application reveals that her own talents were not mechanical, but artistic, and that she much preferred her previous job as a "textile painter," doing hand-paintings on scarves and ties. She was hoping to find work in commercial art. A member of the YWCA, Montgomery was taking courses in history and English literature at Central Evening High School in Philadelphia, and she lists an impressive array of books read, including George Eliot's *Adam Bede,* Harriet Beecher Stowe's *Uncle Tom's Cabin,* and Jack London's *Call of the Wild.*

Her first-person narrator transforms by the end of the poem into a collective "we." And despite differences of gender and race, she describes a solidarity among the working class who "now work hand in hand in industry / A mass trying hard to control machinery." This discursive working-class solidarity presents a paradox, at times demonstrating a liberating equality between the sexes, and at other times acting to silence women's and African American voices within masculinist discourse.

Feminist scholar Cheris Kramarae argues that interpersonal communication, an important focus of many women's lives, is not typically considered in technological planning or evaluation because technology reflects the patriarchal social relationships in which it is embedded (11). However, Kramarae also points out that this patriarchal power centers around the needs of an elite group of white males. Thus working-class men as well as women have suffered from an inability to communicate on the clamoring shop floor. With sound and other sensory imagery, the women denounce their deafening workplaces in over half of their poems. In the following example by Mary Nero written in 1938 for *Shop and School,* the noise not only prevents the women from talking to each other, but worse, it prevents them from thinking. Typically, the poet deconstructs conceptual hierarchies central to masculinist thought by uniting the physical and material with the mental and refusing to value the mental over the material.

### Mass Production

Machines and workers;
Grating noise, steady noise.
A humming, a murmuring,
Machines and workers.

Snap machines, button machines,
Hurrying girls, stumbling girls,
Owners, managers—
Rushing the work.
Workers hurrying
To earn more pay;
Work, Work!
Clattering, grinding—
Work, machines, noise, heat,
Heat, noise, machines, Work.

Day in, day out,
Week after week,
No break, no stop—
Numbing our souls,
Drugging our minds,
Rasping our nerves.
How long can we last?
How long before our souls die?
Work, noise, machines, heat,

Heat, machines, noise, work.
Shall we die without one protest?
Have we no soul?
Do we not feel?
Do we not see?
Piles of work
Pressing down;
Waves of heat
Engulfing, drowning.
Bosses, owner
Rushing, pushing.
Roaring, deafening;
Year in, year out,
Workers' souls dying?
Dying, Dying?

(16)

Although not feminist, the poem is gendered by its insertion of "hurrying girls, stumbling girls" into the textualized manufacturing process—an insertion that "the bosses" would no doubt prefer to avoid, for the idea of young women working was still not an accepted one, much less "girls" working with machines. Yet Nero was most likely speaking for all workers, female and male, in her poem of rage. Thus her use of the term "workers," which echoes the masculinist rhetoric of the workers' movement, seems more appropriate than not. Indeed, as has been noted, the lack of feminist perspectives among working women of the 1930s, both black and white, has been a subject of much concern to scholars. As Kramarae points out, common experience with certain technological processes may at times unite working-class women and men—perhaps even across race—thus reducing the motivation for feminist, gendered or racially marked renderings of that experience (7). Sharon Hartman Strom explains that "the failure of feminists to remain visible in the thirties meant that working-class women had no public sanction for articulating feminist ideas" (367). On the other hand, the androcentric discourse of worker empowerment came to them through all sorts of cultural media.

### Nature: Scene of Harmony and Wisdom

The women wrote numerous odes to nature, extolling the beauty of green meadows, the tranquility of cool gardens, and the radiant glow of sunsets. Trees were also frequently the focus of celebratory poems, perhaps because so many of the women worked in defoliated urban environments and were denied the pleasure of luxuriant shade. Helen Cooper, the author of the following poem, written for the 1936 *Shop and School,* genders a tree feminine and declares a sisterly bond with it, signaling the metaphorical identification with nature typical of the working women.

### A Tree and I

I know now why a tree and I
Seem so much akin.
The same stuff runs in both of us;
We're sisters under the skin.

(15)

Affirming their unity with nature is important for the Summer School students. Since the "same stuff runs in both of us," nature's vast creative, fortifying, and regenerative powers now flow through the working women. Like Nero, Cooper deconstructs masculinist oppositions; in her identification with the tree and nature, she does not relegate the "body-nature" side of the traditional polarity to a status inferior to the "mind-culture" side. Instead she celebrates the corporeal and natural as a fundamental and life-affirming component of her identity.

Also typical of the workers' nature poetry is this ode to a tree by Betty Katz, included in the 1932 *Shop and School.*

### Tree, Beautiful Tree

Tree, beautiful tree,
As I lie under thee,
You intoxicate me,
Your height makes me see
The beauty above thee.
Branches so loose and free
Make me forget the slavery
Far behind.
The leaves full of fragrance
And delight
Awaken in me
Desire for right,
Whisper, telling me
Of secrets beyond thee,
O glorious thing of nature,
I love thee.

(48)

To a certain extent, the working women appropriate the romantic discourse regarding nature that was culturally available to them. Thus nature is depicted as a repository of truths and wisdom and as constituting a domain less sullied than the humanly constructed one of industrial capitalism. A "machine in the garden" motif resonates throughout the nature poetry as an outdoor realm of harmony, and beauty is often contrasted with an oppressive and alienating shop floor. The poets also link industrialization to the destruction of nature and, because of their grueling working conditions, the destruction of their own bodies.

However, the women workers go beyond customary romantic perspectives when they present nature as more than a harmonious setting and source of wisdom, but as a catalyst necessary for intellectual growth, fruitful contemplation, and collective reflection and action. Nature is not passive in this construct but a subjectivity active in the development of human thought, the "desire for right," and the search for knowledge. Nature thus becomes an ally in the worker students' quest for social, political, and economic justice. As the last poem included in this article will attest, the women believe that the Bryn Mawr educational project succeeds in part because of its inspirational natural surroundings. Again, nature and culture are not presented as polarities, but as interdependent areas of life. The women often express a utopian longing for unity between mind and body, culture and nature, for a community in harmony with its natural surroundings, where a collectivity arranges meaningful work and other creative activities that engage hands and brains.

### Poems of Politics and Social Themes

The next poem, from the 1936 *Shop and School,* portrays antagonisms between working- and upper-class white women by textualizing the rhetoric of class that has been clearly inscribed on their bodies. The poet, Thelma Brown, was an "American born" white student from Roanoke, Virginia. Because her application was accessible, we learn a great deal about her background: that she was thirty years old and an officer of the United Textile Workers Union. She had served as president of her YWCA Club and vice chairman of its Workers Education division. Politically progressive, she also directed a Pioneer Youth Club. Her reading for the year included a variety of left-leaning publications: the *New Republic,* the *Call* (Socialist Party weekly), the *Daily Worker* (Communist Party daily), and *The Case for Industrial Organizations.* Brown commented in a postscript that the following poem passed "through my mind as I sat in a conference at Hollins College" organized to introduce college girls to working girls (20).

## Thoughts

I work, you play,
You have everything,
I have nothing.
Why should I sit here, afraid to take my coat off?
Is it because I smell so strong of acid?
Why don't I take my gloves off?
Is it because my hands are so rough and dirty looking?
Why do I keep my hat on?
Is it because my hair smells like a wet dog?
Acid again. Acid that smells like burning sulphur.
There are fumes of sulphur in Hell.

You daughters of the rich,
You walk so easy and sure of yourselves,
You don't smell at all.
Your hands are well kept,
Your hair shines with cleanliness,
Your eyes are bright and eager looking.
But who makes your sweetness, your cleanliness possible?
Is it not workers like me?
I work, you play,
You have everything;
I have nothing.

(20)

Written as an internal dialogue, Brown's poem forcefully denounces the upper-class students she addresses in her poem. The physical toll of capitalist injustice is written on the working woman's body through unpleasant smells and dirty hands—results of the truly hellish work she must carry out. Foucault's panoptic gaze comes to mind as her poetic persona's self-monitoring inhibits her movements and actions. Since her body is marked as working-class, she refuses to take off her hat, coat, and gloves in front of the upper-class girls. And as is the case in many other poems, Brown's basic message is Marxist: The exploited labor of the working class makes possible a pampered lifestyle for daughters of the bourgeoisie.

### A Poem of Politics and Aesthetics

In 1927, Smith organized the publication of *The Workers Look at the Stars* as a fund-raising project for Vineyard Shore, a residential school for women workers modeled after the Bryn Mawr Summer School. The publication was a small but attractively bound, thirty-two-page booklet of poetry written by the women workers at the Bryn Mawr Summer School during its first six years. It contained twenty poems, four of which were written by Smith herself and included at the request of the students.

The penultimate poem in the booklet is worth particular attention since the poet, Constance Ortmayer, similar to Cooper above, places several areas of life that are typically thought of as distinct and oppositional in "harmonious combination" (H. Smith, *Workers* 29). In her highly conceptual articulation of the relationship between economics and poetry, she again steps beyond cultural givens and provides an extraordinary example of the Summer School's pedagogical success.

### Economics in Poetry

The wonders of nature, the violence of the elements,
The dreams of lovers, the sacrifices of the strong,
The tears of mothers, the laughter of children,
Battles, Wars, Music . . .
All these are supple clay in the hands of the poet,
Clay with which he molds beautiful figures,
Phantom figures of every shape and form;
Figures that are all the more wondrous because
We cannot touch them. No, nor really see them,
For the poet builds them, molds them, fashions them
To live in our minds.
Many of them are transient dwellers.
Some find their way to our hearts, to live
As long as our hearts live.

But economics, the means and ways by which we make our living,
Millions of us, working, sweating, striving, to what end?
So that we may eat and clothe our bodies.
And why do we eat and clothe our bodies?
So that we may have the strength to work, sweat and strive for another day.
Thus the routine continues day after day, year after year,
With only short periods of respite.
This is not beautiful, but it is part of economics.
Buying and selling, weighing, packing, shipping
Iron, steel, lumber, factories, machinery, money
Stocks, bonds: These are not beautiful,
But they play their part in what we call economics.

Economics, prosaic economics is not pliable clay
For the poet to mold. No, it is rock,
Grey, drab, sullen rock, ugly rock,
And most poets pass it by.
"We can mold no fine figures from this," they say,
"No phantom figures of beauty to dwell in the minds of men."

But a few men have tried and a few have succeeded.
They have chosen new tools to work with,
Have laid down the trowel and taken the chisel.
They have chiseled deep into the rock,
The sullen grey rock of economics.
They have hacked and have pounded
And have fashioned a figure,
A figure to live in the minds of men,
A great rugged giant with huge bulging biceps,
Massive broad shoulders and heavy square jaw;
A brute of a figure that a few men have made
To live in the hearts of men.
We shall smoothen and soften the roughness about it,
And some day perhaps like Pygmalion's Galatea,
It will slowly awaken.
Then it will live in the hearts of us, souls of us,
Part of us, all of us.
We shall thank the few poets,
The poets who saw the cold rock, the sullen grey rock,
But did not pass it by.

(29)

Her noticeably polyphonous text incorporates a number of cultural voices in a strategy of discursive appropriation that again transcends dualities such as work/art, mental/physical labor, male/female, public/private, and mind/body. As is typical of much Summer School poetry, Ortmayer makes her points about art, the working class, and its envisioned empowerment by textualizing the body. What is not so typical is her regendering of the body, feminizing it. The effect is "transgressive" as bell hooks uses that term, that is, "a movement against and beyond boundaries" (12).

Listening closely to the discourses in the poem, we hear echoes of Carl Sandberg's "Chicago" in Ortmayer's description of economics as the "great rugged giant with huge bulging biceps." She undoubtedly had Sandberg in mind as a poet who did not "pass by" the "grey rock" of economics but used it in creating a poetic tribute to the working people of a dynamic city. This metaphoric equivalence between economics and the worker recalls theoretical Marxism, in which the working class becomes the physical embodiment of revolutionary theory. Like many of her classmates, Ortmayer probably had direct or indirect contact with Marxism, given its prevalence in working-class culture of the 1920s and 1930s. Another cultural text used by Ortmayer comes from Greek mythology and supplies the narrative image she uses for her transformative project. Mythology was a common subject in many high school or middle school curriculums of the 1920s and was studied in some Summer School classes as well.

Ortmayer artfully appropriates these discourses and uses them in her corporeal metaphor. An emphasis on the body, its pain but also its strength, is crucial to Ortmayer and the poet of her poem since bourgeois discourse tends to erase workers' physical presence and oppression. Both poets give textual embodiment to the working class, providing a physical description of the worker and underscoring the monotonous aspect of mechanized physical labor. Proud and aware of the important role played by the working class in the area of economics, Ortmayer gives equal weight to the routine physical labor of the working class and the more abstract maneuvers of capital as she juxtaposes "weighing, packing, shipping," with "money / Stocks, bonds." Ortmayer also criticizes bourgeois poetic creations as abstract "phantom figures," which live in our "minds." Transgressing the mind/body duality, she feels that the new poets have now begun the construction of a new "body" of poetry, albeit a masculine one with "Massive broad shoulders and heavy square jaw," which lives in a more bodily or material realm, in the "hearts of men," rather than in their minds. This textual embodiment of the working class inserting itself into the more public world of economics parallels Ortmayer's creative act of placing her poem into the public realm and commenting on the public discourse of economics.

There are other discursive transgressions occurring in the poem. In Ortmayer's use of a collective speaking subject and in her veiled criticism of the romantic poet who "molds beautiful figures," she rejects the unitary "I" of bourgeois subjectivity for a collective "we" who speaks with a more democratic and gender-inclusive voice. Finally, in Ortmayer's most impressive discursive maneuver, she regenders the working-class and creative artists, feminizing them and their accomplishments. While masculine poets have indeed written about a new masculine worker—"A brute of a figure a few men have made / To live in the hearts of men"—they seem to have also inspired the poem's collective persona to speak/write/act as "women." A regendering takes place as the male creators become an expanded, feminized "we" who "shall smoothen and soften the roughness" until, like "Pygmalion's Galatea," the working class is feminized and can live "in the hearts of us, souls of us," "all of us," as a more inclusive working class. Thus Ortmayer has taken the words of others and shaped them into her own transgressive creation, which enlarges the boundaries of human agency to include the working class and women in the creative project of building a new society.[8]

## Poems about Education: In Tribute to the Summer School

The working women generously praised Bryn Mawr in their poetry and expressed great sadness when their eight-week sessions were about to end. Below, poet Mary Sekula celebrates the Summer School in the 1932 *Shop and School* for its inspiring environment, both natural and intellectual, and for her increased ability to think tolerantly and critically. Yet, this final poem in my sample also aches with loss as the poet contemplates leaving the scholarly and aesthetic abundance that has been hers.

### I Have Stolen Away

I have stolen away from my friends, and from the busy street.
From the grind of the wheel, and the sweltering heat;
I have come to visit you, and what you've in store for me.
To tell you of my past Bryn Mawr, and my future through you to see.
  But now I must go.

From near and far, you have friends that come to you
From across vast lands, and deep blue seas, that separate in two;
To you it does not matter the color, race or creed
You teach them all one lesson "Think," and plant in them the seed.
  But now I must go.

You have in me awakened many a memory;
Some are filled with laughter, others sympathy.
If I could but commune a few words with thee,
I would tell you of my spirit, that stands silently with me.
  But now I must go.

Your wisdom is surrounded by nature's soft toned beauty,
The trees they bow their branches, as though to say,"We greet thee."

I love you, Bryn Mawr, as I love a friend.
Though I'll try not to be selfish, and let others have a share,
    But now I must go.

Perhaps there may come a time
When again my spirit will feed,
Bathe itself in thy beauty,
And humble workers meet.
    But now I must go.

                                                        (14)

Sekula's poem contains many of the themes and techniques that are common throughout the working women's poetry. First of all, like many of the others, she uses strategies of transcendence and transgression to breach cultural constraints. Her title emphasizes her break with the social norms prescribed for the working class as she "steals" the temporal, natural, and discursive space to grow and bond with other working women. Indeed, by appropriating knowledge and discourse usually denied to these "humble workers," they have "stolen away," to critique their past and present, while imagining a better future.

Though the barriers broken at Bryn Mawr are many, they are typically pulled together again in a poetic synthesis of a more satisfying order. Thus, the harsh conditions of mechanized industry, "the grind of the wheel, and the sweltering heat," are denounced and then supplanted by "Nature's soft-toned beauty," which surrounds the campus and fosters a more satisfying intellectual and manual industry. Sekula also refers to differences of "color, race or creed" that are acknowledged at the Summer School and overcome to a certain degree. And again, the natural and human realms recombine as Sekula uses the oft-repeated trope of personifying a tree, which greets her like a friend.

Yet as the relentless refrain "But now I must go" illustrates, Sekula feels a dismaying need to return to work. Her emphasis on the temporal, hurried, and pressured aspects of industrial life, which we also see in many of her classmates' poems, seems to confer a more enduring, even timeless quality to the Summer School experience. Bryn Mawr has offered an escape from the stultifying, stress-filled factory to a realm where heart, mind, and body are united in meaningful work, a realm with a spiritual dimension for some. Sekula, for example, points out that her spirit "stands silently with" her, no doubt the same spirit that classmate Marjorie Moss refers to in the poem that begins this chapter. Both believe that a "spirit of Bryn Mawr" animates the graduates as they go forth to create the future they began to envision at the Summer School. Indeed, these women workers have been in a world apart, and its model and memory will transcend the mechanized working environment they must revisit.

## LESSONS OF TRANSGRESSION, TRANSFORMATION, TRANSCENDENCE

Perhaps the most salient characteristic of the working women's poetry is its transgressive nature. Poet after poet expresses the desire to transcend her daily living situation and build a new, more satisfying society. As in other areas of Summer School work, the material environment is privileged, whether as the lived experience that must be escaped or the future that is desired and has to be built. Marjorie Moss summons a "New Dawn," affirming the need for a material transformation of the everyday through spiritual rejuvenation and expansion. Helen Roseman longs to be away from the dreary reality of her job, only feeling "happy when the time passes by." Mary Montgomery's "Change in Universe" deals with cataclysmic transformation. In "Mass Production," Mary Nero anguishes over the death of a transcendent human essence, the worker's "soul." In "A Tree and I," Helen Cooper leaves the realm of the human for the natural, as does Betty Katz in dreaming of "secrets beyond thee." Thelma Brown implicitly calls for an economic revolution in "Thoughts," while Constance Ortmayer recombines disparate elements of her existence in "harmonious combination," even going so far as to regender androcentric cultural givens.

Ultimately, the texts of these working women both impress and surprise: impress because the writing seems genuine, informed, imaginative, far-reaching, and transformative; surprise because, even today, the economics of literacy does not allow us to expect such textual achievement from workers. However, as Deborah Brandt has carefully demonstrated, certain "encounters with literacy sponsors . . . can be sites for the innovative rerouting of resources into projects of self-development and social change" (169). The Bryn Mawr Summer School seems to have been such a sponsoring agency for women workers. If lessons can be drawn from the Summer School project, they would come from the pedagogical principles developed and applied there: Students were given a broad education grounded in the liberal arts with a focus on social critique; educators respected and valued students' life experience and related this experience to larger artistic, political, and economic concerns; educational materials and literature were made relevant to students' daily lives and problems; student voices were listened to in matters of pedagogy and administration; students studied in an environment of natural beauty; they were able to produce as well as consume in the educational enterprise; and, most importantly, the Summer School education engaged heart, mind, and body in transformative projects for social good.

## APPENDIX: POETRY AND LITERARY ESSAYS BY WOMEN WORKERS AT THE BRYN MAWR SUMMER SCHOOL

### "Sue"
**Agnes Bole**
*Shop and School,* 1933

Sue was kinda lazy, She jus' always took her time,
And her voice was thick and heavy an' fell in certain rhyme.
Her feet jus' wouldn't hurry none; her eyelids always drooped;
Her carriage when one looked quite close had a certain stoop.
She could hardly hold a job. She'd say in her own way,
"Oh, what's the use of all this work?"
The boss, he usta say,
"See here, Sue, I hates lak tho dooce to have to let you go,
But you's the laziest girl I've met or ever wants to know."
But Sue made up for lack of speed or any fairy-like grace,
For Sue could change the coldest heart with the smile upon her face.
I guess she saved her job that way, oh, at least three times or more,
And when she started out to close the exit door,
The boss jus' said with kind of pomp, "I'll give you 'nother trial."
I often wonder how much control Sue practiced through her smile.

### "Maw"
**Agnes Bole**
*Shop and School,* 1933

Maw was over forty and was a ragman's wife.
Maw could read our teacups and thrill us all alive.
We would sit around at noon hour impatiently and wait
For Maw to start her readings and tell us all our fate.

Maw would frown and read the leaves,
And if she had been right,

We all would have married every man in sight.
Maw would say with quite a sigh
That soon we all would wed.
The fortunes that she used to tell
Almost turned our head.

There used to be some money in each cup of tea
And cars and boats and homes and all such luxury.
We never would have to work so hard
After we were wed.
Maw thought that we believed in everything she said.

And when the bell had sounded
And our work we must resume,
I used to watch the ragman's wife
slowly cross the room.

There was something in her eyes that made me understand
That Maw really lived in some other land
Where cares and strife were laid aside
And thoughts were fancy free.
I often think that she instilled some of her thoughts in me.

## "Under the Greenwood Tree"
## Mary Barnes Curtis
### *Bryn Mawr Echo,* 1928

I would that I might live again
An hour under the greenwood tree
With the branches spreading round about
Seemingly shutting the whole world out
With the carpet of green
And the sunset glow
Lighting each face
As they listen so
To the speaker telling a story so old
Of a world made right by a vote at the poll.

The speaker is gone, the crowd has broken
But gathers again with words unspoken

To settle the question of the world made right
By strike or ballot, struggle or fight.
The lights come on as darkness falls,
And still the argument rambles on:
"I am sure the workers would reach their goal,
If once they got the world in their control."
"That may be so, but I cannot see
How that will win my bread for me."
Thus the argument gathers force
As each one speaks all in one chorus.
The argument may be old or new
But give me again with you, and you
An hour under the greenwood tree
With the carpet of green
And the sunset glow
Lighting each face as they listen so.

### "What Carl Sandburg Means to Me"
**Lucretia Gregorio**
*Bryn Mawr Daisy*, 1924

I was sitting, waiting for a poem to be read, and into my consciousness came the words:

"Hog butcher for the World
Tool Maker, Stacker of Wheat
Player with Railroad and the Nation's Freight Handler;
Stormy, husky, brawling,
City of the Big Shoulders."

Was this poetry? I wondered, as the voice went on. This vivid, vigorous, living picture of Chicago. Tense, I waited for more. It was economics and poetry I sat listening to, and it came like a stirring call. Poetry I had always associated with the dreamers and thinkers of the fine, delicate things of life, words that made beautiful pictures of beautiful thoughts. Sandburg is a poet who sees and puts into living words the actualities of our everyday life. He makes economics a brutal and savage thing; but I'm glad he makes it brag and laugh and fight instead of submitting dull and dispirited to fate. He knows that man is fighting and he makes it a glorious fight. Life is hard and life is cruel, but isn't it better to fight it than fear it? This is how Sandburg makes me feel,— and to think of him is to lift my head.

## "A Boss Hiring a Private Secretary"
**Fay Koenigsberg**
*Shop and School*, 1931

Do you know, Miss Blank, how to write advertisements?
Do you know correspondence, book-keeping, and three foreign languages?
And can you take a fluent dictation?
And toward customers, can you act properly?
Can you dress to suit the reputation of my firm?
Of course, sharp at 8 o'clock you must be on your job—
And you'll stay a little longer because of the telephone calls,
But, to pass the time, you can amuse yourself with the evening news.
You see I am fair—
And, of course, you are willing, reliable, and honest,
I don't have to mention that.
Just one thing more:
We might need you sometimes as a model.
And don't forget to manicure your nails,
That's all, I think.
Pardon me, what's that you say?
Oh, yes, your salary.
You know how business now is bad,
You'll have to consider this.
You girls—you have it easy—
No worries at all, you are getting your salary.
I'll give you fifteen dollars in cash,
And hope that you are satisfied.
If not—there are others.

## "Apples"
**Kate Malkin**
*Shop and School*, 1931

Please tell us, Apples, why are you so red?
Is it because you are ashamed to be sold
By the unemployed for their bread?
Or is it because you are just like us—
Torn off by force without your will,
Packed in boxes and in cans?
Did you too have no chance?

**"Proletarian Literature"**
**Gay McNamara**
*Shop and School,* 1936

Proletarian literature to me means that kind of composition which deals with working class problems and conveys the ideals of needed changes in the social system. It must be a sincere and strong expression, relying more on its honesty than beauty of words alone.

This sort of literature has been criticized from the stand point that it is "propaganda". Admitting that, I would say that most of literature, directly or indirectly, is also propaganda. A novel will present the solution of some problem; it will teach some moral; at least it will picture a certain way of living or thinking. All of this definitely influences the minds of readers.

However, the time has passed when to be a good proletarian novel all a book need do was to involve struggling workers in the blackness of a capitalistic society. With all due respect to Upton Sinclair and his work, I am sure that the later novelists are doing a clearer and deeper sort of writing. His novels definitely contributed much to the growing movement but they were cruder than good literature. The new writing is no longer a "changeling" in this field. These novels and their kind show that working class literature can be powerful, beautiful, and moving. It is taking its place as art, as good literature.

The question arises whether the workers should do this writing. They should certainly develop and encourage this form of expression whenever possible. The problem lies in the fact that the mass of workers have neither the leisure or the inclination to write. Those who can deal with working class problems sympathetically and progressively should be included among the creators of the new literature.

Let our novels, our plays, our poetry be written in the language of workers. It can be simple and understandable and yet so interesting and well-written that it can reach the thinking of the majority of people. True proletarian literature then will carry on the workers' message. That play or novel which can present only hopelessness and defeat is not serving the purpose or meeting the workers' need.

This literature will live and thrive as long as existing conditions continue. It is the effort to be heard of millions of challenging voices. Crush it and it will spring up again, for it is the expression of our present day, the only true literature of the workers of our time.

**"To a Negro"**
**Elsie Moulton**
*Shop and School,* **1934**

> Why, why, why, do they say I am better than you?
> If we were reversed and you could be white
> And I could be black, not one single mite
> Of difference could they find in us two.
>
> Why! Why! Why! You did not come out of the earth.
> Your mother suffered as did my mother too.
> They both had a daughter, one me and one you,
> And so we are equal in birth.
>
> Should a blind man judge between our evils
> Perhaps he'd choose you, perhaps me.
> But whichever he chose, we'd be equal,
> To him two human beings we'd be.
>
> Some folk like the taste of a black grape
> Some prefer grapes that are green
> But come down to brass tacks, both people agree
> That a grape is a grape just the same.
>
> If there be a power above us
> Who says these things should not be
> Let him bring down curses and judgment
> On him who says you are different from me.
>
> If there be no powers above us,
> Then right must find a way through,
> Because, damn them, what is the difference?
> There's none between me and you.

**"What Literature Means to Me"**
**Jeanne Paul**
*Bryn Mawr Light,* **1926**

Literature means to me the key to realms of beauty, dreams and fantasies to worlds of illusions and realities.

Often, after a day's monotonous humdrum work, I have rushed through the crowds of Broadway, mingling with the multitudes in my desire to escape myself. Yet, among the thousands, I have felt alone; as alone as on a deserted island. I wanted something. What? I could not say.

But, with my magic key of literature, I was able to enter into strange lands. Sometimes, in the land of Poetry, I would meet with glorious sunsets, exquisite flowers, singing birds, storms on sea and on land. I would hear the plaintive murmurings of the brooklets, and sink into insignificance before the grandeurs of age-old mountains. And all these would be accompanied by fascinating rhythms that stirred unknown depths within me.

Sometimes, in the land of Novels, I would see strange peoples, witness struggles between heart and mind. There I would hear things which my heart had often felt but could never have spoken. Always, after unlocking the door to these strange lands, I felt that something in me had been satisfied. My possessing this magic key somewhat made up for my dull world.

**"Wavering"**
**Helen Sharkey**
*Shop and School*, 1931

I see sometimes in my dreams
Vast differences it seems
Instead of my clanking, clanging press
I see hills and woods with birds at rest
And instead of the wheels that always turn
I see the radiance of the sunset's burn.
Nor do I try to hear the roaring powers;
Instead I hear the hush of the flowers.
But just for a moment do these molded dreams last
For I hear a noise far worse than the past;
And my dreams all shatter, again I hear
Clanging, turning, roaring and a voice within ear—
(Saying "get busy").

# Material of Desire: Bodily Rhetoric       6
# in Working Women's Poetry

I would like to write a poem,
But I have no words.
My grammar was ladies' waists,
And my schooling skirts.

> —Anonymous dressmaker, *Opening Vistas in Workers' Education: An Autobiography of Hilda Worthington Smith*

In writing this doubly ironic poem about not being able to write a poem, a student at the Bryn Mawr Summer School subverts discursive rules of class and gender that hinder her creativity. In a further ironic move, she explains the materiality of social relations that so limit all working-class women. Physically confined to factories for long, painful hours, the women had little time for intellectual pursuits. Their cultural logic or "grammar" had been largely corporeal, based on their physical exploitation for the benefit of a "lady" of another class. The working women felt discursively deprived, unable to write. In their minds poetry was connected to esteemed literary arts, classical learning, aesthetic sophistication—all discursive markers of the middle- and upper-class education they lacked. Yet remarkably, by the end of their Summer School session, many workers were writing poems, poems the likes of which had never been seen before and rarely since, poems inscribed with working-class, racial, and occasionally gendered identities; at times celebratory, at times defiant and demanding. The Summer School's mix of progressive discursive and material contexts ("material" in the democratic structures established for deciding on issues of administration and pedagogy) enabled the working women to transgress cultural scripts that limited their gender, race, and class. Poetry was the centerpiece of a liberatory writing curriculum. Acting as a discursive bridge, it carried students from the immaterial and ideal world of texts and concepts studied in class back to the material world, which they described in terms of the exploitation, poor working conditions, and prejudicial attitudes they wanted to change. This textual/mental versus material/corporeal dialectic and bridging is especially evident in the bodily motif that pervades the women's poetry. The recovery of this discarded and forgotten discursive "body" of women's work reveals how a pedagogical project may progress from a textual to physical or material context. It is also important in reminding us of the significance of the corporeal realm where we live both the pain and the pleasure of our immaterial rhetorics.

## DISCOURSE AND WOMEN WORKERS:
## PEDAGOGY, POETRY, AND POWER

As we have seen, the students at the Summer School enjoyed a richly progressive discursive environment, which they appropriated for constructing more empowered subjectivities and satisfying cultural traditions. Public discourse of the 1920s and especially the 1930s included much proworker rhetoric as union demands became public issues and even policy. The rhetoric of the New Deal often put workers at the center of its stated benefits. Much leftist ideology reached mainstream discourse through the widespread political work of the Communist, Socialist, and other leftist political parties. Also, the perspectives of the progressive and worker education movements were pervasive in the culture of education, especially at the Summer School. The working women, therefore, found much support at the Summer School and in the wider community for the new cultural scripts they were writing. They also encountered and sometimes wrote against subtexts of racism, classism, and sexism found in working-class institutions as well as those of the larger culture.

### Poetry of Machines and the Body

In their search for "words" and "grammar" to write poetry, women workers at the Bryn Mawr Summer School created a rhetoric that directed public gaze to their exhausting work and located their subjectivity in the public discursive arena. Since these women workers were physically confined to steamy factories for the manufacture of objects they could rarely afford, they chose to textualize their bodies in a rhetoric that exposed the oppressive relationships of power, economics, gender, race, and class that plagued their lives. Fortunately, the Summer School afforded the women workers time to study their role in the national economy—a role they came to understand as even more important than that of the upper-class "ladies" whom they served. Subsequently, through their poetic rhetoric of the body, they were able to speak their desires for material bounty as well as intellectual and aesthetic rewards. In recovering their poetry, we extend the opportunity begun at Bryn Mawr for working women to enter the discursive body politic, a space that remains off-limits to them even today, and even as they continue to perform many of the most tedious and exhausting tasks of global capitalist production.

The mechanized factory, where women and men worked alongside frighteningly powerful and fast-paced industrial machinery, prompted much poetic discourse at the Summer School. It was in this poetry that the Bryn Mawr worker students felt compelled to write their bodies. In fact, two-thirds of the poems dealing with the workplace make mention of workers' bodies. The value of an embodied working-class perspective has been emphasized by Janet Zandy in her anthology of working-class writing, *Liberating Memory*. "The lived experience of working class people encodes a kind of knowledge—especially of the body—that is absent in bourgeois . . . institutions" (2). Similarly, bell hooks writes that "there is a particular knowledge that comes from suffering. It is a way of knowing that is often expressed through the body, what it knows, what has been deeply inscribed on it through experience" (91).

Indeed, the bodily knowledge disclosed in the working women's poetry rhetoricized their texts in complex, paradoxical, and multifaceted ways. The selected poetry that follows illustrates several recurring themes that mark this corporeal rhetoric: First of all, the women felt a need to textualize their bodily presence in the factory, a painful presence capitalist owners still prefer to ignore. Second, the working women used a rhetoric of struggle to record their fight against owners and machines for control of their bodies. Third, they wrote their bodies as sites of social control as well as sites of individual and collective resistance. Also, as subjectivities both written by and writing beyond conventional patriarchal dualities, the women asserted that they were more than "mere" bodies; they had inquiring minds, aesthetic ambitions, and creative abilities. And although most of their poetry was written in solidarity with their white male working-class counterparts, occasional gendered opposition to masculine oppression and racism did surface. Finally, we frequently see women encouraging each other to create an alternative discursive tradition, one denouncing the injustice of their exploitation and celebrating the working class across differences of gender and race.

### Pointing Out Bodies in the Factory

The working women frequently called attention to the fact that their jobs were physically painful and mentally depressing. This discursive rendering of suffering was assertive in an age when public mention of the body was prohibited for women and the working class in general as it named the site of much class and gender oppression. This poem by Mary Feldman, from the 1936 *Shop and School,* exposes capitalism's sacrifice of the worker's body and mind in the production of relatively insignificant articles of apparel.

**Buttons**

Remember the old nursery rhyme,
"Buttons, buttons, who's got the button?"
Remember? Yes, such childish play!
It's play no more with buttons. It's work.
Such back-aching, eye-straining work!
Buttons—large buttons—small buttons
White buttons—black buttons—colored buttons
Buttons for shirts—buttons for sweaters—buttons for coats.
Do people think when they buy buttons
Of the fast, steady, monotonous work?
Buttons pouring out of the machine towards
Me on the ever-moving belt!
I stare at buttons, I sort buttons.
All day long. My eyes ache, so, ache!
Buttons, just buttons!

(6)

Cultural texts were commonly appropriated by the worker writers for use in their poetry. Here Feldman calls on discourse from a more innocent and happier time to provoke her readers into an awareness of the role of human labor in the production process. Perhaps she was also familiar with the Marxist concepts of commodity fetishization, surplus value, and alienation, as her poem also seems to illustrate these ideas. In a highly rhetorical style, she employs textual strategies such as irony, questions, direct address, and exclamations to condemn the subject position workers occupy in the mechanized industrial workplace.

### Bodies Against the Machine: The Machine Against the Body

The women workers also protested poetically against the ways their bodies were subjected to the controlling forces of capitalist patriarchy. Feminist interpretations of Michel Foucault's work are useful in understanding this disciplining of the "docile body" for increased utility and efficiency in assigned cultural tasks. According to Sandra Lee Bartky, the "production of 'docile bodies' requires that an uninterrupted coercion be directed to the very processes of bodily activity...; this 'micro-physics of power' fragments and partitions the body's time, its space and its movements" (qtd. in Diamond and Quinby 62). Indeed, constraints imposed on their time, space, and movement are frequent themes in the women's poetry and can be seen in the 1934 *Shop and School* poem by twenty-eight-year-old Adelaide Burgdorf, a white woman whose application records that she worked as a part-time stock sorter in a button factory in Rochester, New York. Not a union member, she was recruited to the Summer School through her local YWCA Industrial Club, where she had held numerous offices. Previous to her Bryn Mawr experience, she had attended courses in dramatics, English, economics, and history offered through the Y. Her obvious intellectual ability and curiosity must have made her days at the factory tortuous indeed.

### Factories

Grey walls greet me on all sides,
The roar of motors fills my ears,
And all my eyes can see are fast whirling wheels.
Amid the noise and clashing of wheels,
    more speed.
My hands so tired can move no faster.
My eyes droop with weariness,
But I dare not sleep.
I am chained to this huge machine
And it keeps on saying,
    more speed.

Can it be that somewhere beyond all this
Bright flowers bloom and birds sing gaily?
Can I find there food for my body
As well as my soul?
Or must I always go on hearing the wheels say,
    more speed.

(21)

Corporeal representation and transformation are central tropes in this poem. Burgdorf's bodily senses are overwhelmed by the machine, which pushes her. The machine is itself anthropomorphized to represent the embodied owner. When the machine speaks, what is heard is the capitalist's call for "more speed" made material again in Burgdorf's aching hands and eyes. Using conventional cultural dichotomies, Burgdorf presents nature/(woman's) body in opposition to culture/(man's) mind. However, Burgdorf and her fellow poets frequently revalue the maligned half of this dyad. She defends the body in its need for repose and praises the natural realm for offering a revitalizing alternative to urban industrialism, thus deconstructing patriarchal meanings.

In the next poem, from the 1929 *Shop and School,* Mary Kosovicz, a twenty-two-year-old textile worker of Polish origin from Rhode Island describes an incident in which a worker has to fight the machine for control of her body. Kosovicz's application shows that although she left school in the eighth grade, she also had a strong desire to continue learning. Educational Chair of her local YWCA Industrial Club, she had taken five evening classes at the Y, including Greek Mythology, music appreciation, and English literature. She reported having read *A Midsummer Night's Dream, The American Federationist,* and the *Providence News* among other works over the year. She was not a union member.

### The Machine

Hello, you big monster.
I'm not afraid of you today.
Yesterday, you played me a dirty trick
By pulling in my hand,
And crushing it till I screamed.
You laughed and roared on and on.
Louder and louder, just like a wild lion
Full of joy and that has just caught its prey
I was helpless.
To fight you would be like fighting wild beasts.
You don't care what you do to me.
Cripple me for life or take it from me.
There is one who can compete with you
And that is Fate in all her glory.
If it wasn't for her,
I wonder where I would be
When you took the notion, you fierce-looking thing,
That I no longer needed my hand,
Fate stepped in, and said to you,
"You have all he power in this world:
Your gears, your wheels, your huge rollers,
Why! the size of a human being compared to you
Is as great as a mouse compared to him.

This human body doesn't stand a chance with you;
You will go on living and roaring
Long after the human body is dead and buried.

So why should I let you take its life or disable it?
You paid no heed to that, did you? Of course not.
Remember when you pulled that hand of mine
And how I screamed till I could scream no more?
Fate heard me and she stepped in,
Like lightning the power was shut off,
For what reason, no one knows but I.
Today, I am not afraid of you.
I don't hear your terrible noise,
I hear music, louder and louder.
Oh, how I wish to dance to you,
Your roaring wheels and your terrible curse.

(32)

Here the machine is transmogrified into a monster, a wild lion, and a human-like deity similar to those Burgdorf may have studied in her Greek mythology course. She speaks defiantly to the machine, which crushed her hand, and complains that the "human body doesn't stand a chance with you." Although the human body she has in mind seems to be masculine (see "him," in text), she attributes her rescue to a feminine "Fate," again in accordance with Greek myth. Then, "today," likely due to her Bryn Mawr experience, she has courage enough to confront the machine; she is transformed, "not afraid." Her bodily senses are altered. She no longer hears the machine's "terrible noise," but "music, louder and louder." Her new mentality is also embodied in her wish to "dance to you," perhaps as a way of controlling, placating, domesticating the "roaring wheels" and "terrible curse."

**The Body as Site of Liberation**

As we see in Kosovicz's poem above, although women workers were oppressed through their bodies, they also knew them as means of liberation. In her extension of the work of Foucault, Susan Bordo has pointed out: "Where there is power, . . . there is also resistance" (27). Through poetic discourse, the women workers were able to record their bodies as sites of resistance. Mildred Kuhn clearly had her body's liberating potential in mind when she wrote this poem, published in *Shop and School* in 1933.

**Lost**

The loud swish, swish of machines
The stinking, sweating reeking masses,
Voices loud and harsh echoing in my dull dead brain,
My body moving, working, slaving, keeping one small spark alive.
Dimly as tho' miles away, I hear a bell.
No more swishing,
No voices loud and harsh,
Just my body dragging me home.

(17)

Although it is through her bodily senses that Kuhn is assaulted by the roar of machines and the sweaty smells on the shop floor, it is also through corporeal sensation that she hears a liberating bell. And it is her body that drags her home to peace and quiet. Again writing herself in terms of a mind/body duality, she locates the source of oppression on the mind/immaterial/discursive side of the equation: Thus, discursive "voices loud and harsh" echo in her brain. Her body and its materiality, on the other hand, is written in opposition to this oppression. In a deconstruction of patriarchal meanings, she does not accept the conventional masculinist, classist paradigm of valuing the mind over the body. While her brain is "dead," her body keeps "one small spark alive."

**Beyond Bodies**

Thus, the women workers revalue the nature/body side of the masculinist nature/culture duality, affirming the materiality of their bodies and writing in positive terms about physicality and nature. Yet living in a patriarchal culture that stigmatized their women's bodies and devalued or denied their minds, they also felt a need to maintain that they were more than bodies, even more than bodies in opposition to machines. However, this return to a dematerialization and subsequent devaluation of the body takes a very disturbing turn regarding African American bodies as we will see below.

The white women workers' tendency to give equal value and appreciation to both the bodily and the intellectual realm led them beyond an androcentric polarity, dealing a blow to traditional ideologies of middle-class white masculinity and femininity. Such a blow can be seen in the 1930 *Shop and School* poetry of Doris Bowman, a twenty-four-year-old Jewish hat maker originally from eastern Europe who had lived in the United States for eight years. She was an officer of the International Cap and Millinery Union and her local YWCA. Illustrating the familiarity with literary classics typical of the Jewish students, Bowman had read the following works over the year: *The World's Illusion, My Life* by Isadora Duncan, *Anna Karenina, All Quiet on the Western Front, Strange Interlude, Red Silence,* and *Mother and Son.* Also recorded on her application was a lecture she attended in Chicago entitled "Is Man a Machine?"—an indication of the prevalence of mechanistic critiques in intellectual and artistic discourse of the day.

### Hands

Two hands, bare hands—these are
God's gift to every woman born!
Some hands remain as delicate as flowers,
Shapely, white, unscarred by laboring.
Others grow coarse and rough with use,
Worn with the toil of earning daily bread.
But hands are not symbols of a woman's heart and brain—
The power that moves all hands is very much the same
And once the door of art and learning
Swings wide to those who have found it closed
Their willing minds respond, desires awaken.
They venture through the door with eyes alight,
Eager to grasp the gifts so long denied.

(20)

This poem is rather unusual in its references to gender, race, and class. Not content to have women reduced to mere physical objects or body parts, Bowman insists that "Hands are not symbols of a woman's heart and brain." Using a discourse of equal rights, she proclaims that the intellectual "power that moves all hands is very much the same," implying an equivalence across gender and class even while making note of class differences among women by calling attention to those women's hands, which are "shapely, white, unscarred by laboring." As is the case with many of the poems, it evokes chords of solidarity with working-class men whose hands no doubt are also "worn with the toil of earning daily bread" and who long for "the door of art and learning" to swing open. The solidarity may not extend across race, however, as the reference to "white" makes clear.

### Working-Class Bodies, Gender, and Race

For the most part, the textualized bodies in the Bryn Mawr poetry were not marked by gender and almost never by race. Of course, in our androcentric culture, an unmarked reference to the body renders it masculine and white by default, thus erasing the presence of women and racial minorities. It may be however that in some instances, the androcentric discourse of the working women's poetry records the disciplining of the working class across gender, if not racial difference. Lois McNay, for example, has argued that formations such as race and class "may work across gender distinctions, breaking down the absolute polarity between the male and the female body" (37). Also, in equating masculine and feminine bodies and pointing out the oppressive work conditions both endured, the women were actually writing against the contemporaneous ideological construction of difference, which preferred a notion of women as domestic, weak, and not working (Kessler-Harris, *A Woman's Wage* 57).

In any case, poems by African American students are few. I could identify only one in *Shop and School*, and it was discussed in the previous chapter. However, the poem below, written by Kitty LaSota for the 1938 *Shop and School*, could be considered typical of white women's poems on the subject of race. This selection is not meant to allow the white student to speak for African Americans, but to illustrate a representative attitude about race and gender among whites at the school.

### Ave Maria

She stood there
And played.
Her whole being
Was immersed
In the beautiful
And enchanting
Melody.
It was Schubert's *Ave Maria*,
There
At the formal opening
Of the school,
Where we are taught
To love, and respect,
And treat one another
As Christ taught,
Speeches were given
By the director,
A gentle and lovely woman,
Beloved by all.
And a colored girl,
Who was lovingly applauded.

No discrimination,
For she is a human being
With a soul
Not unlike your soul
And my soul.
So we sat and listened
Entranced
To a melody
That did honor
The Blessed Virgin
Who was once Flesh and blood
Like us.
And as the young woman played,
Not only on the strings
Of her violin,
But on the strings
Of our hearts
As well,
I wondered why
Girls and women
Who too are flesh and blood
And have souls
Should be treated
Not humanly,
But unjustly,
By employers,
Why Negroes
Should be discriminated against.
God of creation,
Shed light
And create understanding
In the ignorant hearts of men;
Make them aware that we are all
Equal.
That difference lies only
In the color of skin.

(21)

The bodily presence of a "colored girl" was noteworthy and celebrated in LaSota's poem. But the tragedy of this liberal perspective is that the "negro" had to be disembodied for others to accept her humanity. Thus, LaSota disparages the materiality of the body in an attempt to devalue the "difference [that] lies only / In the color of skin." As abolitionists had done one hundred years before, LaSota draws heavily on religious discourse and appropriates conventional dualistic thinking to buttress her argument for racial equality. Since all of humanity has an immortal soul that is superior to the body, all are worthy of respect and equal treatment while on earth. Her frequent allusions to transubstantiation, the change from the material into the immaterial, also sustain her argument. As bodies and souls of Christian icons come and go in their quest for higher states of being, both the singer and her audience are similarly transported. The "colored girl's" body is left behind, as "her whole being is immersed" in the heavenly melody. The audience is likewise "entranced" in a beyond-the-body experience. But in a typical move towards working-class solidarity, LaSota points out the commonality of feminine experience across race and class because (white) "girls and women / Who too are flesh and blood / And have souls" are also dehumanized and treated unjustly. Whether or not her vision of solidarity includes men is not clear, as it is difficult to know just how gender- and class-specific LaSota's comment about the "ignorant hearts of *men*" is.

While the African American body was accorded the conventional but genocidal cultural script of being erased in order to be accepted, in a few instances, white poets did emphasize their specific bodily knowledge to argue in favor of their gender and class. In "A Mother's Misery" by Molly Ferrara, published in the 1934 *Shop and School,* we have a poignant account, in terms of a white woman's corporeal existence, of the troubles and travails experienced by a working-class mother and her family during the depression. Forced to work soon after her baby daughter was born, the woman in this poem literally embodies the double material burden capitalism inflicts on the working mother as she struggles to meet the demands of both industrial and bodily production.

### A Mother's Misery

Stitch twice and then turn under.
Baby feeling better? Wonder—
Two long seams; now stitch again.
Call the doctor: Yes but then—
Watch your seams now, not too wide.
Oh! for money for help at her side.

Sweat a-dripping from your brow.
You think Mary. I know how.

Maybe Jim has found a job.
Little Nan will cease to sob.
Wonder what I could do and how.
Bronchitis, pneumonia, the grippe?
See what I've done; now rip and stitch.
My it's warm! It's sweltering! Stifling!
Sleeves are done; just put on piping.

Adjust this kerchief, I must, for then
It is sweet nectar nature provides,
But circumstances to you have denied.
Three weeks old! My joy, my pride!
Oh! to hold you to my side,
Tugging gently at my bosom,
Suckling lips, reluctant, loosening.
Little lids slowly lowering;
Slumberman around is hovering.
Then I'd tuck you safe in bed.
I have done just as you said!
Child of mine, oh, to be dead!
God! oh God! Please do not take her.
I can't help if I forsake her.
Every day I toil to earn
Food and clothes for my new-born.

(7)

In a machine rhythm of point-counterpoint, Ferrara's internal dialogue textualizes the split consciousness that results from mechanized and alienating work. As her thoughts turn from "Baby feeling better" to "now stitch again" and back to "My joy, my pride!" we see the difficulty of her endeavor. Once again the woman worker complains about the sensory assault inflicted on the corporeal and natural realm by machines. She celebrates the organic domain of which her body is a part as unsullied and life-sustaining, dispensing the "sweet nectar nature provides." Supporting this rhetorical strategy of revaluing the natural realm is the discourse of domesticity, a patriarchal subtext that nevertheless underscores the injustice of having to work with young children inadequately cared for at home.

### Recovering Workers Bodies: Material and Discursive

In hopes of building a working-class or alternative discursive tradition,

Josephine Kiezulas, writing in the 1937 *Shop and School,* reminds her readers of their common labor history—all through discursive interpretations of bodily experience.

### Lawrence, Massachusetts

A phantom hope lurks behind its hills.
A voice is heard from a distance.
From mill to mill the echo falls
To all to leave their chains—
The speeded looms and spindles, the bosses' scowl
No voice complains of aching backs.
Our discontent has no meaning
For we are not better than the machines at which we work.
The phantom's name we know so well,
But can we speak it without fear
The Law says: "Yes"—Our jobs say: "No."
We want our jobs. We need them.
And yet we also need this ghost
To help us live as well as labor.
Bread and work are not alone a full and useful life.
In 1912, 1919 and 1931 we shouted its name,
And sang of it in soprano and bass
In our picket lines.
And with our whole hearts we yelled
Unionism—Unionism—Unionism.
We yelled so loud that like a shot
It echoed throughout the land.
But the memory of bloodshed and brutality
Has muffled the voices.
You read of us in books and yet wonder
Why we won't accept with open arms—Unionism.
Now this same ghost lurks once more
And beckons to our young who know
So little of their past.
What will come, we know not.
Oh, God, may we but have this favor.
That those who are heaped in riches
Give us the chance to use our might intelligently.
Bread and work are not alone a full and useful life.

(10)

Chastising her audience of working women for forgetting their union past in fear, Kiezulas again equates workers with machines: "We are no better than the machines at which we work," she laments. Obviously a fervent union advocate, the poet reminds workers of events mainstream historical discourse prefers to erase. Again valuing the material realm, she insists on the materialization of the "ghost" of unionism. From the titular reference to the "Bread and Roses" strike among women textile workers in Lawrence, Massachusetts (also called "The Uprising of the Thirty Thousand" of 1909) to the Triangle Shirtwaist fire of 1912, which took the lives of 146 young women workers, Kiezulas tries to reconstruct the discursive record of "bloodshed," "brutality," and victory involved in building the labor movement. We see the same complaints and textual strategies found in the poetry of other women workers as Kiezulas points out the disciplining effect of "speeded looms." We have the same anger at the sensory assault of the factory. The same "aching backs" and "bosses' scowl." The style is dialogic, with voices clamoring for domination and public space: "But can we speak it without fear?" The Law says: "Yes"—Our jobs say: "No." And echoing the refrain of a popular women's labor movement song, "Bread and Roses," the poet declares that workers need more than a decent wage: "Bread and work alone are not a full and useful life." Kiezulas wants workers to "live as well as labor." To do so requires a militant attitude and Kiezulas calls for that in words echoing Marx's call to get rid of workers' "chains." While for the most part, the poem is gendered female in its history of women who work at "looms and spindles," a collective "we" narrates and calls for a return to the (supposed) cross-gendered solidarity of the past when workers "sang of" unionism "in soprano and bass."

# Afterword: Questions of Agency and Voice

> Here in Bryn Mawr we have found a voice with which to relate our individual experiences and we have found a wide common interest in the desire to bring humanity to a better basis. From east to west of this large country unemployment and poverty are the specters in every worker's home. The employed fear them and those who actually endure them know the effect on body and mind. . . .
>
> From that recognition we realize the fitness and the purpose of our Summer School. Social control and economic planning questions have not been confined to the classrooms. Why are we so poor in a world of plenty? Why can't we make the things that people want when the material is at hand? Why should the workers of one country destroy the workers of another, and why, having made the world safe for democracy, should it be so difficult for the oppressed to make their voices heard? All these questions have been asked on the Bryn Mawr campus this summer and this magazine shows how we tried to answer them.
>
> —Jane McCall, *Shop and School*, 1932

Another question that may come to mind after reading such an affirmation concerns how representative the texts from the Bryn Mawr Summer School are. Does a "true" working women's voice emerge from exposure to a variety of cultural scripts, each vying for discursive allegiance? It is difficult to assess the "authenticity" of the workers' voices presented here, if one can still converse in such terms. Put more poststructurally, the degree of agency involved in the students' discursive productions is uncertain. To what extent the students shaped or were shaped by their discursive environment is difficult to assess. Certainly there may have been an element of "teacher pleasing" in their writing. As has been noted, they were influenced by discourse from the labor movement, left-wing political ideologies, religious affiliations, and later, the rhetoric of the New Deal administration, which had filled the public domain. Undoubtedly, an heteroglossic variety of discourses operated on and through the women workers. Nevertheless, the writing examined in this study was selected for publication in *Shop and School* and other magazines by an editorial board, consisting of students and a faculty adviser, presumably because of its representative or exemplary quality. This, plus the fact that the poetry, at least, was written as an extracurricular endeavor rather than as an assignment, seem to increase its validity as highly authorized discourse.

Unfortunately, except for the studies published by the Women's Bureau of the Department of Labor, the original audience for this writing was most likely fairly small. A few anthologies of workers' poetry were published over the years by the Affiliated Schools for Women Workers, and these may have gone out to union and YWCA classes. Smith also published a booklet of workers' poetry as a fund-raising project for the Summer School in 1927 (*Women Workers*). And an occasional poem or piece appeared in the regular Bryn Mawr undergraduate newspaper. Also, a more personal mode of distribution occurred at the end of the summer, when each Summer School graduate was given her copy of *Shop and School* to take with her to the wider world, where perhaps the essays, poetry, and plays were read by family members and other acquaintances in church, union, or workplace. In spite of its relatively small audience, the publishing and exchange of their writing must have been rewarding to the women in a number of ways: Through it they registered and validated complaints, feelings, and desires; they created images of better lives and healthier bodies; they built collective solidarity; they issued inspirational calls to action; they boosted morale and found the courage and conviction they needed to fight for justice on the shop floor and the picket line. Indeed, through their writing, the working women constructed stronger public and private voices for themselves and began to participate in a worker's movement and culture that would make their lives easier and satisfy many of their most profound desires.

Yet the Summer School had its critics on the left and right. Each side accused the school of instilling inappropriate cultural scripts in the minds of the working women. Early in the Summer School's history, many labor unions and leftist political groups voiced suspicion about the motives of the educators. Could an elite institution like Bryn Mawr truly be interested in the future of the working class? Wouldn't the worker students be encouraged to adopt upwardly mobile attitudes and abandon their class identification? On the other side of the political fence, the Bryn Mawr Board of Trustees believed the Summer School too closely connected to a militant labor movement and the political left—the students had even demanded a Marxist on the faculty. When newspapers reported that two faculty members attended a rally in support of a strike in New Jersey, the Bryn Mawr

College trustees withdrew their support for the school, claiming that such action breached an earlier agreement. Ironically, at about the same time that the Summer School lost the support of the Bryn Mawr Board of Trustees, organized labor took a conservative turn and withdrew funding for the Brookwood Labor College and other independent efforts at worker education including the Bryn Mawr Summer School. In spite of this loss of support, the Summer School was able to continue, eventually as a co-ed labor school, in Smith's family mansion on the Hudson River until finally closing its doors in 1954.

During its seventeen-year existence, the Bryn Mawr Summer School for Women Workers offered its students a haven for body, mind, and soul that served them well for the rest of their lives. At Bryn Mawr, they celebrated their working-class roots; improved their ability to speak, read, and write for the betterment of their class; learned practical subjects such as English and labor economics as well as the critical thinking and aesthetic pleasures of the liberal arts. They produced a body of working-class literature of their own as well as documentary essays, journalism, and statistical accounts, giving rare voice to working-class women, a voice so rare that, because of the Summer School publications and archives, we may have more working-women's discourse from the 1920s and 1930s than we do from the last two decades of the twentieth century.

In summing up the benefits of the Bryn Mawr experience for working women, the words of economist and faculty member Amy Hewes, written in 1956, offer an apt tribute to its effect on the material culture of its day:

> The individual histories of hundreds of former worker-students at the Bryn Mawr Summer School, if they were available, would be a telling measure of the school's influence. The names of many are well known among trade unionists. A number have become successful mediators in state and federal services; others have held positions in state departments of labor, and a large number have promoted workers' education or themselves become successful teachers. (*Early Experiments*)

Perhaps the Summer School will become relevant again in the new millennium as compositionists begin looking for alternatives to an acontextual, post-process approach to teaching writing. Instead of today's "discursive turn," the Summer School exemplifies a "materialist turn," materialist in that the primary pedagogical focus is on "material culture," which in the broadest sense includes the lived experiential conditions in which students learn and work, as well as the exploitative economic relationships that still prevail in our currently globalized capitalism. This materialism is "dialectical" in that "reality" is believed to be discursively constructed, but the dialectic rests for a time, a stasis prevails, as it did at the Summer School, when specific textualities, subjectivities, ideologies, and economic systems are located (also discursively) in their particular time and space for analysis, critique, and change. The Summer School students appropriated discourse and reconstructed discursive subjectivities, often as collectivities, thus expanding the force and power of their own discourse. The increased agency experienced by the students led to changes in the material conditions of teaching and learning as they voiced their desire to be part of the curricular and administrative structure of the school.

The curriculum was critiqued and amended in terms of who the students were and what they needed. The pedagogy at the Summer School was self-reflexive in that the process of evaluation and change never stopped, but it evolved as the economic, political, and demographic context of the Summer School evolved. Thus, an awareness of the social constructedness and historically determined nature of class, race, and gender played a large part in demystifying the means of production and the working women's place in this dynamic. These concepts are still the important ones for students to learn today.

*Notes*

*Works Cited*

*Index*

# Notes

## INTRODUCTION: FEMINISMS, RHETORICS, AND MATERIALISMS AT THE BRYN MAWR SUMMER SCHOOL FOR WOMEN WORKERS

1. The late Alan France formulated a "materialist rhetoric" for the composition class, which has much in common with my description of the Summer School's materialist pedagogy.

## 1. THE BRYN MAWR SUMMER SCHOOL FOR WOMEN WORKERS

1. Smith was also to become director of the Worker Education Project in Roosevelt's Works Progress Administration. Much of the following information comes from her 1929 book describing the school's early success, *Women Workers at the Bryn Mawr Summer School.* My account is also based on records of the school's various administrative and curricular activities, which Smith and subsequent directors carefully preserved. These records, as well as student publications, application forms, course syllabi, and committee minutes, are found in archival collections located at Bryn Mawr College, Rutgers University, Cornell University, and the University of Wisconsin; more specifically, Bryn Mawr College Archives, Bryn Mawr College; the Affiliated Schools for Workers Collection, MC 1168, Special Collections and University Libraries, Rutgers University Libraries, Rutgers University; Inventory of the American Labor Education Service Papers, boxes 1–78, the State Historical Society of Wisconsin; American Labor Education Service Records, boxes 1–36, Kheel Labor-Management Documentation Center, Martin P. Catherwood Library, New York State School of Industrial and Labor Relations, Cornell University. In addition, I received much inspiration and information from Rita Heller's definitive dissertation, as well as from her film *Women of Summer,* which depicts the school's history through a moving 1984 reunion of many Summer School students and faculty. I also interviewed two Summer School faculty: the late Alice Hansen Cook, then eighty-nine years old and a renowned labor educator; and Ester Peterson, who was ending her illustrious career in labor and public service as President Clinton's representative to the United Nations. Two Summer School students, Garineh Narzakian and Mary Scafidi, then in their late seventies and living in the Philadelphia area, were also interviewed.

2. This department's collaborative and democratic practice has been described by JoAnn Campbell in "Women's Work, Worthy Work: Composition Instruction at Vassar College, 1897–1922."

## 3. LIBERATING VOICES: AUTOBIOGRAPHY AT THE SUMMER SCHOOL

1. Kennan's syllabi and assignments are located in files containing business records, correspondence, publications, course materials, curricula, student works, and photo-

graphs donated by Hilda Worthington Smith to the Institute of Management and Labor Relations, Rutgers University.

2. Compare this assignment with the somewhat less "critical" autobiographical assignments taken from "first units of contemporary composition readers," which "suggest the hegemony of the autobiographical essay" (Linda H. Peterson 170):

1. Write an autobiographical or narrative essay tracing a particular problem that you had to face while growing up in your family.

2. Write an account of a memorable experience in your childhood or high school years, such as meeting an influential person, taking an unusual vacation, living through a notable event in local or national history, experiencing an accident or other crisis.

3. The theme of great expectations fulfilled or unfulfilled has been used time and again in literature. Does that theme offer a way of writing about something of your own experience? If so, write about it.

4. Narrate a memorable "return" you have made—to home, to a former home, to your high school, to an old workplace. Concentrate on rendering details that reveal your feelings.

5. "I burned at the injustice of it and felt the heat of an uncomfortable truth." If you remember a similar experience, write a narrative that discloses both the experience and the truth on which it was based.

3. Because of a dispute with the Bryn Mawr College Board of Trustees, the Summer School was not on the Bryn Mawr campus in 1935. I have not been able to obtain an issue of *Shop and School* for that year.

4. Similar assignments were found in Dorothy Weil's English syllabus of 1927 and William Card's syllabus of 1936, both of which are located in the Smith papers at the Institute of Management and Labor Relations, Rutgers University.

### 4. MATERIAL TEXTS: LABOR DRAMA AT THE BRYN MAWR SUMMER SCHOOL

1. Congressperson Martin Dies of Texas was staunchly anti-communist, anti-labor and anti-immigrant. He later chaired the House Un-American Activities Committee.

2. Below is a partial record of plays seen from 1924–1938.

> 1924—Susan Glaspell, *The Inheritors,* Hedgerow Theater, Rose Valley
> 1925—Henrik Ibsen, *The Pillars of Society,* Hedgerow Theater, Rose Valley
> 1926—Lady Gregory, *Spreading the News,* read by tutors
> 1928—Susan Glaspell, *The Inheritors,* Hedgerow Theater, Rose Valley; George Bernard Shaw, *Arms and the Man,* Hedgerow Players; Henrik Ibsen, *Pillars of Society,* Hedgerow Players
> 1929—George Bernard Shaw, *Misalliance,* by the Hedgerow Theater, Rose Valley; George Bernard Shaw, *The Devil's Disciple,* by the Hedgerow Theater, Rose Valley
> 1930—Tom Tippett, *Mill Shadows,* reading
> 1936—Brookwood Labor College, *Free Tom Mooney,* reading
> 1937—Theodore Dreiser *The [sic] American Tragedy,* Hedgerow Players; Edna St. Vincent Millay, *Aria da Capo,* Hedgerow Players

1938—L. D. Kennedy, *The Frodi,* Hedgerow Theater, Rose Valley; Richard Maibaum, *A Moral Entertainment,* The Federal Theater Project; Marc Blitzstein, *The Cradle Will Rock,* reading

The plays listed below were frequently recommended on syllabi and reading lists to students in English classes:

1921—John Galsworthy, *Justice, Strife, The Silver Box, The Mob;* George Bernard Shaw, *Man and Superman, Pygmalion, Major Barbara;* Israel Zangwill, *The Melting Pot;* Edward Sheldon, *The Boss, The Nigger;* Gerhart Hauptman, *The Weavers*

1926—Karl Kapek, *R.U.R., The World We Live In*

1927—Henrik Ibsen, *The Doll's House, Enemy of the People, The Pillars of Society*

1934—Eugene Brieux, *Maternity, Damaged Goods;* John Golden, *Precedent;* Eugene O'Neill, *Beyond the Horizon, The Hairy Ape;* Elmer Rice, *The Adding Machine;* Paul and Claire Sifton, '1931; Israel Zangwill, *The Melting Pot*

1935—Albert Maltz, *The Black Pit;* Clifford Odets, *Till the Day I Die, Waiting for Lefty;* Paul Peters and George Sklar, *Stevedore;* Elmer Rice, *Street Scene, We the People;* Ernst Toller, *The Machine Wreckers, Man and the Masses;* George Sklar and Albert Maltz, *Peace on Earth*

1937—Paul Green, *In Abraham's Bosom;* John Wesley, *They Shall Not Die*

1938—Susan Glaspell, *Trifles*

3. For an excellent discussion of the relationship between drama and carnival in a specific context, see Randy Martin.

4. In 1932, Angelo Herndon, a nineteen-year-old communist, organized an interracial hunger march in Atlanta, Georgia. He was arrested for "attempting to incite insurrection," a capital crime. His defense became a *cause celebre* in the 1930s. Nevertheless, a white supremacist judge and jury sentenced him to twenty years in prison. After a lengthy appeals process, the Supreme Court reversed his conviction in 1937. (Naison 307).

5. The gloss on this in the original read: "The Guffey-Snyder Act of 1935 provided for government regulation of the mining industry. Miners rights to organize and bargain collectively were extended; production, work hours and wages were regulated. It was declared unconstitutional in 1936."

### 5. WOMEN WORKERS AND LITERARY DISCOURSE: TRANSGRESSIVE READING AND WRITING

1. For more studies of working-class women's literature, see work by Constance Coiner, Paul Lauter, and Janet Zandy.

2. These works are listed in the Hewes and Cerney report. The short summaries were written by students, presumably to help in choosing those less familiar.

3. The Summer School English department issued a "Suggested Reading List" of one hundred works of fiction, drama, poetry, biography, and nonfiction; contemporary literature predominates. The works are arranged in categories pertaining to social problems. Students wrote the one-sentence summaries included beside the works less familiar to them. I have included these summaries below. Among the thirty-seven works

under "Labor," the largest category, is Sherwood Anderson's *Marching Men* ("Workers in Chicago learning to march together as a first step in solidarity"), as well as *I Went to Pit College* ("A college girl reports on the West Virginia coal fields") by Lauren Gilfillan and *The Autobiography of Mother Jones* and other works that could be classified as proletarian fiction; under "War" were eleven works, including Ernest Hemingway's *A Farewell to Arms* and Paul Eric Remarque's *All Quiet on the Western Front;* "Fascism" included works such as Sinclair Lewis's *It Can't Happen Here* and Eva Lips's *Savage Symphony* ("A German woman describes the nightmare of Nazi fascism"); "Socialism and Communism" contained John Reed's *Ten Days That Shook the World,* and N. Krupskaya's (Lenin's wife) *Memories of Lenin;* under "The Race Question" we find Sterling Brown's *The Negro in American Fiction,* Angelo Herndon's *Let Me Live* ("The autobiography of a class conscious Negro, written in jail"), and Richard Wright's *Uncle Tom's Children;* "Folk Ways and Regional Literature" included Michael Gold's *Jews Without Money* ("A vivid description of Jewish working class life on the East side of New York") and James T. Farrell's *Studs Lonigan* ("An Irishman 'without money' in Chicago"). Notably absent from this list are works on the "woman question."

However, another annotated reading list was initiated at Brookwood Labor College in 1931 by teachers at the Eighth Annual Conference of Teachers in Workers' Education—several of these teachers were Bryn Mawr Summer School faculty. While the focus was also on studying "social problems through literature" and the list did not include a section on women's problems, Elinor Black writing in the introduction does address this omission: "This list . . . will need to be supplemented by more complete lists—some already in existence—on specific topics such as the South, The Position of Women, The Immigrant in America, etc." (2).

4. Other poets read included Wilson Wilfred Gibson, Charlotte Perkins Gilman, Vachel Lindsay, Edgar Lee Masters, Edwin Markham, John Masefield, Edna St. Vincent Millay, and Louis Untermeyer. Also studied was the proletarian verse of Lola Ridges, that found in the 1929 *Anthology of Revolutionary Poetry* by Marcus Graham, and in Genevieve Taggard's anthology *May Days.*

5. The Joint Administrative Committee was the governing body of the Summer School and included equal representation from the faculty, Bryn Mawr trustees, organized labor, and the student body.

6. I provide an account of the poetry of the body in my next chapter.

7. Examples include E. M. Forster's short story "The Machine Stops," about "what will happen when our machine civilization is carried to the extreme of mechanizing all parts of life, and scorning humanity and nature" (*Suggested Reading List* 6); Elmer Rice's *The Adding Machine,* the "tragedy of Mr. Zero, who has passed a life of deadly monotony until he is supplemented by a more efficient adding machine" (11); and Ernst Toller's *Machine Wreckers.*

8. Constance Ortmayer eventually became a sculptor herself and a member of the faculty at Rollins College in Florida.

# Works Cited

Alpern, Anna. "The Symbolic Jacket." *A Scrapbook of Industrial Workers' Experiences* 1932: 52–53.

Altenbaugh, Richard J. *Education for Struggle: The American Labor Colleges of the 1920s and 1930s.* Philadelphia: Temple UP, 1990.

Andrews, William L. "The Changing Moral Discourse of Nineteenth-Century African American Women's Autobiography: Harriet Jacobs and Elizabeth Keckley." *De/Colonizing the Subject.* Ed. Sidonie Smith and Julia Watson Smith. Minneapolis: U of Minnesota P, 1992. 225–241.

Baden, Anne D. "Drama." *Shop and School* 1938: 46.

Bakhtin, M. M. *The Dialogic Imagination.* Ed. Michael Holquist. Tran. Caryl Emerson and Michael Holquist. Austin: U of Texas P, 1981.

———. *Rabelais and His World.* Trans. Helene Iswolsky. Bloomington: Indiana UP, 1984.

Belenky, Mary Field, and Blythe McVicker Clinchy, Nancy Rule Goldberger, and Jill Mattuck Tarule. *Women's Ways of Knowing: The Development of Self, Voice, and Mind.* New York: Basic, 1986.

Berlanger, Kelly, and Linda Strom. *Second Shift: Teaching Writing to Working Adults.* Portsmouth: Boynton, 1999.

Berlin, James A. *Rhetoric and Reality: Writing Instruction in American Colleges, 1900–1965.* Carbondale: Southern Illinois UP, 1987.

Berman, Edward, Helen Herrmann, and Susan Shepherd. "English Syllabus." Bryn Mawr: Bryn Mawr Summer School for Women Workers, 1932.

Bizzell, Patricia. "Power, Authority, and Critical Pedagogy." *Journal of Basic Writing* 10.2 (1991): 54–70.

Black, Elinor G., ed. *Suggested Reading List: Novels, Plays, Biographies, Poetry Dealing with Social and Economic Problems.* New York: Affiliated Schools for Workers, 1933.

Blackburn, Regina. "In Search of the Black Female Self: African-American Women's Autobiographies and Ethnicity." *Women's Autobiography: Essays in Criticism.* Ed. Estelle C. Jelinek. Bloomington: Indiana UP, 1980. 133–48.

Bordo, Susan R. "The Body and the Reproduction of Femininity: A Feminist Appropriation of Foucault." *Gender/Body/Knowledge: Feminist Reconstructions of Being and Knowing.* Ed. Alison M. Jaggar and Susan R. Bordo. New Brunswick: Rutgers UP, 1989. 13–31.

Bowman, Doris. "Hands." *Shop and School* 1930: 15.

Brameld, Theodore. Preface. *Workers' Education in the United States.* New York: Harper, 1941. v–xi.

Brandstein, Rae. "Help Wanted." *Bryn Mawr Daisy* 1924: 4–5.

Brandt, Deborah. "Sponsors of Literacy." *College Composition and Communication* 49 (1998): 165–85.

Brown, Thelma. "Thoughts." *Shop and School* 1936: 48.

*Bryn Mawr Daisy* 1922. Bryn Mawr Summer School for Women Workers.

*Bryn Mawr Daisy* 1924. Bryn Mawr Summer School for Women Workers.

Buhle, Mary Jo, Paul Buhle, and Dan Georgakas. *Encyclopedia of the American Left.* Urbana: U of Chicago P, 1992.

Burgdorf, Adelaide. "Factories." *Shop and School* 1934: 21.

"Calendar." *Bryn Mawr Daisy* 2.4 (1922): 15.

"Calendar." *Bryn Mawr Daisy* 1924. Bryn Mawr Summer School for Women Workers. N. pag.

"Calendar." *Shop and School* 1929: 16–24.

"Calendar of Events." *Shop and School* 1937: 36.

Campbell, JoAnn. "Women's Work, Worthy Work: Composition Instruction at Vassar College, 1897–1922." *Constructing Rhetorical Education.* Ed. Marie Secor and Davida Charney. Carbondale: Southern Illinois UP, 1992. 26–42.

Carter, Jean. "Labor Drama." Introduction. *Affiliated Schools Scrapbook* 1 (Mar. 1936): 1–4.

———. "Labor Drama." *Journal of Adult Education* 7 (Apr. 1935): 179–82.

———. *Mastering the Tools of the Trade: Suggestive Material for Experimental Use in the Teaching of English in Workers' Classes.* New York: Affiliated Schools for Workers, 1932.

———. "Report to Faculty of Bryn Mawr Summer School of Plans Following Staff Conference Held on the Campus, May 15–16, 1937." Bryn Mawr: Bryn Mawr Summer School for Women Workers, 1937. 1–6.

———. "Syllabus—English." Bryn Mawr: Bryn Mawr Summer School for Women Workers, 1933.

———. *This America: A Study of Literature Interpreting the Development of American Civilization.* New York: Affiliated Schools for Workers, 1933.

Carter, Jean, and Marguerite I. Gilmore. "Report of the Directors." Bryn Mawr: Bryn Mawr Summer School for Women Workers, 1938.

Carter, Jean, and Hilda W. Smith. *Education and the Worker Student: A Book about Workers' Education Based upon the Experience of Teachers and Students.* New York: Affiliated Schools for Workers, 1934.

Clodfelter, Ruby. "Negro Literature and Art." *Bryn Mawr Daisy* 1924. Special poetry number. N. pag.

———. "New Viewpoints." *Bryn Mawr Light* 1925: N. pag.

Cloud, Dana L. "The Materiality of Discourse as Oxymoron: A Challenge to Critical Rhetoric." *Western Journal of Communication* 58 (1994): 141–63.

Coiner, Constance. "Literature of Resistance: The Intersection of Feminism and the Communist Left in Meridel Le Sueur and Tillie Olsen." *Left Politics and the Literary Profession.* Ed. Leonard J. Davis and M. Bella Mirabella. New York: Columbia UP, 1990.

———. "U.S. Working-Class Women's Fiction: Notes Toward an Overview." *Women's Studies Quarterly* 23.1/2 (1995): 248–67.

Coit, Eleanor. Foreword. *This America: A Study of Literature Interpreting the Devel-*

*opment of American Civilization*. New York: Affiliated Schools for Workers, 1931. N. pag.

Connors, Robert J. "The Rise and Fall of the Modes of Discourse." *College Composition and Communication* 32 (1981): 444–55.

Cook, Alice Hansen. Personal Interview. 16 June 1992.

"Course of Study." Bryn Mawr: Bryn Mawr Summer School for Women Workers, 1922.

Crowley, Sharon. *Composition in the University*. Pittsburgh: U of Pittsburgh P, 1998.

———. "The Material of Rhetoric." Afterword. *Rhetorical Bodies*. Ed. Jack Selzer and Sharon Crowley. Madison: U of Wisconsin P, 1999. 357–64.

Culley, Margo. "What a Piece of Work Is Woman!" Introduction. *American Women's Autobiography: Fea(s)ts of Memory*. Madison: U of Wisconsin P, 1992. 3–31.

Davies, Margaret Llewelyn, ed. *Life as We Have Known It by Cooperative Working Women*. New York: Norton, 1975.

Diamond, Irene, and Lee Quinby. *Feminism and Foucault*. Boston: Northeastern UP, 1988.

Doyle, Clar. *Raising Curtains on Education: Drama as a Site for Critical Pedagogy*. Westport: Bergin, 1993.

Dramatics Project Group Bryn Mawr. *Labor Dramatics: Scrapbook of the Dramatic Project Group at the Bryn Mawr Summer School*. Bryn Mawr: Bryn Mawr Summer School for Women Workers, 1933. N. pag.

Ebert, Teresa L. "For a Red Pedagogy: Feminism, Desire, and Need." *College English* 58.7 (1996): 795–819.

Ede, Lisa, Cheryl Glenn, and Andrea Lunsford. "Border Crossings: Intersections of Rhetoric and Feminism." *Rhetorica: A Journal of the History of Rhetoric* 13 (1995): 401–42.

Elliott, Grace. "My Attitude Toward the Negro." *Shop and School* 1931: 5.

Eisenstein, Sarah. *Give Us Bread but Give Us Roses: Working Women's Consciousness in the United States, 1890 to the First World War*. London: Routledge, 1983.

Epstein, Ruth, Margaret Sofia, and Jean Carter. "Calendar." *Shop and School* 1930: 50–54.

Eudovich, Faye. "Thoughts on Utopian Education." *Shop and School* 1930: 22.

"Experiments in Labor Dramatics at the Bryn Mawr Summer School for Women Workers in Industry." Bryn Mawr: Bryn Mawr Summer School for Women Workers, 1932.

Feldman, Mary. "Buttons." *Shop and School* 1924: 5.

Ferrara, Molly. "A Mother's Misery." *Shop and School* 1934: 56.

Fickland, Eloise. "Looking Back." *Shop and School* 1933: 32.

Fincke, William Mann. "The Place of Literature in Workers' Education." *Affiliated Schools Scrapbook* 1.2 (1936): 10–12.

———. "Written Words." *Journal of Adult Education* 7 (Apr. 1935): 179–92.

Flynn, Elizabeth A. "Composing as a Woman." *College Composition and Communication* 39 (1988): 423–35.

Foley, Barbara. *Radical Representations: Politics and Form in U.S. Proletarian Fiction, 1929–1941*. Durham: Duke UP, 1993.

Fox-Genovese, Elizabeth. "My Statue, My Self: Autobiographical Writings of Afro-American Women." *The Private Self: Theory and Practice of Women's Autobiographical Writings*. Ed. Shari Benstock. Chapel Hill: U of North Carolina P, 1988. 63–89.

France, Alan W. *Composition as a Cultural Practice.* Westport: Bergin, 1994.

Friedman, Daniel. "A Brief Description of the Workers' Theatre Movement of the Thirties." *Theatre for Working-Class Audiences in the United States, 1930–1980.* Ed. Bruce A. McConachie and Daniel Friedman. Westport: Greenwood, 1985. 110–19.

Friedman, Susan Stanford. "Women's Autobiographical Selves: Theory and Practice." *The Private Self: Theory and Practice of Women's Autobiographical Writings.* Ed. Shari Benstock. Chapel Hill: U of North Carolina P, 1988. 34–63.

Gagnier, Regina. "The Literary Standard, Working-Class Autobiography, and Gender." *Revealing Lives: Autobiography, Biography and Gender.* Ed. Susan Groag Bell and Marilyn Yalom. Albany: State U of New York P, 1990. 93–114.

Gere, Anne Ruggles. *Interior Practices: Literacy and Cultural Work in U. S. Women's Clubs, 1880–1920.* Urbana: U of Illinois P, 1997.

Gerhart, Wilma. "My Last Job." *A Scrapbook of Industrial Workers Experiences* 1932: 33.

Giroux, Henry A. *Theory and Resistance in Education: A Pedagogy for the Opposition.* Boston: Bergin, 1983.

Goldberg, Edith. "My Autobiography." *Echo* 1928: 25.

Goldfarb, Lyn. "Memories of a Movement: A Conversation." *Sisterhood and Solidarity: Workers Education for Women, 1914–1984.* Ed. Joyce L. Kornbluh and Mary Frederickson. Philadelphia: Temple UP, 1984. 326–42.

Goldstein, Michael, and Douglas McDermott. "The Living Newspaper as Dramatic Form." *Modern Drama* 7 (1965): 82–94.

Gordon, Sarah. "A Typical Day in My Life." *Shop and School* 1929: 27–28.

Grala, Victoria. "Dramatics." *Shop and School* 1937: 34–35.

Greenstein, Rose. "Sacrifice." *Shop and School* 1930: 30–31.

Gregorio, Lucretia. "What Carl Sandburg Means to Me." *Bryn Mawr Daisy* 1924. Special poetry number. N. pag.

Hantz, Rose. "The Banana Argument." *Shop and School* 1932: 62.

Hapke, Laura. *Daughters of the Great Depression: Women, Work and Fiction in the American 1930s.* Athens: U of Georgia P, 1995.

Heller, Rita. "Blue Collars and Blue Stockings: The Bryn Mawr School for Women Workers, 1921–1938." *Sisterhood and Solidarity: Workers Education for Women, 1914–1984.* Ed. Joyce L. Kornbluh and Mary Frederickson. Philadelphia: Temple UP, 1984. 110–45.

———. *The Women of Summer: The Bryn Mawr Summer School for Women Workers, 1921–1938.* Diss. State U of New Jersey, 1986.

Heller, Rita, and Suzanne Bauman. *The Women of Summer.* Film. National Endowment for the Humanities, 1985.

Herndl, Diane Price. "The Dilemmas of a Feminist Dialogic." *Feminism, Bakhtin, and the Dialogic.* Ed. Dale M. Bauer and S. Jaret McKinstry. Albany: State U of New York P, 1991. 7–25.

Herrmann, Helen. "Joint Meeting of Curriculum Committee and 1933 Bryn Mawr Faculty in New York City." Bryn Mawr: Bryn Mawr Summer School for Women Workers, 1933.

Herstein, Lillian. "Equal Is Equal Brothers: Lillian Herstein, American Federation of Teachers (1886–1983)." *Rocking the Boat: Union Women's Voices, 1915–1975.* Ed. Brigid O'Farrell and Joyce L. Kornbluh. New Brunswick: Rutgers UP, 1996. 10–33.

Hewes, Amy. *Early Experiments in Workers' Education.* New York: American Labor Education Service, 1956. N. pag.

——. "Syllabus Economics II." Bryn Mawr: Bryn Mawr Summer School for Women Workers, 1922.

Hewes, Amy, and Isobel M. Cerney. "Report on English in the Hewes-Cerney Unit." Bryn Mawr: Bryn Mawr Summer School for Women Workers, 1937.

Hewes, Amy, and Students. *Changing Jobs: A Study Made by Students in the Economics Course at the Bryn Mawr Summer School under the Direction of Amy Hewes.* Bulletin of the Women's Bureau No. 54, United States Department of Labor. Washington, D.C.: United States Government Printing Office, 1926.

——. *The First Job: A Study Made by Students in the Economics Course at the Bryn Mawr Summer School under the Direction of Amy Hewes.* Bulletin of the Women's Bureau, United States Department of Labor. Washington, D.C.: United States Government Printing Office, 1922.

——. *The Savings of Women Workers: Study by Students in Bryn Mawr Summer School, under the Direction of Amy Hewes.* Bulletin of the Women's Bureau, United States Department of Labor. Washington, D.C.: United States Government Printing Office, 1927.

——. *Women Workers and Family Support: A Study Made by Students in the Economics Course at the Bryn Mawr Summer School under the Direction of Amy Hewes.* Bulletin of the Women's Bureau No. 49, United States Department of Labor. Washington, D.C.: United States Government Printing Office, 1925.

——. *Women Workers and the N.R.A.: Study by Students in Bryn Mawr Summer School, under the Direction of Amy Hewes.* Bulletin of the Women's Bureau, United States Department of Labor. Washington, D.C.: United States Government Printing Office, 1934.

——. *Women Workers in the Third Year of the Depression: Study by Students in Bryn Mawr Summer School, under the Direction of Amy Hewes.* Bulletin of the Women's Bureau No. 103, United States Department of Labor. Washington, D.C.: United States Government Printing Office, 1933.

Hollis, Karyn L. "Autobiographical Writing at the Bryn Mawr Summer School for Women Workers." *College Composition and Communication* 45 (1994): 31–60.

——. "Literacy Theory, Teaching Composition, and Feminist Response." *Pre/Text* 13 (1992): 103–16.

——. "Material of Desire: Bodily Rhetoric in Working Women's Poetry at the Bryn Mawr Summer School, 1921–1938." *Rhetorical Bodies: Towards a Material Rhetoric.* Ed. Jack Selzer and Sharon Crowely. Madison: U of Wisconsin P, 1999.

——. "Plays of Heteroglossia: Labor Drama at the Bryn Mawr Summer School." *Popular Literacy.* Ed. John Trimbur. Pittsburgh: U of Pittsburgh P.

Holt, Mara. "Knowledge, Social Relations, and Authority in Collaborative Practices of the 1930s and the 1950s." *College Composition and Communication* 44 (1993): 538–55.

hooks, bell. *Teaching to Transgress.* New York: Routledge, 1994.

Humphreys, Haroldine. "The Play Spirit in Acting." *Bryn Mawr Alumnae Bulletin* 2 (Oct. 1922): 16–17.

Jackson, Marion. "It Set Me Thinking." *Shop and School* 1936: 9–10.

——. "The Rest Room in My Shop." *Shop and School* 1936: 15.

Jelinek, Estelle C. *The Tradition of Women's Autobiography: From Antiquity to the Present.* Boston: Twayne, 1986.

Johnston, Ellen. *The Autobiography, Poems, and Songs of "the Factory Girl."* Glasgow: William Love, 1867.

Kates, Susan. *Activist Rhetorics and American Higher Education.* Carbondale: Southern Illinois UP, 2001.

Kennan, Ellen. "Autobiography." "English Syllabus." Bryn Mawr: Bryn Mawr Summer School for Women Workers, 1926. 1.

———. "Autobiography." "English Syllabus." Bryn Mawr: Bryn Mawr Summer School for Women Workers, 1934. 1.

———. "Report on English in Williams-Kennan Unit, 1935." Bryn Mawr: Bryn Mawr Summer School for Women Workers, 1935.

———. "Syllabus—English." Bryn Mawr: Bryn Mawr Summer School for Women Workers, 1931.

Kennan, Ellen, Elinor Goldmark Black, and Grace Hawk. "Syllabus—English." Bryn Mawr: Bryn Mawr Summer School for Women Workers, 1930.

Kennan, Ellen, and Grace Hawk. "Syllabus—English." Bryn Mawr: Bryn Mawr Summer School for Workers, 1927.

Kent, Thomas, ed. *Post-Process Theory: Beyond the Writing Process Paradigm.* Carbondale: Southern Illinois UP, 1999.

Kessler-Harris, Alice. "Problems of Coalition-Building: Women and Trade Unions in the 1920s." *Women, Work and Protest: A Century of U.S. Women's Labor History.* Ed. Ruth Milkman. London: Routledge, 1985. 110–38.

———. *A Woman's Wage: Historical Meanings and Social Consequences.* Lexington: U of Kentucky P, 1990.

Kiezulas, Josephine. "Lawrence, Massachusetts." *Shop and School* 1937: 10.

Kornbluh, Joyce L., and Mary Frederickson. *Sisterhood and Solidarity: Workers Education for Women, 1914–1984.* Philadelphia: Temple UP, 1984.

Kosovicz, Mary. "The Machine." *Shop and School* 1929: 44.

Kramarae, Cheris. *Technology and Women's Voices: Keeping in Touch.* New York: Routledge, 1988.

Kruger, Rose. "Literature." *Bryn Mawr Daisy.* 1924. N. pag.

Kuhns, Mildred. "Lost." *Shop and School* 1933: 34.

Lamousen, Nina. "What Do You Think?" *Shop and School* 1934: 20.

LaSota, Kitty. "Ave Maria." *Shop and School* 1938: 41.

Lauter, Paul. "Working-Class Women's Literature: An Introduction to Study." *Radical Teacher* Mar. 1980: 16–26.

Lemons, J. Stanley. *The Woman Citizen: Social Feminism in the 1920s.* Charlottesville: U of Virginia P, 1990.

Lockwood, Helen Drusilla. *Tools and the Man: A Comparative Study of the French Workingman and the English Chartists in the Literature of 1830–1848.* New York: Columbia UP, 1927.

MacKaye, Hazel. "Plays for Workers." *Workers' Education* 4 (May 1926): 11–18.

Martin, Randy. *Socialist Ensembles: Theatre and State in Cuba and Nicaragua.* Minneapolis: U of Minnesota P, 1994.

Marx, Karl. *Capital.* Vol. 1. Trans. Ben Fowkes. New York: Random, 1977.

Maynes, Mary Jo. "Gender and Class in Working-Class Women's Autobiographies."

*German Women in the Eighteenth and Nineteenth Centuries: A Social and Literary History.* Ed. Ruth-Ellen B. Joeres and Mary Jo Maynes. Bloomington: Indiana UP, 1986. 230–46.

——. "Gender and Narrative Form in French and German Working-Class Narratives." *Interpreting Lives: Feminist Theory and Personal Narratives.* Ed. Personal Narratives Group. Bloomington: Indiana UP, 1989. 103–17.

McConachie, Bruce A., and Daniel Friedman. *Theatre for Working-Class Audiences in the United States, 1830–1980.* Westport: Greenwood, 1985. 121–42.

McDermott, Douglas. "The Workers' Laboratory Theatre: Archetype and Example." *Theatre for Working-Class Audiences in the United States, 1830–1980.* Ed. Bruce A. McConachie and Daniel Friedman. Westport: Greenwood, 1985. 87–95.

McNamara, Gay. "Proletarian Literature." *Shop and School* 1936: 19.

McNay, Lois. *Foucault and Feminism: Power, Gender and the Self,* Boston: Northeastern UP, 1992.

"Minutes: Instruction Committee Meeting." April 30, 1932. Bryn Mawr: Bryn Mawr Summer School for Women Workers.

Mirza, Heidi Safia. "Mapping a Genealogy of Black British Feminism." Introduction. *Black British Feminism: A Reader.* Ed. Heidi Safia Mirza. London: Routledge, 1997: 1–28.

Montgomery, David. *Workers' Control in America.* Cambridge: Cambridge UP, 1979.

Moore, Mildred. "A History of the Women's Trade Union League of Chicago." MA thesis, U of Chicago, 1915. Cited in Diane Kirkby, "The Wage Earning Woman and the State: The National Women's Trade Union League and Protective Labor Legislation 1903–1922." *Labor History* 28.1 (1987): 54–74.

Naison, Mark D. "Herndon Case." *Encyclopedia of the American Left.* Ed. Mari Jo Juhle, Paul Buhle, and Dan Georgakas. Urbana: U of Chicago P, 1982. 307.

Nochlin, Linda. "The Paterson Strike Pageant of 1913." *Theatre for Working-Class Audiences in the United States, 1830–1980.* Ed. Bruce A. McConachie and Daniel Friedman. Westport: Greenwood, 1985. 87–95.

Nussbaum, Karen. "Women in Labor: Always the Bridesmaid." *Not Your Father's Union Movement.* Ed. Jo-Ann Mort. New York: Verso, 1998. 55–68.

O'Farrell, Brigid, and Joyce L. Kornbluh, eds. *Rocking the Boat: Union Women's Voices, 1915–1975.* New Brunswick: Rutgers UP, 1996.

Orleck, Annelise. *Common Sense and a Little Fire: Women and Working-Class Politics in the United States, 1900–1965.* Chapel Hill: U of North Carolina P, 1995.

Ortmayer, Constance. "Economics in Poetry." *Workers Look at the Stars.* New York: Vineyard Shore Workers' School, 1927. 29–30.

*Outcrop* 1929. Bryn Mawr Summer School for Women Workers.

Palmer, G. L., ed. *A Scrapbook of the American Labor Movement: Compiled by the Trade Union Problem Unit in the Bryn Mawr Summer School, 1930.* New York: The Educational Department, Affiliated Summer Schools for Women Workers in Industry, 1931.

Palmer, Gladys L., and Andria Taylor Hourwich, eds. *A Scrapbook of the American Labor Movement.* New York, The Educational Department, Affiliated Summer Schools for Women Workers in Industry, 1932.

Parrish, Beulah. "Those Mill Villages." *Shop and School* 1930: 6.

Perkins, David. *A History of Modern Poetry: From the 1890s to the High Modernist Mode.* Cambridge: Harvard UP, 1976.

Perlman, Elizabeth. "Machinery as a Friend and Enemy." *Shop and School* 1932: 5.

Peterson, Esther E. "Bryn Mawr Summer School, 1937: Dramatics." Bryn Mawr: Bryn Mawr Summer School for Women Workers, 1937.

———. "Dramatics and Recreation." Bryn Mawr: Bryn Mawr Summer School for Women Workers, 1936.

———. "The Medium of Movement." *Journal of Adult Education* 7 (Apr. 1935): 182–84.

Peterson, Linda H. "Gender and the Autobiographical Essay: Research Perspectives, Pedagogical Practices." *College Composition and Communication* 42 (1991): 170–83.

Pharo, Florence M. "Syllabus—English." Bryn Mawr: Bryn Mawr Summer School for Women Workers, 1930.

Plunder, Olga Law. *Monograph on Methods of Teaching English to Workers' Classes.* New York: Affiliated Summer Schools for Women Workers in Industry, 1931.

Porter, Ester. "Dramatics: Material for Recreation." Bryn Mawr: Bryn Mawr Summer School for Women Workers, 1934. 63–65.

Prelude. *It's Unconstitutional.* Bryn Mawr: Bryn Mawr Summer School for Women Workers, 1936.

Previti, Jennie. "Mother Goose Depression Nursery Rhymes." *Shop and School* 1933: 16.

Ransdell, Hollace. "Amateur Dramatics in the Labor Movement." *Affiliated Schools Scrapbook* Mar. 1936: 2–4.

Ratcliffe, Krista. "Review: Material Matters: Bodies and Rhetoric." *College Composition and Communication* 64 (2002): 613–23.

"Recommendations of Student Body, Bryn Mawr Summer School, 1936." Bryn Mawr: Bryn Mawr Summer School for Women Workers, 1936.

Richardson, Elaine. "'To Protect and Serve': African American Female Literacies." *College Composition and Communication* 53 (2002): 675–704.

Rose, Shirley K. "Reading Representative Anecdotes of Literacy Practice; or 'See Dick and Jane read and write!'" *Rhetoric Review* 8 (1990): 244–59.

Rowbotham, Sheila. *Woman's Consciousness, Man's World.* London: Penguin, 1973.

Roydhouse, Marion W. "Partners in Progress: The Affiliated Schools for Women Workers, 1928–1939." *Sisterhood and Solidarity: Worker's Education for Women, 1914–1984.* Ed. Joyce L. Kornbluh and Mary Frederickson Kornbluh. Philadelphia: Temple UP, 1984. 189–221.

Rury, John L. *Education and Women's Work: Female Schooling and the Division of Labor in Urban America, 1870–1930.* Albany: State U of New York P, 1991.

Russell, David R. "Activity Theory and Process Approaches: Writing (Power) in School and Society." *Post-Process Theory: Beyond the Writing Process Paradigm.* Ed. Thomas Kent. Carbondale: Southern Illinois UP, 1999. 80–96.

———. "Writing Across the Curriculum in Historical Perspective: Toward a Social Interpretation." *College English* 52 (1990): 52–73.

Ryan, Barbara. *Feminism and the Women's Movement: Dynamics of Change in Social Movement Ideology and Activism.* New York: Routledge, 1992.

Sayre, Henry M. "American Vernacular: Objectivism, Precisionism, and the Aesthetics of the Machine." *Twentieth Century Literature* 35 (1989): 310–42.

Schneider, Florence Hemley. *Patterns of Workers' Education: The Story of the Bryn*

*Mawr Summer School.* Washington, D.C.: American Council on Public Affairs, 1941.

Selzer, Jack. "Habeas Corpus." *Rhetorical Bodies.* Eds. Jack Selzer and Sharon Crowley. Madison: U of Wisconsin P, 1999. 3–15.

———, and Sharon Crowley, eds. *Rhetorical Bodies.* Madison: U of Wisconsin P, 1999.

*Shop and School* 1926. Bryn Mawr Summer School for Women Workers. N. pag.

*Shop and School* 1934. Bryn Mawr Summer School for Women Workers.

*Shop and School* 1938. Bryn Mawr Summer School for Women Workers.

Sirc, Geoffrey. "Gender and 'Writing Formations' in First-Year Narratives." *Freshman English News* 18 (1989): 4–11.

Smith, Emma. *A Cornish Waif's Story: An Autobiography.* London: Odhams, 1954.

Smith, Hilda Worthington. Foreword. *The Workers Look at the Stars.* New York: Vineyard Shore Workers School, 1927. 3–4.

———. *Opening Vistas in Workers' Education: An Autobiography of Hilda Worthington Smith.* Washington, D.C.: self-published, 1978.

———. "The Student and Teacher in Workers' Education." *Workers' Education in the United States.* Ed. Theodore Brameld. New York: Harper, 1941. 181–202.

———. "Summary of Three Periods of Discussion Groups on Workers' Education." Bryn Mawr: Bryn Mawr Summer School for Women Workers, 1936.

———. *Women Workers at the Bryn Mawr Summer School.* New York: Affiliated Summer Schools for Women Workers in Industry and American Association for Adult Education, 1929.

Smith, Sidonie. *A Poetics of Women's Autobiography: Marginality and the Fictions of Self-Representation.* Bloomington: Indiana UP, 1987.

———. "Resisting the Gaze of Embodiment: Women's Autobiography in the Nineteenth Century." *American Women's Autobiography: Fea(s)ts of Memory.* Ed. Margo Culley. Madison: U of Wisconsin P, 1992. 75–110.

Stambaugh, Ruthella. "The Chronicle." *Bryn Mawr Echo* 1928: 39–43.

Strickler, Frank. "Affluence for Whom?—Another Look at Prosperity and the Working Classes in the 1920s." *Labor History* 24 (1983): 5–33.

Storm, Sharon Hartman. "Challenging 'Women's Place:' Feminism, the Left, and Industrial Unionism in the 1930s." *Feminist Studies* 9 (1983): 359–86.

"Suggested Reading List." Bryn Mawr: Bryn Mawr Summer School for Women Workers, 1937.

*Suggested Reading List: Novels, Plays, Biographies, Poetry dealing with Social and Economic Problems.* New York: Affiliated Schools for Workers, 1933.

Susman, Walter I. *Culture as History: The Transformation of American Society in the Twentieth Century.* New York: Pantheon, 1973.

Thurlwell, Mabel. "Calendar." *Bryn Mawr Daisy* July 1924. N. pag.

Trimbur, John. "Review: The Politics of Radical Pedagogy: A Plea for 'A Dose of Vulgar Marxism.'" *College English* 56 (1994): 194–206.

Varnum, Robin. "The History of Composition: Reclaiming Our Lost Generation." *Journal of Advanced Composition* 12 (1998): 39–56.

Walsh, Margaret. "The Heart and Soul of the People." *Bryn Mawr Echoes* 1927: N. pag.

Weedon, Chris. *Feminism, Theory and the Politics of Difference.* London: Routledge, 1997.

———. *Feminist Practice and Poststructuralist Theory.* Oxford: Basil Blackwell, 1987.

Weinblatt, Sophie. "My Recollections of a Massacre." *Bryn Mawr Light* 1926: N. pag.

Wells, Susan. "Rogue Cops and Health Care: What Do We Want from Public Writing?" *College Composition and Communication* 47 (1996): 325–41.

Wolfe, Lillian. "How and Why I Chose My First Job." *Bryn Mawr Daisy* 2.1 (July 8, 1922): 8–9.

Woodward, Kathleen. "From Virtual Cyborgs to Biological Time Bombs: Technocriticism and the Material Body." *Culture on the Brink: Ideologies of Technology*. Ed. Gretchen Bender and Timothy Druckrey. Seattle: Bay, 1994. 47–67.

Wosnak, Wanda. "Childhood Recollections." *A Scrapbook of Industrial Worker's Experiences* 1932: 54.

Wylie, Laura. "English Literature." "Syllabus." Bryn Mawr: Bryn Mawr Summer School for Women Workers, 1926.

Young, Richard E. "Paradigms and Problems: Needed Research in Rhetorical Invention." *Research on Composing: Points of Departure*. Ed. Charles Cooper and Lee Odell. Urbana: NCTE, 1978. 29–47.

Zandy, Janet, ed. *Calling Home: Working-Class Women's Writings, An Anthology*. New Brunswick: Rutgers UP, 1990.

———, ed. *Liberating Memory: Our Work and Our Working-Class Consciousness*. New Brunswick: Rutgers UP, 1994.

———, ed. *What We Hold in Common: An Introduction to Working-Class Studies*. New York: Feminist, 2001.

# Index

academic discourse, 93–94

Affiliated Summer Schools for Women Workers, 21, 43, 121

African Americans, student views of, 26, 31, 125, 160–62

African American students, 16–18, 90, 125, 160; autobiographies of, 69–72, 77–80; double oppression and, 70–71; and subjectivity, 70, 78–80

agency, 9, 48, 68, 118, 166

agitprop theater, 95, 96

Agricultural Adjustment Act, 13

American Federation of Labor, 15, 38

*America You Called Us* (student play), 99

anarchists, 85–86

Andrews, William L., 70

assignments, 63–66, 82, 127, 174n2

audience, 2, 7, 51, 72, 167; for labor dramas, 8, 96–97, 110–11

autobiographies, 7, 51, 61–62, 174n2; by African American students, 69–72, 77–80; androcentric, 62, 76, 81; assignments, 63–66; and bourgeois ideology, 62–63, 65, 79; collective subjectivity in, 73–74, 83–84; critical perspective of, 64–66; extratextual context of, 83–84; feminism in, 74–76; human relationships in, 80–82; left-wing rhetoric in, 73–74; materialist pedagogy and, 68, 76; models for, 82–83; narratives of education, 77–80; narratives of work and union, 72–76; narratives on family and childhood, 67–72; and reconstruction of subjectivity, 81–83; research on, 80–84; topics, 66–67; Victorian conventions in, 70–71, 79

Bakhtin, Mikhail, 69, 73, 107

Bartky, Sandra Lee, 154–55

Bentley, Phyllis, 121, 131

Berlanger, Kelly, 38

Berlin, Jim, 6, 34–37, 41, 46

Bizzell, Patricia, 83

bodily discourse, 51, 151–52; and common labor history, 163–65; factory setting and, 153–54; intellectual realm and, 158–59; machinery and, 152–57, 163; public arena and, 152–53; and textual embodiment, 139–40; of working-class bodies, gender, and race, 159–63

body: African American, 160–62; disciplining of, 154–55; feminization of, 139–41; industrial context of, 8–9; oppression of, 6, 109, 137; as site of liberation, 157–58; suffering and, 153–54

Bordo, Susan, 157

bourgeois ideology, 4, 131, 140; antiworker, 109–10; autobiographies and, 62–63, 65, 79

Bowman, Doris, 158–59

Brameld, Theodore, 46

Brandt, Deborah, 143

"Bread and Roses" strike, 165

Brookwood Labor College, 31, 38, 43, 47, 105, 120

Brown, Thelma, 136–37, 143

Bryn Mawr Summer School for Women Workers, 1, 15–19 (*see also* curriculum; faculty); alumnae, 16, 18, 80; class context of, 2–4; controversies surrounding, 21–22, 51–52; criticism of, 167–68; discursive environment of, 151–52; diverse student body of, 12, 16; goals of, 19–21; guest lecturers at, 10, 25–26, 43, 52; historical context of, 6, 11–13; Joint Administrative Board, 16, 20, 125; and materialist pedagogical enterprises, 6–7; mission statement of, 20; poetry about, 141–43; social science workshop at, 54–56; student role in, 6, 16, 21, 25, 125; teaching writing at, 38–46; withdrawal of support for, 9, 18–19, 38; workers' education movement and, 37–38

Buck, Gertrude, 19

capitalism, 3, 12, 48
carnivalesque, 107, 109
Carter, Jean, 7; *Education and the Worker Student,* 20–22, 39, 126–28; interview with, 58–59; "Labor Drama," 97–98; on labor drama, 97–99, 101, 106; *Mastering the Tools of the Trade,* 41–42; *This America,* 121
Cerney, Isabel, 121–22
"Chicago" (Sandburg), 124, 139–40, 146
Chodorow, Nancy, 81
clarity, 35, 45
class issues, 2–4, 7, 11–12, 48, 52; in poetry, 136–37; vs. gender and race, 131–34
Clodfelter, Ruby, 124–25
Cloud, Dana L., 7, 49–50
*Club Worker,* 38
Cohn, Fannia, 14
Coit, Eleanor, 43, 46
collaborative work, 24
communications movement, 41
composition pedagogy, 6, 62
consumers, 6, 8, 48
Cook, Alice Hansen, 62
coping strategies, 18
"Cornish Waif's Story" (Smith), 63
cross-class alliances, 11–12
Crowley, Sharon, 1, 2, 4–5, 48
Culley, Margo, 70
cultural materialism, 5
current-traditional rhetoric, 6, 33–36, 46
curriculum, 8; assignments, 63–66, 82, 127, 174n2; development of, 22–23, 120; dramatics, 100–101; goals of, 20–21; interdisciplinary approach, 1, 11, 22–23; reading lists, 120, 122–23, 131, 175–76n3; student forums, 28–29; student input, 16, 25, 125; subject matter, 39–40

Dewey, John, 19, 36
dialectical materialism, 168–69
discourse (*see also* literary discourse): androcentric, 62, 76, 81, 159–60; appropriation of, 107, 139–41, 169; bourgeois, 62–63, 65, 79, 109–10, 131, 140
discursive turn, 48–50, 168
discursivity of materiality, 5
Doyle, Clar, 111–12
"Dramatics and Recreation" (Peterson), 99–100
dualisms, 4, 9, 51, 135, 140

Ebert, Teresa, 7, 48, 49
economics, 12–13; student views of, 25, 28, 138–40
*Education and the Worker Student* (Carter and Smith), 20–22, 39, 126–28
election script, 96
English composition (*see also* autobiographies; pedagogy): and current-traditional rhetoric, 6, 33–36, 46; labor drama and, 102–3; student views of, 25, 33; usage conventions in, 34–35
*English Journal,* 36–37
Equal Rights Amendment (ERA), 4
essays, 7, 35, 36–37, 48
European Folk High Schools, 121
experiential writing, 128, 134
extratextuality, 4–7, 23, 83–84

faculty, 17, 19–23; autobiographies and, 62–63; awareness of worker perspectives, 20–21, 39–40, 62–63; controversial issues and, 21–22, 51–52
Federal Theater Project, 96, 106
feminism, 1; in autobiographies, 74–76; and class distinctions, 2–4; industrial, 2–3, 13–15, 80; social, 4, 80
field trips, 52
Fincke, William (Bill), 44, 120, 127
Flanagan, Hallie, 96
Florida State College for Women, 37
Flynn, Elizabeth, 80
Foley, Barbara, 128
folk literature, 121, 127
Foucault, Michel, 154
Fox-Genovese, Elizabeth, 70, 71, 72
free-market ideologies, 12–13
Friedman, Daniel, 95, 96
Friedman, Susan Stanford, 81

Gagnier, Regina, 63, 68, 79, 83
gender, 2–3, 7, 81; bodily discourse and, 159–63; in poetry, 131–34
Gere, Anne Ruggles, 38
Glenn, Cheryl, 1
Gordon, Sarah, 74–76
Grala, Victoria, 96–97, 98
Gregorio, Lucretia, 124, 146
guest lecturers, 10, 25–26, 43, 52

Hanson, Alice, 23
Herstein, Lillian, 17–18, 23

heteroglossia, 69, 107, 111
Hewes, Amy, 2, 23, 44–45, 121–22, 168
historical context, 5–6, 11–13
hooks, bell, 117, 139, 153
household employees, 29–31
Hudson Shore Labor College, 18–19, 168
Humphreys, Haroldine, 102

idealist pedagogies, 4–5
immigrants, 12, 14–15, 123, 158–59
industrial feminism, 2–3, 13–15, 80
Industrial Workers of the World, 95
*Inheritance* (Bentley), 121, 131
"In Search of the Black Female Self" (Blackburn), 70
interdisciplinary approach, 1, 11, 22–23, 99–100, 102–3
International Ladies Garment Workers Union (ILGWU), 14–15
International Peace Festival, 102
*It's Unconstitutional* (student play), 8, 104–10, 112–16

Jackson, Marion, 77–80
Jelinek, Estelle C., 80
Jewish immigrant women, 14–15, 123, 158–59
Johnston, Ellen, 63
Joint Administrative Board, 16, 20, 125
*Journal of Adult Education*, 97–98, 127

Kates, Susan, 47
Kennan, Ellen, 63–66, 82
Kessler-Harris, Alice, 13–15
Kramarae, Cheris, 132–33
Kruger, Rose, 124

laboratory notebooks, 24, 44–45
labor colleges and schools, 10, 18–19, 21, 29, 38, 43, 101–2, 119, 121 (*see also* Brookwood Labor College; Bryn Mawr Summer School for Women Workers)
Labor Department, 7, 45
labor drama, 8, 23–24; academic discourse and, 93–94; audience, 8, 96–97, 110–11; in curriculum, 100–101; genres from the working class, 95–100; improvisation, 98–99; interdisciplinary efforts, 99–100, 102–3; legacy of, 111–12; literary criticism and, 110–11; living newspaper, 93, 96, 103, 106; making political material, 101–10; official vs. unofficial discourses, 107–9;

and reconstruction of subjectivities, 97–100; "Trade Party" and, 104–5; workers' culture and, 94–95
"Labor Drama" (Carter), 97–98
*Labor Dramatics,* 103
Ladies Waist and Dressmakers' Union, 72
"language handicapped" students, 23
Lantern Ceremony, 102
Lauter, Paul, 73
League of Workers' Theatres, 95
learning, 21
leftist ideology, 14–15, 73–74, 152, 167; literary discourses of, 121–22, 126, 131
*Liberating Memory* (Zandy), 153
Lindsay, Tillie, 44
literacy skills, 37
literary criticism, 62, 80–82, 110–11
literary discourse, 117–19 (*see also* bodily discourse; discourse; poetry); construction of subjectivities and, 119–20; empowerment of workers and, 82–83, 118–23; interactive discussion, 120–21; reading in discussion groups, 121–22; syllabi, 120–23; transgressive, 117, 118, 124–25, 139–40, 143–44, 151; by women workers, 128–43; women workers on, 123–26
"Literary Theory, Teaching Composition, and Feminist Response" (Hollis), 83
living newspaper, 24, 93, 96, 103, 106
Lockwood, Helen, 19, 119–20

machine imagery, 130–32; bodily discourse and, 152–57, 163
Marx, Karl, 131
Marxism, 48–49, 140, 154
mass recitation, 95–96, 105
*Mastering the Tools of the Trade* (Carter), 41–42
material culture, 5, 34, 36–37, 47
materialist pedagogy, 4–7, 19, 46–48, 168–69 (*see also* labor drama; pedagogy); autobiographies and, 68, 76; development of, 23–24; elements of, 50–52; post-process critique and, 48–50; for working women writers, 126–28
materialist turn, 168
materiality of discourse, 5
Maynes, Mary Jo, 3, 79
McConachie, Bruce A., 96–97
McNamara, Gay, 125–26, 148
Mirza, Heidi Safia, 50

*Monograph on Methods of Teaching English to Workers' Classes* (Plunder), 40–41, 46
Moore, Mildred, 2
Moscow Blue Blouses, 95
Moss, Marjorie, 117, 118, 142–43
"Mother Goose Depression Pantomime" (Previti), 104

narrative voice: collective "we," 73–74, 79–80, 83, 129, 132; individual "I," 7, 68, 71, 79–80, 83, 129, 132, 140
National Committee for Household Workers, 30
National Industrial Recovery Act, 13, 104–5
National Women's Trade Union League, 16
National Youth Administration, 13
nature, poetry about, 134–36
New Deal, 13, 152
*New Theater,* 95
North American women, 14–15

Odets, Clifford, 96
official vs. unofficial discourses, 107–9
Orleck, Annelise, 2–3

pacifist movement, 58
Palmer, Gladys, 42–44
Parrish, Beulah, 67–68, 71
participatory pageant, 94–95
"Partners in Progress" (Roydhouse), 3–4
*Paterson Strike Pageant, The,* 95
pedagogy, 6, 11, 143–44 (*see also* English composition; materialist pedagogy); discursive turn, 48–50, 168; emphasis on life experience, 20–21, 36, 39–40, 128, 134; post-process approach, 7, 46, 48–50, 168; process approach, 6, 33–34, 48, 127–28; of production, 50–51; workshop/process approach, 127–28
Penn State Conference on Rhetoric and Composition, 4
people's literature, 121
Perkins, David, 129
Perkins, Frances, 45
Perlman, Elizabeth, 131
Peterson, Ester, 98, 99–100, 101, 104–6
Peterson, Linda H., 80, 81, 83
Pharo, Florence M., 102
"Place of Literature in Workers' Education" (Fincke), 120
Plunder, Olga Law, 40–41, 46

*Poetics of Women's Autobiography, A* (Smith), 62
poetry, 3, 8, 51, 122–23 (*see also* student poetry); about African American students, 160–62; bodily discourse and, 140, 151–53; class issues in, 136–37; about education, 141–43; gender and, 131–34, 159; machine imagery in, 130–32, 152–53; on nature, 134–36; of politics and social themes, 136–41; race and, 131–34, 160–62; topics, 129–30; as transgressive, 143–44, 151; on unions, 163–65; by women workers, 128–43
poetry classes, 8, 36
political action, 47
post-process approach, 7, 46, 48–50, 168
poststructuralism, 4, 49, 62, 81–82, 118
Previti, Jennie, 104
process approach, 6, 33–34, 48, 127–28
production, pedagogy of, 50–51
progressivism, 12, 36, 152
proletarian literature, 125–26
*Prolet-Buehne,* 95
public arena, 1, 23, 47, 68, 152–53; student poetry and, 118–19

racial issues, 7, 12 (*see also* African Americans; African American students); bodily discourse and, 159–63; male ethnic prejudice, 14–15
Rand School of Social Science, 74
Ratcliffe, Krista, 5
reading lists, 120, 122–23, 131, 175–76n3
reality, 168–69
red pedagogy, 49
red scares, 12
Reed, John, 95
religious discourse, 160–62
resistance, body as site of, 157–58
Richardson, Elaine, 18
*Rocking the Boat: Union Women's Voices* (Herstein), 17–18
role-playing, 98
Roosevelt, Franklin D., 13
Roydhouse, Marion W., 3–4

Sacco, Nicola, 12, 67, 85–86
Sandburg, Carl, 124, 129, 139–40, 146
Scott, Fred Newton, 19
Scottsboro Case, 28–29, 78
scrapbooks, 24, 42–44
Selzer, Jack, 4–5

sexism, in unions, 13–15
Shapiro, Hilda, 17
*Shop and School,* 7, 36
Sirc, Geoffrey, 81, 82
sketch, 128
Smith, Emma, 63
Smith, Hilda Worthington, 16, 63, 67, 97, 119, 173n1; on controversy, 21–22; as drama director, 99, 100, 101; *Education and the Worker Student,* 20–22, 39, 126–28; on goals of Summer School, 19–20; interview with, 3–4; on pedagogy, 39, 63; *A Poetics of Women's Autobiography,* 62; on statistical reports, 45–46; *Women Workers at the Bryn Mawr Summer School,* 167, 173n1; *The Workers Look at the Stars,* 137–38
Smith, Sidonie, 62, 68, 76, 81, 82
social atom phenomenon, 79
social constructivism, 81, 119–20, 169
social discourse, 36–37, 49–50
social feminism, 4, 80
social literacy, 18
Social Sciences Workshop, 24, 54–57
Social Security Act, 13
social/transactive rhetorics, 6, 35
strikes, 12–14; students and, 87–90; student views of, 56–57, 87–88
Strom, Linda, 38
Strom, Sharon Hartman, 134
struggle, rhetoric of, 153
student-centered approaches, 11, 21, 40–41
student poetry, 144–50, 151 (*see also* poetry; student writings); "Apples" (Malkin), 147; "Ave Maria" (LaSota), 160–62; "A Boss Hiring a Private Secretary" (Koenigsberg), 147; "Buttons" (Feldman), 154; "A Change in the Universe" (Montgomery), 132, 143; "Economics in Poetry" (Ortmayer), 138–41, 143; "Factories" (Burgdorf), 155–56; "Hands" (Bowman), 159; "I Have Stolen Away" (Sekula), 141–42; "Lawrence, Massachusetts" (Kiezulas), 163–65; "Lost" (Kuhn), 158; "The Machine" (Kosovicz), 156–57; "Mass Production" (Nero), 133–34, 143; "Maw" (Bole), 144–45; "A Mother's Misery" (Ferrara), 162–63; "My Job" (Roseman), 130, 143; "A New Dawn" (Moss), 117, 118, 142–43; "Sue" (Bole), 144; "Thoughts" (Brown), 137, 143; "To a Negro" (Moulton), 149; "A Tree and I" (Cooper), 135, 143; "Tree,

Beautiful Tree" (Katz), 135, 143; "Under the Greenwood Tree" (Curtis), 145–46; "Wavering" (Sharkey), 150
students: application forms of, 21; forums for, 28–29; international, 25, 29, 55, 60; leadership roles for, 1, 7–8, 28; and political activism, 167–68; social roles for, 47–48; strikes and, 87–90; studies by, 2, 7, 23–24, 44–46, 54–56; as teachers, 28–29
student speakers, 43
student writings (*see also* autobiographies; student poetry): *America You Called Us* (play), 99; "Before and After I Came to Bryn Mawr" (Dominick), 27; "Childhood Recollections" (Wosnak), 91–92; "A Day on Strike" (Daum), 56–57; "Editorial" (Meltzer), 27–28; "The Funeral of Sacco and Vanzetti" (Daun), 85–86; "The Heart and Soul of the People" (Walsh), 31–32; "The Household Employees Come into Their Own" (Rhones), 29–30; "It Set Me Thinking" (Jackson), 77–80; *It's Unconstitutional* (play), 8, 104–10, 112–16; "Jean Carter—An Interview" (Petelson), 58–59; "Looking Back" (Fickland), 69–72; "Mother Goose Depression Pantomime" (Previti), 104; "My Great Grandmother" (Thompson), 90; "My Last Job" (Gerhart), 86–87; "On the Job" (Panglo), 88–90; "An Open Letter" (Arslanian), 24–26; "Proletarian Literature" (McNamara), 125–26, 148; "Right or Might?" (Murawski), 58; "Sacrifice" (Greenstein), 72–74; "Six Weeks' Gleanings" (Baker), 26; "The Social Science Workshop" (Collins), 54–56; "The Social Science Workshop and the Worker" (Lockstein), 57; "Sold Out" (de Nicholas), 87–88; "The Symbolic Jacket" (Alpern), 52–54; "This America" (Brown), 84–85; "Those Mill Villages" (Parrish), 67–68; "A Typical Day in My Life" (Gordon), 74–76; "Unemployment as It Is Studied at Bryn Mawr" (Taublieb), 59–60; "Use It or Lose It" (Van Duvall), 30–31; *The Wage and Hour Bill* (play), 93; "What Carl Sandburg Means to Me" (Gregorio), 124, 146; "What Do You Think" (Lamousen), 110–11; "What Literature Means to Me" (Paul), 123, 149–50
studies, by students, 2, 7, 23–24, 44–46, 54–56
subjective/expressionistic rhetorics, 6, 35, 36

subjectivity, 7, 47, 51, 76, 169; in African American writing, 70, 78–80; collective, 36, 62–63, 68, 73–74, 83–84, 110, 140, 169; construction of, through literary discourse, 119–20; discursive, 62, 81–82; public arena and, 152–53; reconstruction of, 81–83, 97–100, 118–20

suffering, 153–54

Supreme Court, 104–5, 106

Susman, Warren, 130

"Symposium on Creative Expression" (Fincke), 127

Taylor, Warren, 37

Teacher Education Project (WPA), 101

technology, 60, 130–33

*Ten Days That Shook the World*, 95

texts, 4; social discourses and, 49–50; subjectivity and, 81–83; textual embodiment, 139–40

*This America: A Study of Literature Interpreting the Development of American Civilization* (Carter), 121

Thomas, M. Carey, 16, 17

Thurlwell, Mabel, 2

"Trade Party," 99, 104–5

transgression, 8, 117–18, 124–25; discursive appropriation, 139–41, 169; poetry and, 143–44, 151

Triangle Shirtwaist fire, 72–74, 165

Trimbur, John, 48–49

unions, 12; poetry on, 163–65; sexism in, 13–15; students in, 25, 30, 88–90; student writings on, 25, 58–59, 72–76

unit system, 23, 66, 101

"Uprising of the 20,000," 13

Vanzetti, Bartolomeo, 12, 67, 85–86

Varnum, Robin, 46

Vassar College, 19, 100

vernacular literature, 119

visual elements, 24, 44–45, 54–56

voice, 9, 166, 168

vulgar marxism, 48–49

*Wage and Hour Bill, The* (student play), 93

*Waiting for Lefty* (Odets), 96

waitresses, 18

Weedon, Chris, 81–83

Wells, Susan, 118

Women's Bureau, 45

women's clubs, 38

women's movement, 11–12

Women's Trade Union League, 2

*Women's Ways of Knowing* (Belenky), 69

*Women Workers at the Bryn Mawr Summer School* (Smith), 167, 173n1

word usage, study of, 41–42

Workers Education Bureau, 21

"Workers Education in United States" (Smith), 21

workers' education movement, 14, 20–21, 37–38, 152

*Workers Look at the Stars, The* (Smith), 137–38

workers' theater movement, 8; agitprop theatre, 95, 96; debate within, 110–11; goals of, 97–100; at labor colleges and summer schools, 101–2; mass recitations, 95–96; participatory pageants, 94–95

working-class culture, 94–95, 97, 127

Works Progress Administration, 13, 101

Wylie, Laura, 19, 120

Young, Richard, 34–35

Y.W.C.A. Industrial Girls' Clubs, 31

Zandy, Janet, 72, 80, 153

Karyn L. Hollis is an associate professor of English at Villanova University, where she directs the undergraduate concentration in rhetoric and writing. She has published articles on literacy, service-learning, writing center work, and feminism and composition. Her current research concerns the opportunities labor unions present for working-class activist literacy.

# Studies in Rhetorics and Feminisms

S tudies in Rhetorics and Feminisms seeks to address the interdisciplinarity that rhetorics and feminisms represent. Rhetorical and feminist scholars want to connect rhetorical inquiry with contemporary academic and social concerns, exploring rhetoric's relevance to current issues of opportunity and diversity. This interdisciplinarity has already begun to transform the rhetorical tradition as we have known it (upper-class, agonistic, public, and male) into regendered, inclusionary rhetorics (democratic, dialogic, collaborative, cultural, and private). Our intellectual advancements depend on such ongoing transformation.

Rhetoric, whether ancient, contemporary, or futuristic, always inscribes the relation of language and power at a particular moment, indicating who may speak, who may listen, and what can be said. The only way we can displace the traditional rhetoric of masculine-only, public performance is to replace it with rhetorics that are recognized as being better suited to our present needs. We must understand more fully the rhetorics of the non-Western tradition, of women, of a variety of cultural and ethnic groups. Therefore, Studies in Rhetorics and Feminisms espouses a theoretical position of openness and expansion, a place for rhetorics to grow and thrive in a symbiotic relationship with all that feminisms have to offer, particularly when these two fields intersect with philosophical, sociological, religious, psychological, pedagogical, and literary issues.

The series seeks scholarly works that both examine and extend rhetoric, works that span the sexes, disciplines, cultures, ethnicities, and sociocultural practices as they intersect with the rhetorical tradition. After all, the recent resurgence of rhetorical studies has not so much been a discovery of new rhetorics; it has been more a recognition of existing rhetorical activities and practices, of our newfound ability and willingness to listen to previously untold stories.

The series editors seek both high-quality traditional and cutting-edge scholarly work that extends the significant relationship between rhetoric and feminism within various genres, cultural contexts, historical periods, methodologies, theoretical positions, and methods of delivery (e.g., film and hypertext to elocution and preaching).

Queries and submissions:
Professor Cheryl Glenn, Editor
  E-mail: cjg6@psu.edu
Professor Shirley Wilson Logan, Editor
  E-mail: Shirley_W_Logan@umail.umd.edu

Studies in Rhetorics and Feminisms
Department of English
142 South Burrowes Bldg
Penn State University
University Park, PA 16802-6200